Distorted Images

Cinema and Society Series
General Editor: Jeffrey Richards

Published and forthcoming:

DISTORTED IMAGES
British National Identity and Film in the 1920s

Kenton Bamford

I.B.Tauris *Publishers*
LONDON · NEW YORK

Published in 1999 by I.B.Tauris & Co Ltd
Victoria House, Bloomsbury Square, London WC1B 4DZ
175 Fifth Avenue, New York NY 10010

In the United States and Canada distributed by St. Martin's Press
175 Fifth Avenue, New York NY 10010

ISBN 1 86086 358 2

A full CIP record for this book is available from the British Library
A full CIP record for this book is available from the Library of Congress

Library of Congress catalog card: available

Typeset in Garamond by Ewan Smith, London
Printed and bound in Great Britain by WBC Ltd, Bridgend

Contents

Illustrations

Abbreviations

BFI	British Film Institute
CEA	Cinematograph Exhibitors' Association
Kine Weekly	*Kinematograph Weekly*
Kine Monthly	*Kinematograph Monthly Record*
Pictures	*Pictures and Picturegoer*

Acknowledgements

The inspiration for this book came from those historians who dared to take British film seriously. My editor, Philippa Brewster, has kept me in line and I have been fortunate in my association with Annie Pinder, whose generosity of spirit and hard work enabled me to complete the book on time. My research would not have been completed without the support and encouragement of Sheila Benson and the obdurate belief of my closest allies, Carol-Ann and Niko. Finally, I must thank Gladys Morris, who remembered, always.

General Editor's Introduction

One of the least known periods of British film history is the 1920s. It has inspired markedly fewer books and articles than the subsequent decades and still remains something of an unknown quantity. This is in large measure due to the fact that the bulk of the films from that decade have been lost or destroyed. Yet there is a story to be told and Kenton Bamford has tackled it with vigour and insight. In the absence of the films themselves, he makes full and excellent use of a wide range of contemporary reviews to re-create the trends and debates in the film culture. He also analyses the original source materials on which many of the films were based. The British cinema lived perpetually in the shade of Hollywood and the cinemagoing public opted in their millions for the Hollywood product rather than its native counterpart. Bamford seeks to explain why. One of the principal arguments advanced in favour of British films at the time was patriotism and this took the practical form of special British Film Weeks in cinemas and, later on, protective legislation. But what image of the nation did British films project? Bamford sensitively explores the class attitudes and values that under-pinned the images of Britain and of British men and women. He investigates the culture of the stage and popular fiction on which the cinema fed. He demonstrates that a stilted and stultifying aura of middle-class gentility stifled creativity, innovation and democracy in British films. But the picture is not wholly negative. It remains true that British cinema produced no Eisenstein, Griffith or Gance and no stars to equal

Fairbanks, Pickford or Chaplin. Bamford nevertheless makes out a convincing case for Betty Balfour, a 1920s precursor of Gracie Fields, as the British superstar, and hails George Pearson as an unsung directorial hero of British cinema. There are evidently still cinematic riches waiting to be discovered in 1920s British films.

Jeffrey Richards

Introduction

Film was the major cultural phenomenon of the first half of the twentieth century and Great Britain, with its dominant western cultural tradition and identity, should have been in a position to participate fully in what amounted to a revolution in mass entertainment. That it failed to do so raises many questions. The power of the American film industry undoubtedly weighed against Britain's chances; the booking and marketing practices adopted by the American industry were such that American production companies operated in a near-monopoly situation, with British films fighting for even a small share of the home market.[1] But that begs another question: when legislation enforced a quota of British films on renters and exhibitors why did British audiences retain their preference for American films? From the end of the First World War British audiences were encouraged, with almost evangelical fervour, to believe that 'British is Best', that if they took the time to watch British films they would be convinced of the error of their ways and shift their support to British productions. This did not happen.

The qualities supposedly invested in British films, which defined their difference from American and European films and their superiority to those films, are what concerns this book, for in the battle for screen time the British film industry employed a nationalist offensive, pitting itself, its values and its product against the invasion of foreign films and the values displayed in those films. Given that so many films of the period have either disappeared or been destroyed, the task of defining 'typically British' is problematic.[2] Partly to compensate for that loss, the original sources have been consulted as well as any other material which may shed light on the specificity of Britishness – what were perceived to be the particular qualities of a British film – for if the cinema was, for so many, a theatre of dreams, why did British audiences favour the American dream? Was it possible, as the Sex Pistols claimed in their alternative version of the British National Anthem, that there was no hope in England's dreaming?

Part I

British and Best?

1

Branding British Films: 'Quite English, you know ...'

W riting in 1919, the editor of *Cinema Chat*, a publication claiming a circulation of 115,000 copies a week, voiced the opinion that 'it is not so very long ago that we used to sneak into a picture house in mortal dread of being seen by anyone who knew us'.[1] One explanation for such an attitude resides in the origins of the film industry; these lie in the livelier, more democratic side of theatre, where the circus, music halls, fairs and cheap stock-companies co-existed, and in the initial stages of the film industry techniques common to those forms of entertainment were utilized – farce, melodrama and mime were integral elements of early films. For a time music-hall acts and rudimentary films shared venues and billing, but with the growing popularity of films as a singular source of amusement it became apparent that a profit could be made from showing films on their own. Prior to 1914 some £15 million had been invested in exhibition alone and in the years immediately following the First World War there was a huge boom in all aspects of the industry.[2] However, in keeping with sound economic principles, much of the investment was in property. As many as fifty new film concerns a month were announced in 1919, the majority being exhibitors.[3] William Fox, visiting Britain to promote his productions, no doubt boosted the confidence of exhibitors by assuring members of the Cinematograph Exhibitors' Association (CEA) that they were the only men in the industry making money.[4]

The principal reason the film industry attracted a mass audience was that it provided a cheap, if not the cheapest, form of entertainment. However, the scale of investment necessarily involved in meeting the increasing demand for film required a different kind of investor from those who had pioneered the industry: bankers, industrialists, theatre-owners, Members of Parliament, print magnates – these were the men who shaped the industry in the immediate post-war years.[5] They were a far cry from the itinerant actor-managers who found that films paid better than staged melodrama and the local entrepreneurs who could make a quick profit from renting both films and premises cheaply. Increasingly, at the local level, members of the CEA were likely to be town councillors, Justices of the Peace and members of Boards of Guardians; there were also a number of founders and members of Freemasons' lodges.[6] It was also important for the industry to have local government representation as the industry claimed itself to be 'practically at the mercy of the local authorities ... and the presence at the council table of men who know the trade cannot but make for better conditions all round'.[7]

At the community level the cinema was closely aligned with other aspects of working-class culture: regular fixtures of both cricket and football were played between industry personnel from different areas.[8] The manager of Manchester's Gaiety Theatre courted his audience with a song composed specially for them ('The Ladies of Manchester') and evidently out-performed his competitors when showing a Valentino film by booking an impersonator to give out 'cocoanut kisses' on which the words 'A Kiss from Valentino' were written.[9] Competitions were organized by various production companies with the express purpose of involving audiences with the programmes they saw. For instance, Pathé Pictorial asked for feedback on their short subjects, offering prizes for the best criticism. One such winner was James Wilson, a police constable from Cardiff, whose poem about Pathé's *Jerusalem* won a cash award.[10] Local authorities were also aware of the impact of film on cinema audiences: Cardiff Justices asked exhibitors to display notices prohibiting 'demonstrations of affection' in theatres and the London County Council voted £30 for a survey into eye-strain among cinema audiences.[11]

Increasingly, those with only a peripheral interest in film production sought to use the medium for their own particular purposes. Basil Thomson, Director of British Intelligence between 1919 and 1921, invited Lord Beaverbrook to a showing of *The Land of Mystery* (1920), a film set in Russia, for the express purpose of changing the film's message, which was evidently not hostile enough to the Soviet regime: 'I should like to see it with you because I want the film to convey some sort of lesson to our revolutionaries and at present it doesn't. Probably quite a small alteration would do the trick.'[12] Further up the social scale, the nineteen-year-old Prince of Wales, already a dashing and popular figure in the country, appeared in two films released in 1919: *The Power of Right* and *The Warrior Strain*. Both were anti-German tracts, featuring dastardly Germans being thwarted by heroic young members of the British Cadet Force.[13] King George V's speech to Parliament in 1919 embraced the same kind of issues that appeared in a review of *The Toilers*, a film in which a colliery accident orphans a young man. Promotional material stressed 'the association of industrial strife with poor conditions',[14] a sentiment eloquently reiterated by the sovereign:

> The aspirations for a better social order which have been quickened in the hearts of my people by the experience of the War must be encouraged by prompt and comprehensive action ... We must stop at no sacrifice of interest to stamp out unmerited poverty, to diminish unemployment and mitigate its sufferings, to provide decent homes, to improve the nation's health, and to raise the standard of well-being throughout the community.[15]

The schism between intent and delivery is illustrated by one of the first films to be released in 1919, *Broken in the Wars*, in which the Pensions Minister, John Hodge, was featured.

From the beginning of his tenure as Pensions Minister, Hodge evidently fought a running battle with the Treasury and the Chancellor of the Exchequer, Bonar Law, culminating in a threat to resign should he be forced to 'go to the public and tell them that no concession [on raising pensions in line with the cost of living] can be made'.[16] Hodge thought the government should do something immediately about the desperate straits in which many returning soldiers found themselves and what particularly irked him was the fact that Treasury civil servants, acting without his knowledge, sought to appropriate donations from concerned benefactors. When Sir John Lee, the cotton manufacturer, personally gave Hodge £50,000 to help disabled soldiers, the Treasury demanded the money. Hodge refused to part with it and created a special fund to be administered outside Treasury jurisdiction. More personal donations followed: a concert at the Albert Hall raised £6,000; cinemas all over the country held special matinées at which £121,000 was raised; the Cowen family, which owned the *Newcastle Chronicle*, converted their mansion into a training centre for disabled soldiers; and the King and Queen donated the Corporation of London's silver wedding present, which realized a further £80,000. In recognition of the gift, and as protection against the Treasury, Hodge designated the donations the King's Fund.[17]

Cecil Hepworth, the leading British film producer of the time, had organized a scheme whereby a number of officers returning from France were given training in film production and as the King's Fund was primarily a charity dispensing funds for retraining, he suggested a film be made to publicize the fund. *Broken in the Wars*, featuring three of Hepworth's leading players, Henry Edwards, Alma Taylor and Chrissie White, consisted primarily of one scene in which John Hodge was seen taking tea with the fictional Lady Dorothea. While Hodge and Lady Dorothea are chatting, the Lady's former cobbler, Joe, accompanied by his wife, makes a courtesy call on his patron to inform her of his return from the war. Hodge expresses an interest in meeting the ex-serviceman. Introducing Joe to John Hodge, Lady Dorothea explains: 'How fortunate you have called at this particular moment. Here is Mr Hodge, the Pensions Minister. You have been talking about setting up for yourself in some little business. Mr Hodge is the very man who can help you with his King's Fund.' Just as the Treasury had attempted to limit pension rises prior to 1920 by suggesting that 'Anything further is pure charity, and will come out of the pocket of the general taxpayer',[18] Joe reacts initially with hostility to any offer of help: 'We don't want no charity.' Hodge then explains that he, as a former steel worker, would have been prepared to accept the retraining allowance if he had been in Joe's circumstances, whereupon the disabled cobbler changes his mind and accepts a grant from the fund.

Given the numbers of dead and wounded, given the physical, mental and financial costs of the war, the idea that all could be salved by depending on the kindness of strangers was incredibly simplistic.[19] If the bare facts about Britain's post-war economic position were startling – the government was liable for one million pounds a day in interest payments on the national debt[20] – the situation facing the film industry was even starker. Prior to 1914 American films had captured 50 per cent of the world market; by 1919 their market share had reached 90 per cent. This was not simply a matter of economics; neither was it solely about product superiority. Government sponsorship played at least some part in educating European tastes. During the 1914–18 conflict the Film Division of the American Committee of Public Information supplied 600 projectors on which to show the 14 million feet of film a week shipped for the entertainment of Allied troops and civilians. And if a negotiable peace was stalled among the internecine tableaux of Versailles, America was more prescient in seeking to consolidate its celluloid gains. 'The minute the armistice was signed', an envoy was despatched from Washington to argue the case for the continued dominance of American films. While recognizing that the American share of the world film market would fall once full-scale production resumed in Europe, it was, at the same time, argued that the model of society depicted in American films offered hope for the future:

If a few exhibits in a single ship awoke Japan to the value of Western Civilisation, what effect must our pictures be having as, night after night, they are impressing their stories on the minds of countless millions the world over? This worldwide dissemination of knowledge by means of the motion picture is to be one of the greatest achievements, if not the greatest, of the twentieth century.[21]

Already there was evidence of the particular achievements of the American film industry: the most popular film stars in France were American;[22] it was reported that 'in Petrograd, Charlie Chaplin is a great favourite. The Youth of the city emulate his walk, hat and moustache with great gusto';[23] and the correspondence pages of British film magazines were filled with requests for photographs of the stars of American films – Norma Talmadge, William Farnum, Douglas Fairbanks, Mary Pickford, Sessue Hayakawa and Theda Bara. In the 'Shortly on Show' and 'Topics of the Week' sections of the same magazines there was a preponderance of information on American stars and American films.[24] Magazines specializing in publishing prose versions of popular films, even when British film production had outstripped its pre-war levels, relied heavily on American companies for their content: Fox, Famous Players-Lasky, Goldwyn and Vitagraph were the most prominent sources of material.[25] There were also European films. Sensing a renewed battle, one magazine warned British film producers of 'a new German offensive', namely the production of 200 films in Germany in 1919.[26]

Given the medium, a more appropriate riposte to foreign imports was to be found in publicity material from the Ideal company for a production entitled *Who Loved him Best?* (1919). Much was made of 'the most exciting scene' in which a prize sculpture significantly named 'Militant America' was smashed.[27] The same production company organized the first and certainly not the last 'grand day of British pictures' in which a double feature of British films was presented in an effort to convince audiences that British films were at least the equal of imports.[28]

In 1919 more than 150 British films, shorts and features, were produced; what was of paramount importance was whether or not British audiences would pay to see them. In order to convince the British public that British was best, production companies and British journalists launched a piecemeal propaganda campaign on behalf of the home product. A paragraph from *Stoll's Editorial News* succinctly delineates the theme adopted in the war against American films: 'The best British films are already equal to the best American productions, and a nation which in the past five years has again demonstrated its virility in the wasteful arts of war will prove that in the arts of peace it can hold its own and beat its competitors.'[29] Reviews of a Samuelson production of 1920, *The Last Rose of Summer*, contain the kernel of the argument in favour of home product; a melodramatic tale of a spinster betrayed for the sake of a valuable teaset, it was described as 'a British production of real daintiness'[30] and 'a pleasant story, convincing, and quite English, you know'.[31] If support for such qualities appears unequivocal, it should be noted that some films were still exhibited with little or no on-screen clues to their origins. However, an American review of *Dombey and Son* was quick to spot the film's origins:

> Some pictures are so bad that only fear of the heat keeps the padlock on the profanity chamber, and of this class ... Dombey and Son, offered last week at the Circle is an excellent example ... Triangle fails to give credit to cast, director or cameraman. They are not mentioned and the reason is fairly obvious. All too evident is the fact that this is an import, and worst of all, an English importation.[32]

Such a review suggests that an English film possessed recognizable qualities. Should this be taken as indicative of an inherently English film-making method or vision? The use of 'inherently English' is problematic given that English producers used the same, or similar, technical

equipment as their competitors.³³ There was a worldwide pool of literature from which producers chose their source material and throughout
the period there was a complex cross-fertilization process taking place
in the developing industry with technicians, producers and actors often
making films in England, Europe and North America. Such linkages
existed on a scale which would suggest that silent film had, at the very
least, the propensity to be a universal medium: 'The world today thinks
through its eyes looking at the screen.'³⁴ But the screens of the world
were occupied, for the most part, by American films; the images that
played fitfully across the screens of Britain were predominantly American, and given that audiences showed little inclination to forgo their
American diet it may well have been a legitimate tactic for British
reviewers and publicists to employ jingoism and xenophobia in an
attempt to persuade the British public that British *was* best.

Some of the language of rebuttal was couched in economic terms,
but much of the force of argument in favour of British films appears
to have been based on a perceived or actual sense of social and cultural
superiority: 'English stories with typically English acting and atmosphere'
defined that superiority. One such film, *Sweet and Twenty* (1919), was
praised for its 'artistic portrayal of peaceful rusticity' which was said to
be far superior to the 'exotic sensationalism' of an un-named American
film the reviewer had seen the same day.³⁵ *Sweet and Twenty* was a
somewhat naive story of a disgraced cleric's son redeeming himself in
the colonies and was produced by Sidney Morgan, whose output was
mainly filmed plays and novels at his studio in Shoreham.³⁶ Another
film praised for its Englishness was *Mr Gilfil's Love Story* (1920). Based
on one of the stories in George Eliot's *Scenes of Clerical Life*, it told a
melodramatic tale about a peer's heir being stabbed by his adopted
sister. The singular nature of the film's appeal was its 'pretty English
landscapes; several glimpses of country merrymaking were so good we
would have liked more of them'.³⁷ A typical Hepworth film of the
period, *Sheba* (1919), dealt with the provocative theme of divorce but
was admired not for its subject matter but for its 'Beautiful interiors of
an old English home' and 'delightful woodland scenes and glimpses of
a medieval castle'.³⁸

Such reviews suggest a heritage mentality, a mind-set attuned to
images and values consistent with past glories and vistas from which all
evidence of the present has been removed. Film-makers appeared more
concerned with landscape, architecture and furniture than with cinematic

technique. The producer Walter West, who would suspend production to accommodate his love of horse racing, was clear about the milieu in which his films were set: 'One of the charms of any English house ... is the furnishing and if we are to give the public films picturing the English Baronial residence, and the old country mansions, the style of decoration and furniture must be exactly what one would actually find in some homes.'[39] To decorate the set of *A Dead Certainty* (1920), one of the dozens of films about the 'horsey set' churned out by Broadwest Films in the early 1920s, £600 was paid for an oak writing table, £300 for a settle and £500 for a Hepplewhite suite. A review of the film noted that 'the exterior scenes especially were either dim, flickery or out of focus, and sometimes suffered from all three faults at once' and that 'from the point of view of screen art its only merit is in some of the minor characterisations'.[40] No mention was made of the expensive set decorations and the company's finances were evidently ill-spent in pursuit of baronial authenticity. West's spending was minimal compared to what was on show in *Quinney's* (1919), a story of a Yorkshire antique dealer's determination to marry his daughter into a 'quality' family; this 'sumptuously produced film used £100,000 worth of antiques as properties'.[41] For absolute authenticity the producers of Yvonne Arnaud's first film, *The Temptress* (1920), could not be faulted; they filmed 'lovely interiors' at 'Lord Lambourne's country residence'.[42]

British producers claimed to know how to please British audiences. An unnamed director was quoted as saying: 'if you really wanted to tickle your audience, really get them, you needed to do two things, and two things only. You had to give them sheep. You had to give them running water.'[43] Themes considered cheap and effective were 'children and dumb animals, the countryside and the sea'.[44] Walter West was equally adamant that horses were the magic ingredient which signalled success with the public.[45] Cecil Hepworth's pictures were popular because of 'their portrayal of essentially British character and sentiment, and the unsurpassed beauty of their exterior settings and scenery'.[46] Hepworth had been making films since 1899 and was said to possess 'more knowledge of the technical side of the film business than any other man in this country'. He was clear about how such expertise was to be utilized:[47] 'It was always in the back of my mind from the very beginning that I was to make English pictures, with all the English countryside for background and with English atmosphere and English idiom throughout.'[48] If the cinema was sometimes known as the theatre of dreams, then Hepworth must be seen as one of the principal purveyors of a dream of England which was 'essentially rural and essentially un-changing'.[49] With titles such as *Wild Heather*, *The Forest on the Hill*, *Mist in the Valley*, and *Comin' Thro' the Rye*, Hepworth productions were 'nice stories about nice people, cosy, traditional and even a little smug'.[50] Given that Hepworth admired 'subjects with high ideals and no trucking to the lower tastes or mere silliness of the audiences' it was, perhaps, inevitable that his films should appear smug. Above all else, Hepworth films were explorations of the English countryside. Hepworth was immensely proud of a 7-minute sequence in *Tansy* (1921) in which the star, Alma Taylor, with the assistance of a dog, rounded up a flock of sheep.[51] A review of *Sheba* (1919) waxed lyrical about its atmosphere, using phrases such as 'fruitfulness of Nature' to capture the essence of the film, which appears to have consisted of multiple scenes of Alma Taylor 'seated among rising corn, bathed in the bright spring sunshine'.[52] The plot of *Comin' Thro' the Rye* (1923) concerned a heroine – Alma Taylor once more – who loses the hero to another woman and suffers at some length, and with considerable decorum, in fields and orchards until she receives a letter telling her of her lover's heroic death in battle.[53] A contemporary commentator noted of the film that 'a star role was played by a field in which the rye, as far as I remember, failed to function obediently'.[54]

The novel, by 'Rita', on which *Sheba* was based, was part of an oeuvre of sentimental, sometimes sensational, usually melodramatic, literature, often written by women, which was described as 'belonging to the youth of minds now out of time'.[55] Hepworth's adaptor, Blanche MacIntosh, used a number of such plays and novels as the basis for the company's films. These were writers whom Edmund Gosse mocked for having 'the taint of popularity upon them', and almost all of them wrote novels which were variations on the love-versus-duty theme with traditional values winning out after several hundred pages of temptation. Of Marie Corelli it was said:

> She was just a simple single-tracked … English young woman, with ideas that ran concurrently with tight stays, tailor-made clothes, high chokey collars and boater hats. To smoke a cigarette would have been a sin; to talk slang worse; to say 'damn' impossible, and to mention what is called 'sex stuff' beyond her capacity to under-stand.[56]

In a 1919 film based on Corelli's novel *God's Good Man*, the heroic simplicity of a country parson is contrasted with the flighty behaviour of society types; when asked at a house party if he approves of ladies smoking, the parson replies with some deliberation that he didn't think *ladies* smoked.[57]

Ethel M. Dell, whose novels usually included scenes in which 'women are apt to kneel at open windows, preferably at night – arms flung wide pleading with fate, while birds understand and dogs smile', was an immensely popular writer of the period.[58] At least fourteen of her novels were made into films, with Maurice Elvey being particularly partial to her brand of Edwardian populism. In *Where Three Roads Meet* Dell put her own feelings about the post-war age into the mind of one of her female characters:

> Looking back to the dear pre-war world, she realised how different life had been. There had been time in those days to breathe, to live, to be happy. People had not developed the fighting instinct. Games had been games, not fierce contests for supremacy. And work had been a peaceful thing that brought its own reward, not a mad competition for the highest gain, the shortest hours, the greatest amount of leisure.[59]

This England is a pre-war, comfortable England of traditional values, of fixed social relationships, where poverty, if it exists at all, is picturesque, and where there are no needless excursions down 'nondescript suburban lanes'.[60]

The England depicted on film, the stories which were located within a rural idyll, had much to do with a wider expression of what it meant to be British, or, in the majority of cases, English. The images captured by film-makers were precisely those employed by many public figures of the time: note Stanley Baldwin's sentiment, 'England is the country and the country is England';[61] Kipling's England was 'made up of trees and green fields and mud and the gentry';[62] and Ramsay MacDonald – ever mindful of his Aberavon constituency – littered his speeches with allusions to 'springtime in the sheltered vales and creeks of the West'. Such expressions of national identity bridged political differences: Churchill's England was one of 'landed gentlemen, John Bull farmers, and sturdy yeomen', and in so far as it may have been a tenable expression of an intensely personal idea of what it means to be English, it had little contemporary relevance to the state of the nation.[63] The simplistic idealism of a poet describing brothers dying together in the trenches of the Somme, 'loving still your hills and valleys, Yorkshire moors and Sussex downs', ignored the reality that such men were more than likely to have spent their short lives in cities, living in crowded conditions, working in factories, with little or no access to such scenic embodiments of nationhood.[64]

Reproducing the cinematic myth was common practice among British directors in the immediate post-war period. *The English Rose* (1920), directed by the veteran Fred Paul from an old farce, was 'packed with shots of the open countryside which are very charming, and a generous exhibition of horsemanship'.[65] In the same year, *The Call of Youth*'s only attraction was said to be 'the English background'.[66] Sidney Morgan was acclaimed for discovering Sussex in his production *The Black Sheep* (1920): 'the best recommendation of the film, at this juncture in the history of British productions, is in the many beautiful exteriors.'[67] *When It Was Dark* (1919), 'a soulful blend of sentimentality, surplices, sin and salvation', told an epic tale of right versus wrong: an atheist millionaire attempts, by faking ancient relics, to destroy Christianity. It would appear that the producers of the film had adopted a never-mind-the-story-watch-the-architecture approach to the production, given that a recommendation of the film was based on its appeal to 'those who have an artistic appreciation of historical buildings'.[68] *The Shadow Between*'s chief appeal was 'the charm of the Cornish settings'; its subject matter was that perennial plot about disputed bloodlines and inherited wealth, noted, in 1920, as being 'very conventional drama'.[69] There may well be clues in the notion of 'conventional' with regard to the specificity of British films – a particular attention to, or regard for, convention, which imbued them with 'that hallowed essence of the past lurking in the old family album with brass clasps'.[70] British producers, with their countryside obssesion and reliance on pre-war source material, were attempting, one commentator noted, 'to make the public dance the Valeta when it much prefers the Fox Trot'.[71]

London Pride (1920) directed by Harold Shaw, in whom one reviewer detected 'the same exquisite sensibilities, the same whimsical unexpectedness, the same delicate play of humour, and the same swift inversion of comedy into drama' as J. M. Barrie, was said to be 'pure screen caviar to a public brought up on a photoplay diet of sausage-and-mashed', and although 'the British atmosphere is a big talking point' it was not enough to ensure the film's success.[72] In announcing Stoll's 1919 production of *The Elusive Pimpernel* it was stated that the film would be popular because 'Out of all the wide world, no nation will appreciate the coming of the costume film as will Britain'.[73] The story was described as 'impossible' but the film was praised for 'several fine English garden scenes and a beautiful landscape effect'.[74] A film based on Baroness Orczy's melodramatic swashbuckler which was 'greatest in its scenic productions' must have lacked some of the flavour and thrust of the original, which, from my recollection, is a tense and exciting 'Boy's Own' thriller.

Even when British film-makers availed themselves of American facilities and expertise the results were far from satisfactory. The Samuelson film *Love in the Wilderness* was produced in California in 1920; one review claimed 'it possesses those high qualities of finish that distinguish the American pictures' and, in addition, exhibited one further advantage – 'the correct British touch'.[75] Another review cited the fact that the film did not come up to the standard of the average American or continental production and declared it to be 'mere cuttings from a novel illustrated by moving pictures ... the first 40% of the film is irrelevant'.[76] Perhaps that 40 per cent was the scenic element so typical of British productions, and it may have been this kind of scenic indulgence which prompted the compiler of 'The Film Dictionary' to describe 'Action' as 'the slowest thing about a six-reel story'.[77] If *Love in the Wilderness* was disliked, the same producer's *At the Mercy of Tiberius* (1920) was praised. The film was made at Universal City and 'it will bear comparison with the work of any leading studios in respect of production, quality, acting, and theme'.[78] The film was unusual for a British production in that it was based on an American mystery novel and it could well have been that its star, Peggy Hyland, lent some professional gloss to the production, being as she was a seasoned performer in American films as well as an able screenwriter; the actors in *Love in the Wilderness,* on the other hand, were imported from the London stage.[79] The difference between the two films may also have had something to do with their contrasting themes: *At the Mercy of Tiberius* was a rather melodramatic murder story, with a clever, if improbable, denouement which was eminently visual (the identity of a murderer is imprinted on a window when the killing is illuminated by lightning), whereas *Love in the Wilderness* was a colonial love story in which the pluck of the heroine is matched only by the sacrifices made, and the obstacles overcome, by her lover.[80] Similarly, *The Flag Lieutenant* (1919) was about 'chivalry' and a 'self-denying hero ... elements that always make a strong appeal to the sympathies of the public'.[81] Perhaps the 'correct British touch' resided in the hackneyed themes of many British films of the period – self-sacrifice and the primacy of an unwritten code of honour – as if British producers had taken upon themselves the responsibility previously residing in the Primrose League, which sought to disseminate a code of chivalry among the lower middle classes. Such notions may have appeared less than compelling to audiences familiar with self-sacrifice not as an element of some traditional code of behaviour, but in the more immediate context of day-to-day survival.[82]

In setting their films in a mythical kingdom called Rural England, producers were bound to populate that kingdom with equally mythical characters. The action in *The Sands of Time* (1919) took place in what one reviewer took to be a social vacuum: 'the village atmosphere, socially, is of that democratic kind more common in fiction than in fact, and its inhabitants, irrespective of position, meet on a pleasantly human basis'.[83] Such a statement suggests that equality is an alien concept, a view with antecedents among Victorian critics, Matthew Arnold among them, who saw democracy as a levelling force with entirely negative consequences. Arnold and his colleagues were prepared to cite the condition of the working classes but offered no remedy for that condition, no analysis of the social formation which condemned part of society to 'darken in labour and pain', for it was beyond the parameters of their intention to do anything other than 'add zest to their melancholy or grace to their dreams'.[84] A review of *The Knave of Hearts* (1919) contained similar assumptions. The story concerns an heir whose love of 'strong drink' reduces him to the status of registrar of births, deaths and marriages in Wapping. As well as the obvious temperance message there was the explicit notion that to be forced to live and/or work in Wapping was a severe punishment for a person of his particular class.[85] His redemption depends on personal choice; sobriety leads, inevitably, to a happy ending, but such an obvious plot device could not change the customary squalor of those whose social destiny it was to live and die in Wapping. British film producers offered little in the way of grace to aid the dreaming of their working-class audiences: on offer were visions of an unchanged and unchanging world where charity begat gratitude and passivity, where class division was mollified by paternalism and where the sun shone with artificial brilliance on characters whose privilege commandeered centre-screen.

If the English countryside was one aspect of an unwritten production code it was the most visible part of a composite vision in which was inherent an overtly antagonistic attitude towards an age in which materialistic values were seen to be pre-eminent. The continued presence of characters, of heroes and heroines, depicted as members of the landed gentry implicitly suggested an acceptance of the moral and material supremacy of old money. This does not mean that members of the aristocracy were always virtuous; films such as *I Will* (1919) caricatured the 'silly ass' types in much the same way as comedians such as Jack Hulbert did in a later period, although their characterization is more often than not reminiscent of the good-natured depictions of Major Ponto, Lady Angelina Skeggs and Lord Gules – characters inhabiting the County of Mangelwurzelshire in Thackeray's *Book of Snobs*.[86] However, the delicate balance between presenting a positive image of that class and, at the same time, making that image entertaining was sometimes difficult to maintain; parts of *Duke's Son* (1920) worried one reviewer: 'I feel real regret that Lord Francis Delamere ... who started life with such high ideals ... should become a professional card-sharper – even though he always insisted on being strictly honourable when playing with friends.'[87]

I Will, a collaboration between Hubert Herrick, Kenelm Foss and Guy Newall, was a film in which tradition and social change collide in a rural setting. The film was advertised by Ideal as 'the story of a Nobleman's heir who ... is thoroughly spoiled ... [who] developed into an aimless, idle fop. But there is good British blood in him, and he becomes converted into a fine specimen of manhood, the transformation being largely wrought by the influence of the family motto "I Will".'[88] The film was praised because 'the screen is used as a medium for obtaining real life effects, and these effects never miss fire'. The acting of the two stars, Ivy Duke and Guy Newall, was applauded but other cast members were said to be 'too distinguished to play country types'.[89] The publicity photographs for the launch of the film showed the stars in a rural setting: Ivy Duke posing with her dog, Guy Newall and Ivy Duke 'just returning from a gallop on the downs'.[90] As the film was 'full of lovely pictures of English landscapes, English characters, and honest sentiment', it would appear safe to assume that it may be regarded as an archetypal example of films of the rural idyll genre.

The plot of the film concerned an heir to a country title falling in love with the daughter of a socialist who lives in a nearby village. The foppish heir – Eustace Algernon Dorsingham – is much given to that form of speech which was reproduced as 'By jove ... I nevah heard a gell talk that way before'. Although Ida, played by Ivy Duke, possesses a 'severe little socialist face', Eustace falls in love with her at first sight, and, overcome by passion, attempts to kiss her. This rather obvious attempt at seduction is stopped by a blow from one of Ida's friends. This has a salutary effect on Eustace; he takes up boxing and successfully beats up Ida's erstwhile protector. Ida is still not impressed. Sensing there is more to Ida's rejection than a wanton disregard for his charms, Eustace disguises himself as a yokel and goes to work as a day labourer on a farm. In the farmyard the plight of the socialist, eloquently named Bart Surge, is a topic for gossip:

> 'Socialist indeed – with his silly talk of equality and his blessed bits of sermons and spoutings! Not but what [he] ain't sincere, and eaten up with his opinions. But it takes all sorts to make a world and there be rich and poor, hardworking and shiftless, so long as there's a sky above it ... he's lying sick, with his books and his tracts unsold and the rent unpaid for months. All through Socialism!'

Worried by Eustace's continued absence from the family mansion, his parents instruct the butler to follow their son. The butler observes his young master's agrarian antics, reporting that Eustace has become an ersatz yokel and is using his wages anonymously to support the socialist cause. Doctors are immediately summoned from London to pronounce on the young man's sanity but when it is learned that Eustace has saved the Surge family from starvation and has taken up boxing to protect family honour, his parents realize their son is simply preparing himself, albeit in a slightly eccentric manner, for the time when he will assume the responsibilities incumbent on him as heir to a country estate. To the surprise of socialists and gentry alike, Ida not only accepts the continued benevolence of her reformed suitor but, in time, agrees to marry him. The message of the film was said to be that the family motto 'I Will' was a force for good in more ways than one. *I Will* was a comedy, but it was clear in its assertion that an alien ideology will always be rendered obsolete by the natural order of English social relations.[91]

In *The Auction Mart*, a British Actors' production of 1920, a character named 'Monna Lisa' is exposed to degrading influences because she believes that 'life is a market and everything is up for sale'. Monna leaves home to seek work and excitement in the city but is forced to return after her father suffers a seizure on discovering that his precious daughter has become a night-club dancer. Monna then renounces 'exciting times' in order to devote herself to caring for the man whose health has been ruined by her profligacy. The message was familiar, although its presentation prompted one reviewer to comment that 'the film company held the public in contempt'.[92] *For Her Father's Sake* (1921), a film awash with sentiments similar to those in *The Auction Mart*, was regarded as suitable for 'audiences who like their entertainment according to tradition'.[93] But what was that tradition? In both films daughters were expected to act in accordance with parental demands, their expectations apparently defined by obligation. Surely this was a case of British film-makers retelling the past and calling it the present. In 1914 the music-hall star Vesta Victoria introduced a song into her act which defended women's right to paid employment; she did so because of opposition from middle-class opinion which sought to limit women's access to the workplace, and the lyrics illustrate the polarity which existed between opinion and the reality of many women's lives:

> She's no lady, some people say,
> Just because she goes to work
> For her living every day;
> But there's no lady
> More independent than she
> She's just as much a lady
> As a lady ought to be![94]

The British-born star of American films, Olga Petrova – Muriel Harding to her friends – attempted a comeback in Britain after the popularity of her primitive *femme fatale* act waned in the face of competition from the likes of Pola Negri and Nazimova. In an article for *Cinema Chat* she was outspoken in championing women's rights and she can scarcely have endeared herself to those producers over whom the Edwardian tradition hovered like a cloud in one of their beloved English summer skies:

> I am emphatically a feminist – a Radical feminist. By which I mean that I believe in the equality of the sexes. I think that a woman has her work to do, and should be allowed to do it without

hindrance. She should be permitted to work out her salvation, independent of masculine intervention ... I haven't a great deal of patience with the stories of women who are wronged. I do not think there is any excuse for that type of woman. It is merely weakness. That is what I would like to prove to the public. That a woman is not a weaker vessel. That she has within herself the power to make her way, to carve out her destiny without degrading herself and becoming a chattel.[95]

In 1919 Walter West directed *The Gentleman Rider* for a production company set up by his wife, and star of the film, Violet Hopson. A review noted the novelty of 'the first film to be made under the management of a British star';[96] another review criticized the film for its lack of realism: 'I cannot understand how a woman can be left in sole charge of a racing stable, but this certainly does occur in The Gentleman Rider.'[97] Such an assault on perceived notions of the capacities and potential of women may have been only a temporary aberration on the part of the star, because in deference to the milieu in which the film was set it contained 'no deaths, murder, suicides, ship-wrecks or fires, for Miss Hopson contends that an English racing film should uphold the oldest and best traditions of the British turf'.[98] There was, evidently, some difficulty in marketing the film and it was shown in Canada and India before obtaining a release in Britain; there is no evidence suggesting that those responsible for booking the film were wary of doing so because of its portrayal of a woman in a non-traditional role but some speculation as to the film's reception may be indulged given the opinion cited.[99]

In film magazines of the period there was a recognition of the changes taking place in society, especially with regard to women's visible presence both in the workplace and as consumers of mass entertainment. An article in *Cinema Chat* posed the question, 'Do Business Girls Make Good Wives?', answering in the affirmative: 'Who can understand the ups and downs of office life better than the girl who has worked in one herself? Sometimes the ex-business girl can give helpful advice ... the girl who has been through the mill herself gives loving sympathy to the husband who is still there.'[100] The same magazine offered cooking advice to its readers, 'Meals for the Batchelor Girl',[101] and suggested 'a new and promising career for girls: Women as Engineers'.[102] Magazines carried advertisements funded by the National Council for Combating

Venereal Diseases posing questions such as 'Are you having a good time?': 'Girls who allow men, whom they scarcely know, to give them a good time are doing a dangerous thing. The man may be all right, but unless the girl has exceptional powers of taking care of herself, she may find that she has yielded to temptation with the most disastrous results.'[103] This begs the question: If men are 'all right' surely a woman would be safe from 'disastrous results'? In *A Little Child Shall Lead Them* (1919), 'the influences of Shakespeare, W. S. Gilbert and a treatise on Eugenics are to be traced in the plot' and the film was labelled 'domestic propaganda', with its intent being to persuade women that 'duty towards the race ... is one of the chief responsibilities of marriage'. The film was also said to be 'wholly on the side of the angels', and undoubtedly the English embodiments of such creatures were those held responsible for 'the unchallenged purity of countless happy homes', a state of grace protected by the press, which refrained from publishing the intimate details of divorce actions.[104]

The producers of *Unmarried* (1920), a film dealing with the problem of illegitimacy in a Derbyshire village made for the National Council for the Unmarried Mother and her Child, cast Lady Duff Cooper, Lady Juliet Trevor, Lady Greenwood, the Earl of Craven and other society figures as extras in an attempt to gain cachet for the film's message.[105] The film's principal actors were important figures on the London stage – Gerald du Maurier, Malvina Longfellow, Mary Glynne, and Edmund Gwenn – but their presence could not salvage the film: 'Neither as propaganda nor as entertainment can Unmarried be regarded as a milestone in the British films' progress. The authors ... seem to have been in two minds as to the correct proportions of jam and powder, and the film is so abrupt and disconnected in places as to suggest that this uncertainty of aim continued during production.'[106] *Damaged Goods* (1919), described by one reviewer as a 'masterpiece', was another film that sought to confront the issue of moral decline that was thought to be demonstrable by, among other things, women cutting their hair, wearing skirts which showed more than their ankles, and applying lipstick and rouge, the former being associated at best with the stage, at worst with prostitution.[107] The film, as the title suggests, attempted to reinforce the message which also appeared in advertisements of the period – a message directed specifically at women: 'Marriage: The Best is Yet to Be.'[108] It is ironic that 'cinema entrance halls were much used for the display of reprieve petitions' for the illicit lovers Edith Thompson and

Frederick Bywaters, both of whom were under sentence of death for the murder of Mrs Thompson's husband.[109]

The Christmas period in 1920 saw the opening of the St Martin-in-the-Fields crypt for the benefit of 'many women and girls up from the country, having failed to find a bed in a hotel or hostel, or missed the last train home, or indeed have been reduced to their last penny'.[110] The fact that women were becoming more independently mobile may be attributed, in part, to their wartime experiences as well as to the fact that the burgeoning retail sector, especially in London and the large provincial cities, was a magnet for a considerable proportion of young women whose natural place of employment in the past would have been in domestic service. There was a shortage of domestic labour in this period and it would appear that retail employment was preferred to in-house service by an increasing number of young women who valued the freedom provided by employment in which hours were fixed and in which fewer restrictions were put on leisure time. One magazine commented that a lack of ladies' maids was due to many 'girls taking up hair dressing, manicure and face massage', occupations which were given impetus by the changing images and fashions portrayed in Hollywood films.[111] These young women were the patrons of picture houses and dance halls, and as such possessed the potential to elevate a piece of dance music to popularity and to make stars of film performers. They would have undoubtedly agreed with the reviewer of *Walls of Prejudice* (1920), an adaptation of a play written by a woman, who suggested that a film about the shame of woman being in business was 'ten years behind the times'.[112] There was, however, criticism of these economically independent young women and it concentrated on their lack of 'ladylike' behaviour and their refusal to function simply as the decorative element in a familial *tableau vivant*. What especially bothered middle-class commentators about working-class girls was 'their display of finery, their love of dancing and cinemas, their loud shrieks of laughter in the streets which serve to draw attention to themselves, their competitive boasting of wild adventures on Monday morning'.[113]

It would be an exaggeration to suggest that all British film-makers produced bodies of work oblivious to the reality of their audience's lives, or failed to deliver something to stir their imaginations on a rainy Monday morning. Neither should it be assumed that all films pandered exclusively to 'the lingering love of the conservative lower classes and the still more conservative Royal Academy for sheep and cows in the twilight'.[114] What was clear, however, as early as 1921, was that British audiences were failing to respond to the pro-British propaganda. One exhibitor identified the problem: 'We don't want piffle up here. We want the goods!'[115] But what 'the goods' meant to audiences meant something different to those who reviewed films. A review of Walter West's *The Great Coup* (1919) demonstrates the fact that at least one British reviewer's approach to film had little or nothing to do with the medium as entertainment:

> it affords the pleasure of seeing a number of well-bred people conducting themselves in the customary refined British way, without fuss or 'swank' amidst appropriate surroundings; here a country-house exterior, paddock, stable or riparian back water, and there a drawing room, dining-room, office or library. These things are incidentally superior to America, because they happen to be British, but that by the way. What most impressed us in this production was the striking fact that the gentlemen removed their hats on entering another man's office, and kept their heads uncovered for quite a reasonable length of time when addressed by a lady. We all know that the British set the fashion in matters of good form, especially as to what is 'done' and 'not done', and it might almost be considered that British films should be permitted to enter certain foreign countries on their merits as social mirrors alone.[116]

When audiences turned their back on such expositions of etiquette there were those who sought to blame a perceived breakdown in public behaviour on non-British films. A new disease was also diagnosed: Mary Pickford Madness. One journalist attempted to associate the social and economic conditions in Britain with the behaviour of the crowds which greeted Mary Pickford and her then husband Douglas Fairbanks on their visit to England in 1920:

> If some of the enthusiasts who spent hours outside the Ritz Hotel waiting to catch a glimpse of the famous couple had put in those self same hours at desk, bench, or in execution of their daily task it would have been better for the community at large and the trade of a country burdened by debt. With working hours at present constituted, we cannot afford to waste precious time by pandering to the vanity of two people who are not such very nice people

after all. The Victorian era may have established some so-called prim ideas of common decency, but nowadays there are times when certain views of the then highest Lady in the land might be resumed with advantage.[117]

In appropriating the language and ideology of the more arrogant and least imaginative members of the upper classes, whose prejudices were informed by *The Times* and the *Morning Post*, the journalist demonstrated, like so many film reviewers of the period, that his sensibilities were out of touch with those to whom the film industry offered an escape from the savage conformity of life in post-war Britain.

Constance Collier wrote, 'the world has changed so much since the war ... that I sometimes think those pre-war days were a book I had read, a romance I remembered', and the British Ambassador to the United States commented that it was 'hard to find ground upon which our civilization can certainly and safely stand in the future, as one sees the direction of force passing from the hands of the people who have long held that power'.[118] The practical distillation of the tension in such statements was the scale of industrial dislocation in Britain; strike activity was rife in almost all sections of the working population: on the railways and London's underground system as well as on the docks; in the coal mines and power stations, even in the police force.[119] There were instances immediately following the armistice when the threat of mutiny among troops awaiting demobilization in France as well as in England forced the government to act with uncharacteristic alacrity.[120] A march to Whitehall by several hundred troops on leave, dubbed the Horse Guards Revolution, was apparently so serious that Lloyd George saw fit to break off peace negotiations in Paris and return to London.[121] But perhaps more consistent with the cultural and social tenor of the times was Bonar Law's response to the pressures of industrial and financial dislocation: 'I don't know where we are.'[122] If other politicians, other public figures, felt similarly ill-at-ease, British film reviewers did their bit to placate any fears.

A review of *Land of Mystery* – the film which British Intelligence sought to alter for propaganda purposes – noted smugly that 'the story centres around one of those revolutions that seem to happen so easily in warm countries'.[123] It was reviewed somewhat patronisingly: 'Were we ever in danger of being killed by the extremists? No, but we saw more than enough to understand what real cause the masses had for complaint, and to realise how lucky were the working classes in dear old much-abused England.'[124] Undoubtedly the plot of *Under Suspicion* (1919) would have provided further reassurance of England's superior social system given that the hero and heroine were subject to all manner of tribulations at the hands of Russian 'revolutionists' before escaping to England where they found true happiness.[125] The plot of the film was of little interest to one commentator, who noted: 'Under Suspicion is another Broadwest film which will show you some lovely frocks.'[126] The booking figures for the film were said to be 'colossal'[127] which may well have been gratifying, not only to Walter West, but also to those who wanted to believe that England was the only place where true happiness could be found, and who suspected that 'the Continent was invented for English people, so that they might enjoy their own country'.[128]

There were sporadic attempts by the British film industry to confront the dilemmas of the age but they did so in a contentious manner, producing images consistent with the insecurities of those who sought to govern rather than displaying anything more than a modicum of understanding of experiences common to a significant proportion of their audience. The political alignment of provincial Exhibitors' Associations was clear: they held 'Strike Commemoration' dinners at which they congratulated themselves on the part their industry played in maintaining law and order[129] and, understandably, offered consolation to cinema-owners who had been forced to close temporarily because of strike action.[130] There were also, though, warnings of caution to the trade: 'it is hoped that the exhibitors will not be led into showing partisanship in the dispute.'[131]

The imported *Strife* (1919) was said to be unfortunately titled, 'leading one to imagine in these days of strikes, riots, civil bloodshed, and industrial troubles, to expect some sordid story of the fight of the workers against the iron-handed capitalist', but exhibitors were in no danger of colluding with the producer in presenting an inflammatory product because the film was 'a plain unvarnished, thoroughly clean and wholesome yarn of a youngster, who having made a fool of himself, makes good as a workman in the great mills to which he is the heir'. The film's depiction of working conditions was said to make it 'a safe card to play in the big industrial towns, and also at those halls whose audiences have a wholesome desire to know how the other half of the world lives'.[132] *The Ugly Duckling*, produced by the Samuelson company in Hollywood in 1920, featured a strike and a telephonist heroine who exonerates a banker's son from a false charge of theft; it was said to be 'rather snobbish in flavour, and with an anti-Trade Union bias which may be dangerous in some districts'.[133] *The Ugly Duckling* could well have played successfully in suburban London and the Home Counties but its anti-trade union bias would not have endeared cinema-owners to their local communities in industrial areas where union membership was seen as the first line of defence against exploitation.

The Cry for Justice (1919) was another film in which a strike was featured, along with the elopement of an extravagant wife with a lord, a murder, and an invention which catapulted the principal characters into the realms of the rich and depraved. The plot was regarded as improbable and the film 'does not help us much along the road towards the ideal we hope to find in the British film, yet it shows that native producers are at least attempting to struggle out of the mire.' One review accused the producer of attempting to squeeze 'a quart into a pint pot' with 'ambition falling far short in its achievement', and if the lurid aspects of the plot are discarded it would appear that the film was a parable about the negative effects of newly acquired wealth.[134] Langford Reed, who was responsible for the scenario of *Lass o' the Looms* (1919) as well as *The Heart of a Rose* (1919) – set in 'the Carnforth steel and iron works where Stephen Carnforth controls the destiny of 700 of his fellow-creatures' – appears to have possessed some understanding of the possibilities afforded by locations familiar to the majority of audiences. Reed wrote, 'the real picture is a success because *it is like life*' and he appears to have made an effort to locate films within a context which touched the reality of working-class lives. Before the war Reed had written a scenario called *The Tragedy of a Strike*, about the effects of a strike by gas and electric workers on a town. The film was made by the Clarendon Company as *The Strike Leader* and re-released in 1920. The climax of the film was coded in such a way as to enlist some sympathy for the principal character, in spite of his role as leader of the strike, by having his son die in a hospital where doctors are unable to operate on the injured child because the strike has cut off the hospital's electricity supply.[135] The conclusion could be drawn that strike action was against the best interests of those who participated in it, and it may be reasonably argued that while the working-class setting of the film may have been authentic the ideology underpinning the action owed more to the mixture of confusion and intransigence which characterized the governing class's attitudes towards industrial action than it did to an understanding of, or sympathy for, the genuine feelings of grievance which induced members of the working-class to take such action. In one sense *The Strike Leader* was prophetic, as in the prelude to the General Strike of 1926 Deptford electricity workers cut off supplies to local hospitals.[136]

Strikes may have affected the exhibition sector of the industry, by delaying film deliveries especially, but British producers soon began to experience serious difficulties of their own: how to sell their films to renters and exhibitors whose chief product was American. There were calls for government intervention, and meetings between renters, exhibitors and producers were held to thrash out a solution, but more often than not these meetings 'devolved into a perfervid display of what popularly passes for patriotism' with nothing practical resulting.[137] Much was said at the time, and repeated as gospel, that British producers were handicapped by the rental arm of the industry refusing them access to the exhibition sector on equal terms with American product, but a random examination of film programmes shows no consistent relationship between the trade show date and exhibition. The Queen's Hall cinema in Cricklewood advertised six British films in its programme of twenty for January 1922;[138] the films are listed below in trade show order:

January 1920	*The Husband Hunter*
November 1920	*The Great Day*
January 1921	*The Skin Game*
June 1921	*The Right to Live*
September 1921	*Squibs*
November 1921	*The Fifth Form at St Dominic's*

This suggests that at least some British films were exhibited shortly after they were trade shown. Perhaps the relationship between producers and rental firms was important with regard to release date; *The Right to Live* and *The Fifth Form at St Dominic's* were produced by I. B. Davidson, who had a backing and distribution deal with the rental firm of Grangers.[139] The much-cited evidence of Hepworth and others claiming up to a two-year waiting period applies to *The Husband Hunter* and *The Great Day*, although they may have been re-issues. If *The Great Day* was not a re-issue it would suggest that even films with American backing could be subject to the anomalies of the industry's booking system; the film was made by the British arm of Famous Players-Lasky, which had been subject to a temporary ban because of infringements to normal booking practices.[140] A first-run cinema, such as the Shaftesbury Pavilion, exhibited fewer British films: its programme for February/March 1922 contained only *The Fruitful Vine*, but this had been trade shown as late as September 1921. In its programme it made some reference to block-booking, expressing the opinion that it was possible to provide good programmes without participating in the practice.[141]

The Broadwest production *Her Son* was completed in June 1920; it was playing in cinemas in August.[142] *A Soul's Crucifixion*, trade shown in January 1919, had been extensively exhibited prior to August of the same year.[143] Two other Broadwest productions, *A Daughter of Eve*, trade shown in August 1919, and *Snow in the Desert*, trade shown in December 1919, were playing in America in May of 1920.[144] British and Colonial's *The Black Spider* was sold to America at its trade show in May 1920 and the company's other products were said to have been sold on 'specially advantageous terms, which proves British films are welcomed there provided that they are the right type'.[145] There were, of course, many British films which did not secure early release dates; a comment, made in 1919, sums up what was regarded as a common experience: 'I feel sorry for the film canvasser who, having taken the exhibitor, his wife and eight children to dinner, and then to the theatre, was rewarded with a thirty shilling contract for May 1921.'[146] It would appear, however, that there were exceptions to the block-booking practices which favoured American product, and that in some instances guaranteed sales and early release dates did little to stabilize the financial position of British producers. If the evidence regarding the Broadwest company is noted – that its product was bought 'before an inch had been turned in the camera' – it may be that it was too easy to blame American competition and American booking practices for British failures when other factors relating to quality and subject matter were instrumental in the failure of the industry to adapt itself to market demands.[147]

The specialist film publications of the period list with desperate regularity the demise of production and rental companies: Leslie All-British Production Studios disappeared as early as 1920,[148] and a receiver was appointed in connection with Broadwest Films in 1921. Walter West continued to function as an independent producer, securing finance from whatever source he could.[149] General Film Renting, a distributing company formed to take advantage of the increased number of British films being made, struggled on for barely two years; the collapse of

British Exhibitors' Films, in 1922, came as 'a great surprise to the trade' and the Imperial Film Company soon followed suit, leaving H. G. Wells to pontificate on the 'damned foolery' of a film company purchasing the rights to some of his books without ever bringing them to the screen.[150] The Hepworth Company closed its renting arm in 1923 as its plans for expansion had been dashed by the failure of a shares issue the year before – 'it was almost still-born', according to Hepworth, so badly was it undersubscribed.[151] Like another large producing company, Ideal, and numerous smaller concerns such as Planet Photoplays and Master Films, Hepworth's company could not survive the slump which followed the post-war boom.[152]

There was 'the cry for "bigger" pictures … on all sides'[153] – from the public, from renters and exhibitors- but it would appear that although certain sections of the trade press continued to praise British films for their 'perfect photography and high ideals', the British industry was incapable of delivering what the market demanded.[154] It should also be noted that the home market alone could not sustain 'bigger' pictures, with the increase in investment that such a notion involved. Even overseas sales could not shore up the precarious finances of British production companies. British renters might pay in the region of £50,000 for the rights to a Chaplin film or a super-production such as *The Auction of Souls*, but American renters were able to secure British films for as little as £800.[155] *The Old Curiosity Shop* (1921) was sold to America for an outright payment of £2,000, and this was thought to have been an especially good sale. The industry appears to have developed in such a way as to be biased in favour of American product, with renters and exhibitors acting against the best interests of the home product although there do seem to be exceptions: the re-issue of *A Welsh Singer*, produced in 1914 and re-issued in 1919, followed an initial run of 1,148 cinemas in Great Britain[156] and *Nothing Else Matters* (1920) was booked for 'about £30,000' at its trade show, which represented a profit of at least 400 per cent. Production companies do not appear to have capitalized on such profits, although perhaps such successes were unusual.[157]

A solution to the fact 'that we are a long way behind the Americans' was, according to one journalist, possible 'if some remarkable film producer or artiste were to arise, or some out-of-the-ordinary mechanical improvement was brought to light in England'; only then would 'British films … achieve world-wide fame'.[158] The industry was awaiting, so it was said, 'a dreamer of actions, daring in conception, bold in decision, of vivid imagination and endowed with boundless enthusiasm and confidence. When such a spirit secures control of the industry, ruthlessly scraps the existing for the specially trained, and withall applies the requisite driving force, the British picture will regain its world-wide supremacy.'[159] There were such spirits entering the industry at this time, but the industry was less than accommodating to those whose ideas were expansive. When the British Actors' Film Company wanted to 'think big!' and increase production, the company's backers departed in haste, frightened by the thought of more than modest investments.[160]

Adrian Brunel, who had been associated with British Actors, met similar resistance when he directed *The Man Without Desire* (1923), featuring Ivor Novello, who was by far the most important British male star of the period. Brunel was unable to obtain finance within the industry and the film was completed only due to the errant vision of the theatrical impresario James White – an ex-bricklayer from Lancashire – who supplied the necessary finance because he believed that the cinema would inevitably supersede the theatre as the true medium of dramatic expression. White was said to have 'barked his wares, like the North-country terrier he was', and, because he had 'little or no refinement', to have alienated the City and Turf types on whom his financial dealings were dependent.[161] Brunel and Novello had similar problems financing *The Rat* (1925), which, once made, was a huge success. Lack of adequate finance was regarded as endemic throughout the industry, as *Picture Show Annual* told its readers: 'One of the chief handicaps under which our producers have had to labour is lack of financial backing.'[162]

Herbert Wilcox, who had begun producing on a modest scale in 1920, was unable to secure British finance to expand his company despite the commercial success of two films he made with American stars: *Flames of Passion* (1922) and *Chu Chin Chow* (1923). On a visit to America, in 1924, to promote *Decameron Nights*, Wilcox met the Giannini brothers, who had pioneered film financing through the Bank of America, which they owned, and was able to secure backing for his future productions; in all, the Bank of America lent him some £7 million in the ensuing years and it is yet another sad reflection on the state of British finance that some years later when Wilcox went, with some eminent and titled associates, to the Governor of the Bank of England in order to raise finance to buy the American company Universal, the Governor's response was said to be 'You're surely not going to interest yourself in that awful industry ... those dreadful people are not your class'. According to Wilcox these words were addressed to his companions; the Governor did not see fit to acknowledge his presence.[163]

The failures of the British industry and the parallel popularity of American films were regarded, by some, as a cultural and economic assault on the nation – 'the battle for English films is the battle for England's soul'[164] – and it is, presumably, why films that presented images consistent with notions particular to England's soul were seen as particularly English. To praise a British film was to describe it as 'dignified and impressive'[165] or 'wholesome, absolutely clean'.[166] When problems were featured it was imperative that they be treated with decorum, in an 'essentially British' way which was 'free from nastiness'.[167] The heroes of these films were indubitably 'all a British Officer should be',[168] 'typically solid Englishmen'[169] or 'perfectly mannered English gentleman'.[170] Furthermore it appeared almost *de rigueur* that these true-blue titled heroes were sustained, at times of conflict, or redeemed when sorely tempted, by quaint family mottoes and a love of the great outdoors[171] and it was only natural that foreigners, if they weren't evil, should be permitted the ultimate sacrifice of giving their lives for these paragons of mannered sobriety.[172] A slightly different attitude to such heroes was taken by American reviewers: 'It is to be noted that all English artists are pure in pictures; they also appear to be somewhat devoid of red blood and backbone.'[173]

It was also in the national interest 'to propagate the charms of English womanhood abroad',[174] with portrayals of British heroines who were duty-bound to submit to the dictates of nature and tradition with fortitude and, when pressed to the edge of capitulation, were able to swoon with prescience.[175] Of course such scenes were notable for their 'masterly restraint',[176] a fact not lost on one reviewer, who noted the tepidity of English love scenes: 'if the various episodes of love-making is a consistent idea of an Anglo-Saxon's conception of ardour and affection, certainly Aphrodite never cast her spell over that island.'[177] And there was that class of heroine whose 'unworthiness' to be married to a millionaire or heir was disproved by the discovery of a titled forebear or a capacity to keep the suitor in the manner to which his social position entitled him to be kept.[178] And when a new kind of heroine was discovered – one whose style was the opposite of Home Counties demure, one whose sentiments were rooted in a class which, in film, existed only for the benefit of comic relief or patriarchal benevolence – it was necessary to bestow upon the actress who played her the sobriquet 'our own', and pit her against the invasion of American films and American culture:

> Betty Balfour, the Cockney Queen,
> Is Britain's hope on the movie screen,
> The Yanks may copy St Paul's great dome,
> But only Betty can show us our home.[179]

If film images may be regarded as reflecting the time and place in which they are produced then the majority of British films asserted the ineffable determinism of a social system shackled to the values of a ruling class which no longer ruled but whose successors to power possessed neither the imagination nor the fortitude to forge an alternative social construct. To this end readers were assured that 'one of the advantages of a British production is the home-like atmosphere which is conveyed by the sight of every-day doings presented in an every-day way'; the 'home-like atmosphere' was indicated, in this instance, by a barrister hero and his wife and action taking place in their comfortable suburban residence and at the Old Bailey. The film was, because it was British, 'conspicuous in its artistic restraint'.[180] A film might be 'mediocre in most particulars' but if it showed 'typical English scenes', such as those of Oxford in *The Princess of New York* (1921), it was thought to be superior, as of right, to American films.[181] What was also significantly un-American about British films was the fact that they reinforced the notion of natural order in a period in which the ideology which perpetuated that notion was threatened not only by those to whom it had ceased to be compelling but also by American films which extolled the virtues of Everyman as opposed to the British cinema's obsession with privileged heroes and heroines.

When a film did other than reflect the status quo it was described as 'a panorama or symposium of the revolutions brought about by the war in social ideas and prejudices'. *General Post* (1920) told the story of a small-town tailor who fell in love with the daughter of a peer. One particular scene 'brought down the house'; it was an episode showing a 'stableman-sergeant imploring heaven for patience to endure the stupidity on the drill-ground of his high-born employer'. The reviewer succinctly noted, 'that is, of course, dramatic licence'. So revolutionary was the film that after saving the peer's son and having being awarded a Victoria Cross for his efforts, the possibility of marrying the titled heroine was mooted; this was said to demonstrate 'the social levelling-up caused by the war', but it should be noted that it was not until the once humble tailor was whispered to be in line for a peerage of his own that permission to marry was granted.[182]

There were few films which allowed such class deregulation; there were few films which did not succumb to the condescension of class insularity which decreed that working-class characters, no matter how hard they struggled to enter the plutocracy, should inevitably return to their own class;[183] that maids who attempted to pose as something other than what they were invariably fell foul of other imposters;[184] and that when fortune, in the guise of luck or inheritance, smiled upon members of the working class they would always make fools of themselves by attempting to be 'toffs'.[185] To suggest that a significant proportion of the working classes were prepared to spend money on films which consistently ignored their existence would be naive. Similarly, it would surely be stretching credulity to imagine that films which did contain such characters, portraying them as objects of derision or caricature, deprived of dignity and subject to the whims of their betters, would meet with continuing approval.[186] To countenance images suggestive of obligatory subservience, to be portrayed as predestined to poverty, immune to sensibility and denied the possibility of self-improvement was tantamount to being willing victims of indiscriminate acts of alienation on the part of British film producers.

It is not unreasonable to suggest that it was precisely this gap between the taste of producers and consumers which caused cinemas to empty when British films were advertised. But surely filling cinemas was what the industry was meant to be doing; American films were doing just that, and cinemas exhibitors booked American films for precisely that reason.[187] It did not matter to audiences or exhibitors that the intellectual and social elites regarded Hollywood as uncivilized,[188] and 'the blood letting, the shooting and thundering of horses hooves [with] the appropriate noises and tempo ... supplied by a versatile pianist' as cheap and vulgar.[189] Audiences wanted entertainment. Evidence suggests that British audiences noted the connection between British films and the class-specific imaginations of those producing them and acted in accordance with their rights as consumers: they chose to spend their money on American films. Warnings were given: 'Don't make the mistake of appealing to your high-class patrons only'[190] – they, after all, provided only a minority of consumers – and the failure of such organizations as the British Film League[191] must surely have rattled the superior sensibilities of those who believed that British audiences were more likely to be entertained by chintz and chivalry than by, for instance, Chaplin's heroic little man whose antics, adversities and small triumphs were derived from experiences common to the majority of audiences the world over.[192] In the case of Chaplin, British *was* best, and in escaping from poverty, in embracing a new form of entertainment, in refusing to allow class to define his talent or his horizons, he was not only able to engender laughter and release, he offered hope. British films offered little of that commodity, reliant as they were on an imprint cast in determinist tones; in a period in which the bloodstained banners of recent victory failed to convince so many that the future offered little more than promissory rhetoric pawned to appease a volatile present, British audiences knew, as they sat in darkened halls, exactly what they wanted: they wanted America – Hollywood, and all it had to offer.

2

Roles for Women: 'Ladies ... right through.'[1]

In an article in *Cinema Chat* entitled 'Sirens of the Screen', the phenomenon of the 'strangely fascinating Vampire Lady' was explored, with reference to Theda Bara, Nita Naldi, Nazimova; no British example was mentioned.[2] There are very few references to British 'vamps' in the cinema magazines of the period, as if there was no place within British films for predatory females. One of the few mentions made of such roles appears in a review of *Odds Against Her* (1919): 'Miss Lorna Della playing the adventuress ... bids to become one of the most promising vampires yet seen on this side of the "herring pond".'[3] Unfortunately, nothing came of that promise and Lorna Della disappeared from British screens after completing the film for Barkers. Barker All-British Productions were hardly likely to embellish the career of any but the most resilient of actors; another of their films, *The Disappearance of the Judge* (1919), was described as technically inept: 'candles are blown out without any alteration in the illumination of a scene, and a close-up of a clock in opulent surroundings reflects in its glass the roof and skylight of the studio in which it was shot.' It would appear that 'rough and ready' was an appropriate description of the Ealing studios output.[4] Predictably, the producing company disappeared.[5]

Ruby Miller, whose early stage work had been with Sir Herbert Tree, playing Ophelia, Viola, Perdita and other classical heroines, was cast as a 'vamp dancer' in the Famous Players-Lasky British production of *The*

Mystery Road; the film was released at the end of 1921 and Miss Miller was not seen on screen again until 1927. She did, however, propose an interesting venture – to adapt a screen role she had played, that of 'Diana' in *The Edge o' Beyond* (1919), for the stage. Such an enterprise is noteworthy: the film had been adapted from a novel written by a woman; the film adaptation was made by a woman, Irene Page; and the production company and direction of the venture was to be the responsibility of Ruby Miller. The actress also toured her own actors' company and introduced new regional plays to London. Such an exhibition of independence and self-confidence runs contrary to much of the received wisdom of the period regarding women, especially given the fact that the most popular and endearing screen creation of the period, *Squibs*, made an impassioned plea for women to stay at home and bear more children.[6]

The acquisition of the British rights to Nazimova films was considered a coup of considerable importance – 'Nazimova is set to become the biggest attraction in the British Cinema World'[7] – and it is a matter of some interest that no type approximating that of the 'vamp' was systematically exploited by British producers. The California-born Violet Hopson was occasionally cast in variations on the role, because of her dark hair and eyes, and because her stage parts had typecast her as 'the dear, delightful villainess',[8] but she resolved 'with a grim determination' to turn her back on such roles and become a screen heroine.[9] Perhaps it was the word's connotations that made it unattractive to British producers and actors; women who continued to work after the war were referred to as 'selfish vampires depriving men of jobs'.[10] A letter to *Pictures*, from Max of Birmingham, who described himself as 'heated – my Bolshevik blood is up' because he was sick of being 'bored stiff' by British pictures, illuminates the difficulty of trying to juggle both acceptable images and popularity: 'One point in favour of British screen actresses (and I do not think that anyone can deny this) is that they are far more refined than many of the Americans. We never find our own film-stars dressed in such absurd and immodest costumes as worn by our Yankee friends.'[11] The joke about 'actresses being either a clergyman's daughter or ... reared in a convent' appears relevant in the context of what kind of roles were considered suitable for British stars; it would appear that the public expected, and British producers and directors attempted to market, that elusive essence, 'typical English womanhood'[12].

Cora Goffin, whose short film career left no mark on British film history, won a screen role because she was 'a representative of typical English girlhood' in almost identical circumstances to those which catapulted the unknown Margaret Leahy to Hollywood after she had won a *Daily Sketch* competition to find 'Who will be the New British Film Star?' A small part in Buster Keaton's *The Three Ages* followed, which demonstrated that however beautiful Miss Leahy was her acting talents were minimal.[13] Athanie Davis, aged seventeen, was offered a film contract on the strength of her having once been chosen as the embodiment of the perfect English child. The organizers of the competition, it may be noted, did not look beyond London.[14] Advertisements mirrored the concern with an assault on British womanhood: an advertisement for a '4 in 1 Hair-Drill Outfit' proclaimed its wares with the slogan 'American Challenge to British Beauty: Are we to lose first place?'[15] To compete with the 'screen beauties' of America, alternative modes of appraisal were employed to extol the virtues of British stars. It was the innate refinement and 'typical British charm' of Violet Hopson which prompted a Brighton film fan to pen a poem called 'The Convert':

> I took my 'maiden' auntie
> To our local kinema,
> She was awfully fond of saying:
> '*How wicked Pictures are!*'
> And telling Picture-goers
> That they wasted precious time,
> And warning children's mothers
> That the Pictures lead to Crime.
> Well, you can guess, dear readers,
> Auntie'd never seen the screen,
> So I talked her into going
> Just to say that *she had been*,
> But Aunt saw Violet Hopson,
> So she changed her point of view;
> And when next I go to Pictures
> Well! *my aunt is coming too!*[16]

Film magazines were enlisted to propagate images consistent with the aspirations of the producers and stars themselves. In an interview with Violet Hopson, a journalist ('Miss Pictures') described Hopson's drawing-room as 'graciously restful and serene as the star herself' and went on to enthuse about 'the woman, as natural and sweetly attractive a person as any heroine'; a woman who baked the cakes offered to the journalist, who was fond of cooking and sewing, and who found it possible 'to look after my home, and to give my leisure time to my husband and son' as well as pursuing a film career.[17] When Hopson was under domestic pressure of some kind, a magazine recorded the fact that she 'has received no less than eight offers of domestic assistance within the last fortnight'.[18] So adept at kitchen chores was Hopson that when filming *Vi of Smith's Alley* (1921) in a jam factory she cut her hand on a jam-jar. To play a Cockney character was also something of a departure for Hopson as she was best known for 'Society parts'; she was, furthermore, an American by birth.[19] A review of the film noted that Amy Verity's acting was above the average but made no comment on the performance of the star.[20] Violet Hopson's public persona was of some social standing: she was invited by local authorities to present military medals, make tours of factories and escort groups of school-children on visits to the cinema and circus.[21] As previously noted, she was the first British star to set up her own production company; perhaps a contributory factor to her popularity was the fact that she consistently acted in, and directed, horse-racing pictures; titles such as *A Fortune at Stake*, *A Turf Conspiracy*, *The Gentleman Rider*, *A Sportsman's Wife*, *Kissing Cup's Race* and *A Gamble for Love* attest to her partnership with Walter West as well as to her predilection for a sport she adored. She was of the opinion that horse-racing films were her 'own particular achievement'.[22]

Violet Hopson's films were apparently very popular in post-war France.[23] Another English actress, Mary Harrold, found success in France playing an Indo-Chinese heroine in Louis Feuillade's serial *Tih Minh*. Feuillade had been enormously successful with his *Judex* films so the opportunity to work on one of his productions must have afforded the actress some satisfaction. Although the series was a considerable success, Mary Harrold appears never to have been given the opportunity to replicate her continental success in England.[24]

The career of Mabel Poulton provides another example of the way in which the British film industry failed to capitalize on whatever initial success it was able to generate. Mabel Poulton worked as a secretary at the Alhambra Theatre in London and when a stage tableau was designed to introduce D. W. Griffith's *Broken Blossoms*, a young woman was needed to impersonate the character played by Lillian Gish. Having failed to find a suitable candidate, the Alhambra manager, Charles Penley, suggested that his secretary fill the part. She did so with considerable success and on the strength of such limited stage experience Penley recommended her to George Pearson, who gave her a small part in *Nothing Else Matters* (1920). Betty Balfour, whose first film it also was, had a similarly small role but between them the two young women stole the film from its star Moyna MacGill.[25] Poulton and Balfour were successfully paired again in *Mary-Find-the-Gold* (1921). As Nell in *The Old Curiosity Shop* (1921), Poulton's portrayal of the tragic heroine was said to be 'much less schmaltzy than she is often made out to be by those who scoff at Dickens for his sentimentality'.[26] Thomas Bentley's production was said to be 'a fine picture of Dickens ... above average ... a sure winner with most English audiences'.[27] The under-resourced Welsh-Pearson company to which Poulton and Balfour were under contract could not afford to produce enough films to keep the public appetite for the two young stars satisfied and attempts were made to find suitable vehicles for Poulton's talents among other production companies. She appeared in *The God in the Garden* (1921), directed by Edwin J. Collins for Master Films, and then disappeared from the British film industry for five years. Her 'steady rise in filmcraft', which culminated in the star part of Tessa in *The Constant Nymph* opposite Ivor Novello in 1928, was accomplished in France under the guidance of Marcel L'Herbier, who, after the success of *El Dorado* for Gaumont, set up his own production company, Cinegraphic, producing a series of films which were, stylistically, decades ahead of the pedestrian British products.[28]

Ivy Close was another actress ill-served by the British film industry; she appeared in a series of eminently forgettable films with titles to match: *The Irresistible Flapper, Expiation, A Peep Behind the Scenes* and *Was She Justified?* In *Nelson* (1918) she supported the stage star Malvina Longfellow but the film was not liked: there was 'no sustained interest ... little character drawing ... Nelson walks on in a few scenes, and dies in another.' Malvina Longfellow evidently 'did little more than pose' and Ivy Close's talents were ignored.[29] In *Darby and Joan* (1919) Ivy Close appeared in what was said to be 'nearly the greatest picture Britain has yet produced' but the acting plaudits went to Joan Ritz, 'as a servant girl ... she is almost the first actress we have observed in British pictures who has what the Americans call "picture sense"'.[30] Joan Ritz appeared in a production of *Hobson's Choice* noted for its copious sub-titles but little else.[31] Ivy Close went to France and was cast by Abel Gance in his mammoth production of *La Roue*. The film took more than a year to make and before extensive cutting ran for approximately eight hours. The extant version is said to be 'a unique fusion of French and Hollywood styles' and Ivy Close was enthusiastic in her praise of her director despite the exacting nature of her work with him.[32] If her film career was less than satisfactory, Ivy Close should be remembered for her direct and indirect influence on the subsequent development of the British film industry; her son Ronald Neame became one of the best cinematographers of the 1930s and 1940s and a polished if sometimes disappointing director thereafter, and Michael Powell, one of the few British directors possessed of a genuine sense of cinema, revealed that a publicity still of Ivy Close in *La Roue* first drew him to 'a life in movies'.[33]

Ivy Close began her film career after winning a *Daily Mirror* beauty competition;[34] Dora Lennox began her career in the same fashion but she was even less successful than Ivy Close despite the fact that one of her films, *Rogues of the Turf*, was featured in the British Film Weeks of 1924.[35] The society beauty Poppy Wyndham appeared in *The Tidal Wave*, an Ethel M. Dell adaptation, which was reviewed with some savagery: 'the acting is unconvincing and the continuity poor'.[36] Lillian Hall-Davis, another beauty queen, had a rather more consistent career during the 1920s, appearing in an average of at least two films a year throughout the decade. She worked on a number of Samuelson productions as well as the first Gainsborough film *The Passionate Adventure* (1924). She appeared in a wide variety of films from *The Right to Strike* (1923) to Marie Stopes' propagandist *Married Love* (1923), often exhibiting little more than her striking beauty and somewhat brittle charm.[37] Miriam Sabbage, who beat 50,000 other entrants to a £1,000 beauty competition judged by members of the Royal Academy, was featured in a Samuelson film, *The Bridal Chair* (1920);[38] a review of the film suggested that the acting was akin to musical comedy without the music.[39] Miriam Sabbage promptly disappeared from the screen. 'Brilliant acting' by Jessie Hackett in the stage production of *The Cinema Star* did not translate to a film career.[40] The dancer Eileen Dennis, whose chief claim to fame was a tour of America during which she performed a variation on Pavlova's 'Dying Swan', was a Hepworth player whose career faltered with the collapse of the producing company.[41]

Perhaps the most famous beauty to be lured into the world of film was Lady Diana Manners, the daughter of the Duke and Duchess of

Rutland. Her marriage to Alfred Duff Cooper, in 1919, had been the social event of the year, with huge crowds turning out to watch the wedding procession.[42] The pioneering English-born producer John Stuart Blackton, co-founder of the American Vitagraph Company, was in England to launch the Prizma colour process in which he had invested. The process worked in artificial lighting only if the actors were made-up to look bilious, but it functioned without any such cosmetic embellishment in natural lighting. To the accompaniment of much 'booming', Blackton chose Lady Diana to star as Lady Beatrice Fair, the heroine of *The Glorious Adventure* (1922); the Honorable Lois Stuart was also included among 'the hundred prettiest women in London' who were to decorate the historical extravaganza.[43] The practice of employing 'names' from the society columns in order to lend some cachet to a film was not the sole prerogative of visiting producers; Poppy Wyndham, the daughter of Lord Inchcape, was featured in a few Broadwest racing dramas, played the lead in the unfortunate adaptation of *The Tidal Wave* and was in *A Son of David* (1920), which was said to be the first film written, produced and acted by Jews.[44] Ideal engaged the Marchioness of Queensberry as one of their leading actresses in *Out to Win* (1923), directed by the American Denison Clift, and the Honorable Mrs Astley, sister-in-law of Lord Hastings, was featured in Stoll's *A Dear Fool* (1921).[45] This was said to be 'equal almost' to an American production and was publicized principally on the merits of its child star George K. Arthur, who had previously scored a success in *Kipps* and who subsequently worked in Hollywood.[46] Josie Collins' success in the most popular musical comedy of the time, *The Maid of the Mountains*, was said to have 'thrown her into the arms of Lord Robert Innes-Kerr';[47] she was unable to repeat a different kind of conquest on film. A review of *The Sword of Damocles* (1920), a vehicle for Collins, complained of her 'very bad' acting.[48]

A journalist visiting location filming of *The Glorious Adventure* described 'Commodore and Mrs. Blackton' directing the action from a high rostrum, and noted the problem that was something of a bogey for British producers working on location – lack of adequate natural light. Lady Diana Manners was described as 'highly satisfying to the eye; for hers is the crystalline, ethereal type of beauty that the camera loves'.[49] The film was said to contain 130 players, including Victor McLaglen as an athletic sub-hero and Gerald Lawrence as the juvenile lead, who was, according to Lady Diana, 'twenty five years older than me'; there were also London's prettiest as 'gyrating dancing girls'.[50] The climax of the film was a staging of the Great Fire of London, but even this event failed to ignite the enthusiasm of the public. The film was said to be slow, at times confusing, and ultimately 'not particularly involving'.[51] Blackton featured Lady Diana in another extravagantly mounted historical pageant, *The Virgin Queen* (1923), which was apparently full of 'grotesque anachronisms' and which, again, failed to interest British cinema audiences.[52] Press coverage of the film praised Lady Diana for her courage in shaving off her eyebrows for her portrayal of Queen Elizabeth I, and even the sight of her daughter sporting a red wig could not dent the Duchess of Rutland's maternal delight. A more jaded commentator 'couldn't understand the world-wide admiration' for Lady Diana's beauty and acting talents.[53] It is also pertinent to note the star's comment with regard to Blackton's status as a film-maker, and the reason for his presence in England: 'Hollywood had risen above Mr. Blackton.'[54] Audience expectation had also left Blackton's talents severely exposed: 'Year by year, the public is demanding better and better stories and year by year, it is showing its inability to be entertained by mere spectacle or lavishness of mounting.'[55]

Another noted beauty to feature prominently during the 1920s was Ivy Duke; she usually appeared with her husband Guy Newall in Home Counties dramas, and on occasion her acting was praised for being 'exceptionally good'.[56] She was also described as 'one of the most memorable personalities on the screen'.[57] Reviewing *The Bigamist* (1921) – costing in excess of £51,000 to produce and regarded as 'the most ambitious British picture yet made' – a critic described Ivy Duke as 'beautifully statuesque'. A clue to her screen persona is to be gained from the comment 'she shows more emotional power than her previous work had led us to expect'.[58] *Kine Monthly* advised bookers to view *The Bigamist* before committing themselves to its rental as it was 'tiresome'.[59] The London reviewer for *Variety* noted that Ivy Duke's performance opposite Lionel Barrymore in *Decameron Nights* (1924) was 'without feeling or expression'; she was, the review continued, 'content to pose with artificial beauty which by no means fits the part', and it would appear that many producers and directors of the period were of the opinion that the presentation of a beautiful face and figure compensated for any deficiency in acting ability.[60]

Ena Beaumont was featured in a number of 'health and beauty' shorts as well as in a few feature films made by the Garrick Company, in which she was a partner. As one of Ally Soper's bevy of bathing beauties she was described as

> a typical British girl … an ardent devotee of punting and skulling. Riding, boxing, and dance also figure amongst the athletic pursuits of this vivacious British screen actress. No doubt the open-air life she leads has done much to develop her perfect figure, the proportions of which are remarkably similar to those of Venus de Milo.[61]

Beaumont may well have looked good in 'the role of a little girl in short skirts and socks', but in *Patricia Brent, Spinster* (1919) her performance engendered inappropriate laughter. A critic observed that 'the general note is one of exaggeration … comparable to a fantasia played fortissimo all through', with the acting types more reminiscent of 'Victorian farce than Bayswater "gentility"'.[62]

The critic James Corbett, in an article entitled 'English Girls on the Screen', was certain that 'America cannot eclipse England in the matter of beautiful girls. Our actresses only want a chance to express their real selves on the screen.' His criticism of English actresses was that their technique was inappropriate to the medium; that 'the English cinema actress is not at ease on the screen. Any tendency to abandon or to impulsive movement seems to conform to an overpowering cast technique.' What Corbett meant by 'cast technique' was the stereotyping of actresses to particular parts. With the majority of parts conforming to drawing-room stereotypes, this would appear to be a self-evident observation.[63] Alma Taylor and Chrissie White were regarded, by their respective producers Hepworth and Henry Edwards, and by journalists and the public alike, as quintessentially English. Their screen image was, therefore, thought to correspond to their off-screen personalities. Both started their careers with Hepworth before the war playing the 'Tilly Girls', a couple of mischievous Cockneys, but by the 1920s their position as embodiments of all that was best about being an English 'lady' was entrenched. A poem written for Chrissie White is succinctly titled 'An English Blossom'; the writer expresses pride in the fact that she is 'ours' and refers to the star as 'the sweetest of English flowers'.[64] In another poem, written in praise of Alma Taylor, the sentiments are located in a shared cultural identity, one that was exploited by the Ideal company among others, which filmed interviews with British celebrities to be shown as short subjects with the title *Our Own People*.[65]

My heroine is English born,
Blue-eyes and fair of face;
In sweetness like a summer morn,
A girl of winsome grace.
There may be girls as lovely, yet
Their names I can't recall,
But one name I shall not forget –
'Our Alma' beats them all![66]

By the end of the Great War both performers were of an age which precluded them from playing ingenue or gamine parts; consequently their publicity photographs portrayed them as County types, dressed in clothing suitable for riding or gardening, which was apposite, as between them they had cornered the British market in country heroines. They both looked eminently suited to playing the hero's sensible sister or the society hostess, although one journalist noted that Alma Taylor had 'never quite shaken off the influence of twice playing the heroine in Comin' thro' the Rye'.[67] It appears that there was almost an embargo on criticism of their acting and an assumption that if they were in a film some guarantee as to its quality was implicit. Of *Wild Heather* (1921) a reviewer noted the 'remarkable instance of Chrissie White's advance in her art', but as the actress had been making films for at least twelve years there must be some room for debate as to the previous standard of her acting.[68] It was left to non-British critics to cast aspersions on, for instance, the acting in the 1923 remake of *Comin' thro' the Rye*: 'actors walk right up to the camera as in the old days and make faces at it, showing plainly they have too much make-up on.' This was, it should be stated in mitigation of Alma Taylor's performance, 'especially true of the men'.[69] Between 1918 and 1924 Alma Taylor appeared in seventeen films, sixteen of them directed by Hepworth; because of the slump in the mid-1920s she disappeared from the screen until 1926, when Hepworth directed *The House of Marney* for the Nettlefold company, which had taken over the studios he had once owned. Intermittent work followed without her career reaching the peak it had sustained before and immediately after the war. In the same period (1918 to 1924) Chrissie White appeared in eighteen films, all of them for the Hepworth Company and all but one directed by her partner 'Tedwards'. The only film in which she did not act with, or was not directed by, Henry Edwards was *Wild Heather*, directed by Hepworth himself. Chrissie

White's film career did not survive Hepworth's failure; she and her partner forsook the screen for the stage, although Edwards later returned to film acting, and directing, with some success.[70]

Great attention was said to be paid by British producers and directors to technique, characterization and mode of conduct, with conduct presumably reflecting middle-class mores, and technique invariably that of the stage.[71] Time after time stage stars were given the opportunity to display their much-touted talents on screen and equally as often their efforts fell far short of American standards. The stage phenomenon Meggie Albanesi, for whom George Pearson appears to have had more regard than his most popular star Betty Balfour, appeared in a handful of films without unduly impressing the general public or critics;[72] in *The Great Day* (1920) she shared the acting honours with Geoffrey Kerr although her performance was regarded as 'below average' by another reviewer.[73] She evidently failed to impress the critics in *Darby and Joan*; as previously noted, Joan Ritz received the acting plaudits for her small role in Percy Nash's production.[74]

Another darling of the West End, Mary Glynne, would have had her name 'blazoned forth throughout the country a moving-picture star of the greatest magnitude had she lived in America' according to *Cinema Chat*,[75] although it was her performance in *Candytuft, I Mean Veronica* (1921) which prompted one critic to write:

> The acting ... serves to strike home a truism, that stage artistes are seldom able to show their ability on the silent screen, Mary Glynne does little more than look pretty ... Candytuft, I Mean Veronica is yet another example of the foolishness of employing expensive stage casts and thinking that their names, despite the fact that they are unknown outside London, will get a thin, badly produced, poorly acted story over. This film is without interest, strength, or humour, although the latter element might be said to be represented by a comic servant and a backboneless clergyman. It is without appeal, but it will not cause a single blush to rise to the cheeks of the most maidenly of prudes.[76]

In *The Call of Youth* (1920), which was said to have an 'exceptionally strong name cast', the acting, including that of Mary Glynne, was said to be 'bad'.[77] Perhaps Glynne's lack of finesse was not all her fault; in the hands of a seasoned professional such as Donald Crisp, who had worked in America with D. W. Griffith, her performance as *The Princess of New York* (1921) was said to provide 'proof of the hidden talent which her British producers have failed to discover'.[78]

There were numerous attempts to 'boom' British stars, with the inevitable epithets to match; Alma Taylor had long since tired of being called 'the English Mary Pickford' and readily admitted that the characters she played bore little resemblance to those portrayed by 'the world's sweetheart';[79] Joan Lockton was also called 'the English Mary Pickford';[80] Queenie Thomas and Mary Dibley were both accorded the status of Queen of the Screen;[81] Joan Morgan – daughter of the director Sidney Morgan – was praised as an 'embryonic Ellen Terry' but her performance in *The Great Well* (1924) was described as 'utterly negligible'.[82] The fact that Miss Morgan could knit and read at the same time was, apparently, something to be said in her favour.[83] Constance Worth, although a West End favourite, prompted a reviewer to enquire as to the nature of her 'artificial facial expressions' in *Fate's Plaything* (1920),[84] and Dorothy Minto, in *The Glad Eye* (1920), participated in a display of what was described as 'a bewildering variety of styles'.[85] Reviewing *The Eleventh Commandment* (1924) a critic noted that 'it was a good example of the problem play treated with decorum ... essentially British and free from nastiness'; he was, however, disconcerted by the performance of one of the players: 'Louise Hampton is something of an enigma ... It is impossible to tell whether she is utterly broken down with grief or merely suffering from the primary stages of some peculiar form of facial paralysis.'[86] The critic and script-writer Langford Reed outlined the reason why so many West End favourites failed to please audiences beyond that limited area: 'The close-up brings the face of the artist so intimately before the Kinema audience that every shade of expression is recorded ... It is the inability to appreciate this fact that has made so many of our big stage stars utter failures in the film.'[87]

There were some stars who possessed screen charisma, but, as with a number of male performers, the British industry simply provided a launching pad for Hollywood. There were a good many close-ups in *The Guns of Loos* (1928), possibly because it was Madeleine Carroll's first feature film and her face photographed well.[88] Later she was more than just a glamorous match for Robert Donat in the classic *The Thirty-nine Steps*, but the 1930s found her in Hollywood. Gladys Cooper was, according to the painter Edward Burne-Jones, 'the perfect living type of golden-hair Anglo-Saxon loveliness' and she played opposite Ivor Novello in two successful films, *The Bohemian Girl* (1924) and *Bonnie*

Prince Charlie (1923). She, however, was of the opinion that 'Film acting is a purely impersonal affair, regulated by producers and photographers. Apparently anyone can be made into a film star, but it is certain that no-one can be "made" into a stage star', and she preferred to display her talents on the stage. Ironically, when her stage career and beauty were eclipsed by younger performers, Cooper made the transition to films with the minimum of fuss, sustaining a long and honorable career in Hollywood.[89]

In 1920, on the strength of a secondary role in George Pearson's *Nothing Else Matters*, the seventeen-year-old Betty Balfour was immediately designated 'the Cinema Star Supreme'; the film was said to contain 'wonderful acting by Betty Balfour as the servant-girl', and was praised for being 'in most respects the most notable film of the year'.[90] The acting was said to be 'excellent and the theme, though slightly conventional in detail, is certain to appeal to the public'.[91] The film was rooted in truly popular culture, being a story about a *ménage à trois* comprising a music-hall star, his wife and a playwright. Betty Balfour was inevitably subjected to the usual comparisons, as she noted in an autobiographical sketch penned for a newspaper: 'Am I George Robey, Charlie Chaplin, Cissie Loftus, or Mary Pickford? I have been described as each in my time.'[92] In one aspect of her career Betty Balfour followed a similar path to Mary Pickford. During the formative part of her career Pickford played a variety of 'poor hard-done-by girls', most of them valiantly working-class,[93] just as Balfour specialized in 'skivvy roles – flower-sellers, kitchen maids and Whitechapel debutantes',[94] with a number of scenarios constructed so as to portray her as a drudge, more often than not working in a cheap boarding-house for a harsh London landlady.[95] In the part of Sally in *Nothing Else Matters* she was made up to appear ugly and slovenly but the director Pearson noticed that 'as soon as she smiled her face became transfigured, and all her ugliness disappeared'. Sensing she had 'tremendous possibilities', Pearson added a close-up of Balfour's smile to the end of the film and it was that one shot that 'evoked more applause than anything else, and it is no exaggeration to say that it definitely marked the turning point in her career'.[96]

Betty Balfour's first stage role was at St Andrew's Hall, Kensington, where, as 'a maid of all work' in *Ali Baba and the Forty Thieves*, she included an impersonation of the music-hall star Vesta Tilley in her performance. She was spotted by the revue producer J. L. Davies, and later by C. B. Cochran, and performed regularly in revues and light comedy productions in London. When she was thirteen she starred in a solo revue at the Coliseum, under the auspices of Cochran, which was followed by an eleven-month tour of the country in *All Women*, a revue entirely performed by women. T. A. Welsh, one half of the Welsh-Pearson Company, remembered Balfour at the Ambassadors Theatre in 1915 and offered her a part in *Nothing Else Matters*. The actress noted the connection between her first stage performance and her first film: 'I had been maid-of-all work in the pantomime – I was maid-of-all-work in this film, too. I seemed fated to mix with pots and pans!' and it was in such roles, set in a milieu familiar to working-class film-goers, that 'she went straight to the hearts of every member of the audience'.[97] It was said that 'she alone personified what the British public wanted', that no other British star possessed her charisma. That the essence of her films was sentimentality, that they were simply stories told with a minimum of fuss, were sufficient to elevate her, in a British poll, to 'Top World Star' of 1924; an achievement of some note given the Hollywood opposition.[98]

When Balfour made *Somebody's Darling* for G. A. Cooper in 1925, it was commented that this was her first 'society picture'; given the previous discussion of the themes particular to the majority of British films, it is of considerable interest that Betty Balfour's career was so dissimilar to that of other British artists.[99] A series of films in which she played a Cockney flower-seller named Squibs quickly consolidated her position as the most important cinema star working in Britain in the early 1920s; *Squibs* was released in 1921, *Squibs Wins the Calcutta Sweep* in 1922, and *Squibs M.P.* and *Squibs' Honeymoon* were released in 1923. George Pearson realized after the success of *Nothing Else Matters*, and the comparative failure of *Mary-Find-the-Gold* (1921), featuring Betty Balfour and Mabel Poulton, that there was a problem with regard to finding suitable material for his star. *Mary-Find-the-Gold* was one of many films of the period in which a young woman was rescued from a precarious city existence by a country sweetheart, but what audiences appeared to want was a screen heroine capable of looking after herself. Balfour's screen persona suited the demands of working-class audiences. She was cheeky, irrepressible; she appeared to be enjoying herself and 'her mobile features, her vivacious gestures, and her natural bent for mimicry' caught the public's imagination.[100] A letter from a 'disappointed picture-goer' highlighted not only Betty Balfour's appeal to audiences but also the lack of appeal which characterized many of the other British film performers of the time:

At the pictures we like to see people giving full play to their emotions ... we like to see the characters in a picture excited when the picture itself gets exciting. In British films they don't; they remain perfect ladies and gentlemen right through the piece. Betty Balfour is the only British film actress who really lets herself go. She is the only British film actress who has attained anything approaching genuine stardom. The moral is obvious.[101]

Given the individuality of Balfour's talent, George Pearson chose to look beyond the usual sources of material for properties suited to her temperament and potential appeal. Pearson was one of the few directors of the period who believed that the medium of film required more than adaptations of plays and popular novels if it was to become an art form in its own right: 'I had a desperate longing for story-matter written directly for the screen medium, not for matter that needed adaptation from another medium.'[102] In the programme notes for the trade show of *Nothing Else Matters*, Pearson stated that the film's scenario had been 'designed for the screen, and the screen only. It makes no claim to literary merit. Whatever merit it may have will depend entirely upon the success it attains in arousing the emotions it aims at stirring', and this attitude to film production set Pearson apart from those producers who were content to transfer stage successes to the screen with little or no adjustment to the new medium.[103]

The scenario Pearson wrote, with Eliot Stannard, concerned the adventures of a Cockney flower-seller in Piccadilly Circus. Her boyfriend was a slow but steady policeman and her father a shady street-corner 'bookie'. Pearson wanted the action and humour to emerge naturally from the potential conflict between Balfour's boyfriend and father, with Balfour acting as catalyst. Pearson's cinematic *raison d'être* was to 'capture life, being lived, not plotted', and this was to give his films with Balfour a sense of reality which was communicated to enthusiastic audiences.[104] How Balfour's character was developed depended, initially, on how it was defined:

Comedy was essential, the humour of the ordinary folk, the laughter of the hard-working people. By sheer luck there was a music hall sketch running that had as chief character a jolly and brazen girl who typified the sort of daredevil our Betty might impersonate. The sketch material was unsuitable to our purpose, but the title suggested much of value. We obtained the right to use it – and nothing more – Squibs![105]

The trade showing of *Squibs* was an enormous success and almost as soon as the film was released there was a demand for more films featuring the same character. *Squibs* was said to be 'the best British film for a very long time, with a real touch of genius in its characterisation and some excellent acting ... Real entertainment and first-class business.'[106] The depiction of working-class life owed not a little to Pearson's predilection for seeing 'life through rose-tinted spectacles' but Balfour made Squibs a 'real character ... and she moved among real characters in a real cockney atmosphere'.[107] Balfour's own admiration for the character she played – 'good-natured, witty, and so thoroughly self-reliant'[108] – undoubtedly imbued the part with sincerity. Pett Ridge wrote the story for another Balfour vehicle, *Mord Em'ly* (1922). He was a novelist with a Dickensian approach to his subject matter and his treatment of working-class life was undeniably sentimental, but he acknowledged its humour and resilience and recognized that living conditions were instrumental in forming what middle-class commentators (and the film industry) regarded as less than desirable character traits. He defended 'lack of deference' among the working class; he defended them against the charge that they were 'loafers'; and he praised the independence of young working women, noting that he had heard 'factory girls describe a play or a film, and give the plot more vividly and more accurately than any dramatic critic'.[109]

Betty Balfour's success may also have had something to do with the fact that she excelled at comedy, a genre undervalued and often derided by British critics. Replying to a request from a reader as to where to send comedy scripts, a magazine editor wrote, 'I am afraid I cannot call to mind any company producing comedies in this country.'[110] This was not entirely accurate, as there were companies, such as Pollack-Daring, which specialized in comedy films; one of its 1919 productions, *Jack, Sam and Pete*, was said to be of 'extraordinary quality',[111] although another reviewer was equally certain that it was 'melodrama of the most lurid type ... the stunts have been used times without number from time immemorial [and] the story is of the "blood" type which has long adorned the counters of stationers' shops, and whose readers will doubtless welcome this picturisation of their pet literature with delight'.[112]

Once Aboard the Lugger (1920), the first film produced by the actor Gerald Ames, was said to be a 'fine British comedy'[113] and Hepworth's *Alf's Button* (1920) engendered laudatory notices for its star: 'There are probably very few artistes (perhaps no English one) who can so well express what they mean by gesture, added to facial expression, as can Leslie Henson.'[114] Given such praise, it is of some note that Henson made only two other films during the decade. The negative review of *Jack, Sam and Pete* reeks of snobbery and anticipates the view 'that England should lift the picture business out of the mire and make it an institution like the Royal Academy'. Arguing against such opinions one commentator derided 'directors [who] have actually told me that they do not consider comedy to be an art'; citing Chaplin and others, he noted that comedy made for success, and went on to say: 'I do not ever remember seeing a funny British film, excepting Betty Balfour, who is in a class of her own.'[115]

It is, therefore, all the more extraordinary, given the anti-comedy cultural bias, that Betty Balfour achieved the success she did; it should also have been a lesson to other producers whose solid, middle-class films, featuring types rather than characters, failed to reach audiences in the way Balfour's films were able to do. What Pearson and Balfour created on screen epitomized a particular strand of national identity; a cliché perhaps, even patronizing, but the working-class heroine, the quirky, cheeky, put-upon girl whose spirit refused to be broken, tapped into the aspirations and preferences of British audiences. Among the many poems written in praise of Balfour the following gives some indication of the rapport which existed between the characters she played on screen and those who viewed them; it also underscores the fact that British audiences were receptive to British stars, in British films, when there was a sharing of values, an under-scoring of connecting identities which added significance to the epithet 'our Betty':

B is for Betty and B is for Balfour,
B is for Blue eyes and Blink eyes as well;
B is for Breathless, her daring adventure,
B is for Britain, of which she is Belle.
B is for Brains and for Blonde hair and Beauty,
And then a big B for she Beats all the rest.
B is for Betty and B is for Balfour,
B is for Beautiful, British and Best.[116]

3

Roles for Men: 'Gentlemen ... right through'

C ommenting on the 1926 Paramount production of *Beau Geste*, which had been named 'Film of the Year' in America, *The Times* reminded its readers that the book upon which the film was based was by the British writer P. C. Wren, that Herbert Brenon, the director, had been born in Dublin and that the cast included Ronald Colman, Victor McLaglen, Ralph Forbes, Donald Stuart and Norman Trevor, all of whom were British.[1] The British film industry was responsible for launching the careers of scores of actors who would then flee to California to make or sustain a career in an industry which was unable to support their talents or their aspirations at home. This did not only apply to actors whose names are still recognized by cinema-goers all over the world; it seemed that almost any actor who gave an indication of talent could rely on an American producer to offer him a contract. Pardoe Woodman, whose brief appearances in adaptations of popular novels by Ethel M. Dell and E. Phillips Oppenheim can scarcely have constituted an auspicious career foundation, especially since he had the misfortune to appear in *The Tidal Wave* (1920) of which it was said the 'waves are the best part of the film',[2] was said to have 'received an offer from Los Angeles'.[3] American producers, 'with their usual foresight', were said to be 'tempting Gerald MacCarthy' to join the ranks of highly salaried British film actors who had been decoyed across 'the Herring

Pond'. Gerald MacCarthy was praised for remaining loyal to 'the British companies from whom, he admits, he learnt most of his screencraft'.[4] The few films he made were for Stoll and Ideal, and given the pedestrian nature of much of their product, it is likely that his cinematic education was rather basic. He appeared in *Demos*, directed by the American Denison Clift, which was said to be a 'first-class' production; his acting in the film was also praised but British films failed to provide him with anything but a transitory and less than brilliant career.[5]

The most unlikely of performers made their way across the Atlantic: the veteran actor Bertram Burleigh returned empty-handed from California and in a display of pique announced the death of the star system.[6] Even that most English of English actors, Stewart Rome, ventured to Hollywood when he was approaching forty.[7] Hayford Hobbs tried, unsuccessfully, to find 'real live businessmen who will pay tempting salaries to artists' – presumably he wished to be tempted.[8] Many British performers also fell victim to Hollywood's often fickle taste for actors and types. After noteworthy performances in *Kipps* (1921) and *The Wheels of Chance* (1922), the diminutive George K. Arthur, no doubt carrying copies of the novels H. G. Wells presented to him 'in astonishment', went to Hollywood, where he worked with Josef von Sternberg on *The Salvation Hunters*, but little else of note.[9] Some questions must be raised as to the extent of his talent and the applicability of his acting style given a review of *Love's Influence* (1922): 'George K. Arthur as the hero shows no dramatic ability and his expressions are for the most part purely facial contortions.' The film was a polemic about the evils of acquired money, which led to 'drink' which, in turn, led to the heinous crime of 'taking women out'. *Variety* expressed the opinion that the film's 'chief charm is that audiences witnessing it can sleep without hindrance'.[10] At the age of sixteen Ralph Forbes starred in *The Fifth Form at St Dominic's* (1921), a public school drama about lost examination papers, school and personal honour. Forbes was 'tall, good-looking … he should develop into a handsome screen idol in future years'.[11] He went to Hollywood, where he was appropriately cast in Brenon's *Beau Geste*, after which he reprised his 'typical Englishman' role in a number of mock-English productions: *Smilin' Through*, *The Barretts of Wimpole Street*, *Elizabeth and Essex* and the Lon Chaney version of *Mr Wu*. During lean periods he reworked his *Beau Geste* persona in lower-case adventures for less than successful production companies, as he did for Monogram in *Legion of Missing Men*.[12]

Granger-Davidson advertised *The Sport of Kings* (1922) under a British bulldog logo with the caption, 'Presenting the Renowned Actor Sportsman, Victor McLaglen: British to the Core and proud of it!'[13] After serving a brief sentence as 'the British Douglas Fairbanks' McLaglen left for Hollywood, and considerable success. The title of his autobiography sums up the career paths of many actors of the period: *Express to Hollywood*.[14] McLaglen was described as a 'breezy, agile young screen actor ... boxer, wrestler, swimmer, horseman, fencer and strong man'.[15] His robust appearances in such films as *The Call of the Road* (1920) and *Corinthian Jack* (1921), which were said to be 'old-fashioned',[16] 'a long way from being a masterpiece',[17] prompted one critic to rhyme, 'more in sorrow than in anger':

A man who's been a pugilist and served behind a bar,
Is just the chap they're looking for to make a film star.[18]

McLaglen's journey to Hollywood was accomplished by way of Blackton's *The Glorious Adventure* (1922) and Gainsborough's *The Passionate Adventure* (1924);[19] other actors of his type were less successful. Reviewing the imported *The Climber*, a critic noted that 'realistic boxing ring scenes appeal to a large public',[20] and there does appear to have been a vogue for films featuring boxers. *The Wonder Man* (1921), starring Georges Carpentier, was said to be 'a good business proposition for showmen',[21] and Bombardier Billy Wells appeared in a handful of films in which his pugilistic expertise was the principal attraction. An American action-man, Charles Hutchinson, was imported to add some variety to Stoll's programme, but his 'thrill-a-minute' adventures were unlikely to create more than a ripple on the lake of that company's stolid output.[22]

In an article in *Cinema Chat* entitled 'Stars That Shine Today', no mention is made of British actors, which, given the fact that the magazine was overtly pro-British, suggests an acceptance of the failure of the British industry to respond to the encouragement it, and other magazines, provided.[23] In another article, entitled 'The Race for the Hero Championship', written later in the decade, Ronald Colman and Ivor Novello were listed as British competitors, although Colman was already working in Hollywood and Novello's fame can hardly be attributed to the British film industry as the films that made him a star were French and American.[24]

The actor Langhorne Burton was said to be the highest salaried British film star in 1921; this may well have been so because he regularly worked for the British arm of Famous Players-Lasky. Burton was then approaching fifty years of age and was far from the 'heroic' type.[25] Another mature thespian, Sir John Martin-Harvey, condescended to parade his histrionic talents before the cameras and was rewarded with a glowing review for the repetition of his stage triumph in *The Breed of the Treshams* (1920), a spy story set in the period of Roundheads and Cavaliers: 'a very good first film, in which a stage star is exploited in a part into which his mannerisms fit so naturally that most of his qualifications usually necessary in discussing a stage player's screen work are uncalled for'.[26] The film was directed by Kenelm Foss, who had strong views about the casting of films: 'he believes in fitting the actor to the part, regardless of the fame or importance, and holds that in film work it is of the first importance that your characters should be appropriately cast.'[27] This statement runs contrary to practice, as in the case of Martin-Harvey, who was approaching sixty when he played Sydney Carton in *The Only Way* (1925), a Dickens adaptation which had been written for the stage. More pertinent were the comments made by Jameson Thomas regarding the reality of acting in British films: 'If one wants to live by playing in British films it is better to be miscast than never be cast at all.'[28] This can hardly have endowed British films, and British heroes, with anything approaching the verve, veracity or appeal of their American counterparts.

Such was the nature of British production, and its reliance on the West End stage for film-players, that one of the most persistent criticisms of British films concerned the inappropriate acting style, or styles, of its leading men. There were those who made the transition from stage to screen with the minimum of fuss, most of them, it should be noted, in Hollywood, which appears to have lacked the stage-centred cultural bias so noticeable in London. Clive Brook worked regularly in British films during the 1920s but it was Hollywood that brought him fame; it was remarked that 'England never properly appreciated him.'[29] Hayford Hobbs, in *When it was Dark* (1919), was praised for resisting 'any temptation to be theatrically effective and is, instead, far more forceful by being consistently natural throughout'; the temptation to decamp to a more lucrative environment was too strong to resist and by 1923 Hobbs was in Hollywood.[30] There were numerous other stage stars of eminent reputation who failed to accommodate their high-octane mummery to the screen; of Arthur Wontner, in *Eugene Aram* (1924), it was noted, 'to be a West End legitimate leading man is one thing, to get it over on the silent screen is another'.[31] The acting of the star of *The Great Day* (1920) was similarly criticized: 'however fine an actor Arthur Bourchier is on the legitimate stage, he quickly proves, like so many other legitimate artists, that the studio is no place for him. He is given to over-emphasis and a persistent rolling of eyes.'[32] The middle-aged Henry Ainley, who passed himself off as a hero behind the foot-lights with the aid of heavy make-up, was another stage star whose screen presence was less than effective:

> those who have served a long apprenticeship before the footlights very often over-act in front of the cameras. This is a criticism which is levelled at Henry Ainley, who is starring in the film ver-sion of Money. The famous British actor is not so at home on the screen as he is on the stage.[33]

In the 1924 *Daily News* poll which Betty Balfour topped as favourite British film star, Matheson Lang was the highest-placed British actor. Lang was not entirely comfortable working in the film industry; his entry in *Who's Who in the Theatre* failed to mention his film work, although that may well have been simply to do with the nature of the publication itself.[34] Elsewhere he voiced the opinion that 'it was still considered a little "infra dig" for a leading actor to play in a film and I had been one of the first actor-managers to do so'. Although his ambivalent attitude to film acting did not bode well for his actual performances, a number of productions in which he was featured were accorded considerable praise.

Lang's initial experience of film came in 1916 with the Broadwest Company, which transported the entire stage cast of *The Merchant of Venice* to studios in Walthamstow, and photographed the play, mostly by natural light, in a glass-roofed studio. Lang's first big success was a screen version of a role he had played on the London stage before the war, *Mr Wu* (1919). On stage he had worn a wig for the part, but the director, Maurice Elvey, insisted that his head be shaved for the cameras.[35] Elvey was praised for being 'a master of detail' and the film was said to be 'without a doubt the finest production we have seen from a British studio for a long time'. Furthermore, the critic noted, 'it is difficult to believe that we are watching British players acting in England'.[36] The success of *Mr Wu* seems to have entrenched Lang's penchant for over-blown characterizations, complete with heavy make-up, which he would repeat throughout the decade in films such as *A*

Romance of Old Baghdad, Henry, King of Navarre, The Wandering Jew and *The Chinese Bungalow*. In common with other recruits from the stage, Lang was in his forties when he played dashing characters like Dick Turpin and Guy Fawkes; he noted that the horse playing Black Bess in *Dick Turpin's Ride to York* (1922) was, like her rider, a seasoned stage performer – she had spent most of her life playing the same part in a stage play of the same name.[37] In his fiftieth year Lang played the swashbuckling hero of *The Triumph of the Scarlet Pimpernel* (1928), and it is not surprising that a director he later worked with revealed that the actor thought it time he was 'modernized'.[38]

Carnival (1921) afforded Matheson Lang the opportunity to reach an international audience. He had co-written the play on which the film was based, had starred in its London production, and it was filmed by a competent director, Harley Knoles, who had directed, among other films in America, a version of James Barrie's play *Shall We Join the Ladies?* Knoles, it was said, was 'somehow not at home in British studios' and it is to his credit that the film was a considerable success.[39] On completing it, Knoles personally took the film to America and sold it, securing a distribution deal with Universal.[40] The film was given a special exhibition at the New York super-theatre, the Capitol – 'an honour reserved for films of exceptional merit'.[41] The play on which the film was based had been a failure when staged in New York but an American review said of the film: 'It can be put down as a success of a high order. If this should turn out to be the case it will probably be the first British-made photo-play to win its laurels in this country.'[42] The plot of the film, which has been repeated many times, concerns an actor playing Othello who becomes convinced that his real-life Desdemona is being unfaithful to him; once more Matheson Lang, as the Moor of Venice, was able to use his beloved stage make-up. He received high praise for his performance – 'Lang as the jealous actor, is splendid' – and a Chicago critic advised American producers that 'they would do well to view this picture for plot and acting; both are splendid', but he was less charitable about the technical aspects of the film itself: 'the photography is rather poor, the settings impossible and the direction, well – typically foreign'.[43] Evidently, working in Europe, and the fact that he had found some difficulty in adjusting to English studio conditions, had led Knoles to imbue the film with a foreign 'look' which was readily discernible.

Despite his success, and his evident prestige in Britain, it would be difficult to regard Matheson Lang as a screen hero; the parts he played were often of heroic proportions but his appeal was of a totally different kind from that of a Chaplin, a Fairbanks or a Novarro, or even a Clive Brook or Basil Rathbone, who had begun to capture some of the playboy and 'cad' roles in British pictures.[44] With Hollywood taking the cream of Britain's young acting talent, the absence of a bank of young actors must have had some influence on the kind of films being made, the roles in the films and the appearance of the films themselves. In *Carnival* Matheson Lang was supported by Ivor Novello, who was the only British actor with a West End base to approach international stardom during this period; of Novello's performance in *Carnival*, *Variety* wrote: 'Novello ... is the best-looking villain ever on the screen, anywhere. He acts his role in a sympathetic, understanding manner.'[45] Like Lang, Ivor Novello was more of a performer than an actor in the classical mould, and his role in *The Call of the Blood*, in 1920, was, at the age of twenty-seven, his first professional acting assignment of any kind.[46] Louis Mercanton, a director whose name is inevitably linked to his 1912 production of *Elisabeth Reine d'Angleterre*, made in London with Sarah Bernhardt,[47] hired Novello on seeing his photograph.[48] Mercanton's hunch that Novello's face would suit the camera was proved right; a review of *The Call of the Blood* noted, 'there is no doubt in my mind that Mr Novello will in a very short time become a film favourite, for he has the face for the screen'.[49] Sarah Bernhardt was quoted as saying *The Call of the Blood* was the best film she had ever seen,[50] and *Kine Monthly* used the film to highlight the advantages cinema possessed in relation to theatre: 'What the stage has never done, and never could do ... is to convey the atmosphere of another zone of the world ... the wonderful scenery and startling scenic effects made an extraordinary appeal to the eye ... [the film] enhances the standard of screen art, and must add to the reputation of any Kinema which shows it.'[51] The same publication commented on 'the remarkable fidelity of the acting';[52] another viewer noticed that Novello was the only cast member to be convincingly Italian – the film was set in Italy[53] – and a coterie of Lords, Ladies and foreign diplomats turned out for the private showing of the film that would spark the Novello phenomenon.[54]

Miarka (1920), again directed by Mercanton, was Novello's next film and it was recommended by *Kine Weekly* 'because of the names of Mercanton and Novello'.[55] With Harley Knoles directing, Novello made *Carnival* (1921) and *The Bohemian Girl* (1922). American reviews of *The Bohemian Girl* were ecstatic; the *New York Evening Mail* assured its readers that 'Ivor Novello gives every indication of becoming another Valentino'; he was described as 'a Greek God who is both handsome and an intelligent actor', and his performance was admired for its 'admirable dignity and restraint'. Novello was contracted to D. W. Griffith at the time and with Griffith's company maximizing the attention being paid him, *The Bohemian Girl* became one of the most popular foreign movies shown in America. Novello's next film was for Griffith, *The White Rose*, and he again received excellent notices. It is illuminating to note that Novello, a novice actor, had reached a position where he was lauded as 'one of the greatest new screen personalities of the year' without his having served a stage-based apprenticeship, and without working with a British director.[56] His first film for a British director was a fortunate choice; *The Man Without Desire* (1923) was supervised by Adrian Brunel, who had a reputation for a light touch and skilful story construction. His work with Leslie Howard, under the banner of Minerva Films, was a serious attempt to raise the standard of British films, although one review of *The Man Without Desire* noticed that 'detail has not worried Brunel too much at times'.[57] *The Times* considered that 'Novello's acting sets the seal on a great achievement by Brunel', and despite the morbidity of the story, about a man who had lived for 200 years, the film was said to have been 'saved by its sincerity and the enthusiasm of all concerned'.[58]

Because of distribution problems, *The Man Without Desire*, *The White Rose* and Novello's second film for a British director, *Bonnie Prince Charlie*, were released within weeks of each other. *Bonnie Prince Charlie* (1923) was a virtuoso part for a young actor and Novello was possibly the only British actor capable of playing the role with any conviction. The director, Captain C. C. Calvert, was a journeyman director who had briefly appeared before the cameras, made documentaries, and was apt to produce old-fashioned films; the nature of the films he made was reflected in reviews: *Walls of Prejudice* (1920) was said to be 'sentimentality of the most hackneyed kind' and *In His Grip* (1921) was described as 'rather slow for popular audience', but showed 'pretty Scottish scenes and good technique'.[59] Although Novello's popularity soared – at the height of the 'Novello Boom' he was, according to *Picture Show*, receiving in excess of 2,000 fan letters a week[60] – there were those who appeared to resent his success. One commentator rather waspishly referred to him as being 'overtly pretty ... his gestures at times remind one of a highly hysterical girl', although stills from *The Man Without Desire* display a real sense of drama and a face spectacularly suited to the demands of the camera.[61] Another reviewer, contrasting the real-life heroics seen in the documentary *Crossing the Great Sahara* with Novello's reel-antics, commented, with some sarcasm, on the nature of fame: 'Hero worship is a strange thing. The most idolised man in London today is Ivor Novello, whose exploits consist of looking well in a uniform, composing indifferent music and acting incompetently.'[62] What appears to have been ill-disguised homophobia did little to dent Novello's popularity and he was the only British male film star to approach true stardom during this period. Even after the collapse of British film production in 1924, *Picture Show Annual* rated Novello and Betty Balfour as stars with drawing power comparable to that of American stars.[63]

Another actor with a reputation for playing the young hero was Owen Nares. He was in his early thirties and usually played juvenile leads in West End productions to some effect: 'his heart-vibrating love-making ... has enthroned him in the hearts of susceptible members of the fair sex, ranging from school girls to society matrons.'[64] While on location filming for *All the Winners* (1920) production was stopped by regular invasions of 'pretty girls with cameras' in search of the film's star.[65] *All the Winners* was, as the title suggests, a horse-racing picture, and, like numerous other films about the racing set, was a story seemingly cobbled together around the staging of an important race.[66] *All the Winners* was based on a provocatively titled novel, *Wicked*, by Arthur Applin, but many other racing films were based on plays, a fact that illustrates the continuing taste for old-fashioned barn-storming productions alongside the more eclectic work of playwrights like Shaw, Galsworthy and Barrie. It would appear that many of these plays were melodramas, with final scenes in which equine pyrotechnics of a less than epic nature anticipated the final curtain. In the lesser halls, where such plays were particularly popular, it was sometimes the local dray horse, in its first stage part, that drew the most applause.[67] There were also a number of films of a similar ilk based on the novels of Nat Gould, who was said to rival Edgar Wallace, Charles Garvice and Ethel M. Dell as the most widely read author in the English-speaking world.[68] *All the Winners*, the first Samuelson production to use newly imported American lighting, was not a great success;[69] one reviewer advised, 'it should not be shown in its present form by an exhibitor with a respect for the good name of his hall'.[70] Another film featuring Nares was *For Her Father's Sake* (1921), and this was said to be a 'conventional Society drama which moves very slowly … audiences who like their entertainment according to tradition may find it interesting'.[71] Of his role, as 'the perfect lover', it was said that Nares 'can make love in the conventional "matinee-idol" style as effectively in the studio as he does behind the footlights, but under the lamps he found he had to hold himself in, so to speak … Screen love-making of the gentle persuasive order is more effective than the hustling cave-man style of wooing.'[72]

Another Samuelson production starring Owen Nares was *A Temporary Gentleman* (1920), based on a play by H. F. Maltby, who wrote mainly contemporary comedies, and who appeared in more than seventy British films, usually as a 'choleric character'.[73] The plot concerned a clerk who has risen to junior officer status during the war, but who finds it difficult to revert to his class position after resuming civilian life; a précis of the plot states 'a clerk's service as a subaltern spoils him for menial work'.[74] The play, and film, commented on the rigidity of the class system; the demobbed hero 'tried one officer's employment bureau after another, but none will have him as he is not public school'.[75] The inviolable rights inherent in attendance at the 'right school' was also the subject of a fable entitled 'The Gates of Heaven', which was a particular favourite of Etonians at the time: an Old Etonian dies and his spirit is met at the gates of heaven by the Chief Justice, who charges him with immorality and idleness. When asked if he has anything to say in his own defence, the Old Etonian replies, 'Yes, I was a Peer and educated at a Public School.' The Chief Justice sighs and says, 'Oh well, open the gates.'[76] In a column in *Cinema Chat*, Constance Burleigh's review of *A Temporary Gentleman* revealed something of the attitudes attendant on those who regarded the resumption of civilian life after the war as simply a continuation of what had gone before, with class defining the presumed coherence of British society:

> Owen Nares was such an amusingly exasperating specimen of a 'one-pip snob' when he became a Temporary Gentleman. [The] end of war found him no longer an officer or gentleman but a shabby civilian with no prospects … when he had the nonsense knocked out of him he became a successful commercial traveller and fell in love with the family parlour-maid, a level-headed but most attractive ex W.A.A.C.[77]

This review contains many elements redolent of class snobbery and condescension: a mere clerk could never be a gentleman, ultra-class aspirations described as nonsense, the return of a woman who had served her country during the war to her natural position of service, at first as an employee, and then as a wife. It is also interesting that the pre-war assumptions regarding the employment of domestic help, even in middle-income homes, remain integral to the view of society expressed by Maltby, as well as the reviewer. No account is taken of the fact that domestic service had ceased to be the major arena of women's employment. Even cinema magazines commented on the declining numbers of young women prepared to go into service and the apparent difficulty of retaining in-house staff: 'If every woman put herself in her maid's place for one half day, her servants would stay longer.'[78] Another review of *A Temporary Gentleman* reminded readers that it had been adapted from a very good play and stated that 'the acting and titling are two outstanding features',[79] but as at least two Samuelson productions were anti-union in bias it would appear that the values particular to Samuelson were those which had not yet been released from pre-war bondage and a reliance, for artistic credibility, on notions of popularity which were particular to metropolitan London. Owen Nares was immensely popular in London; his success was based almost exclusively on his West End appearances, and it is, perhaps, not surprising that his screen performances did not travel well. Even after more than a decade's experience before the camera he was still delivering leading-man performances 'in a stifled drawing-room theatrical style' opposite the new stars of the 1930s such as Gracie Fields, in *The Show Goes On*, and Jessie Matthews, in *There Goes the Bride*, where his overweening mannerisms contrasted markedly with the exuberance of his co-stars.[80]

Stewart Rome was a British leading man who appeared in scores of films throughout the 1920s. He was said to be receiving fan mail at the rate of 600 letters a week shortly after the war, and was purportedly 'one of Great Britain's favourite film stars'.[81] He was initially attracted to the stage by a performance of *The Bellringer of Notre Dame* he attended in a booth at Newbury Fair and his film career began with the Hepworth Company before the war.[82] After his demobilization in 1918 he joined Broadwest, which prompted a civil case in which Hepworth and Rome contested the proprietorial rights to his name. Hepworth argued, unsuccessfully, that as Rome's film career had developed under his auspices the name of Stewart Rome should belong to the company which had promoted it and made it successful.[83] In a pen-portrait, *Picture Show Annual* described Rome as 'perhaps the shyest screen star who ever played for a British film ... an outdoor man who likes nothing better than a tramp over the Surrey hills with his pipe and dog for company'; in other words, a real Englishman, strong, silent, fond of the country life.[84] He evidently possessed an aura of gentlemanly charm, which prompted one commentator to enquire as to how he would adapt to playing anyone who suffered the indignity of having to live in 'a common lodging-house, and when financially embarrassed having stars only for his roof'.[85] Film stills from the period show a middle-aged man with a rugged profile, pipe in mouth – hardly a dashing young hero.

In *A Daughter of Eve* (1919) – a murder mystery resolved by the principal character waking from a dream – Rome was said to 'have improved greatly since we saw him last ... although still given to expansive gestures', and his against-type characterization in *The Great Gay Road* (1920), where his character was forced to reside in a lodging-house, was remarked to be 'masterly'.[86] Rome's career was possibly handicapped by his association with Walter West, whose enthusiasm and expansive nature could not make up for a certain deficiency in style as well as technique. The films were unlikely to be regarded as classics but they were less static than many other British films of the period, with a mobile camera and slow motion to add variety to the product. West's string of race horses were probably the most regular stars of his films. When racing was in abeyance boxing came to the fore.[87] In *The Case of Lady Camber* (1920), Stewart Rome co-starred with another Broadwest regular, Gregory Scott, who was designated 'an aristocrat of the screen'[88] – his 'good looks and charm of manner, both on and off the screen, have gained for him the admiration of so many members of the female sex'.[89] The best thing one reviewer could say of *A Sportsman's Wife* (1921), in which Scott co-starred with Violet Hopson, was that the racing scenes were as well done as ever but that the film needed substantial cutting.[90] In an interview, Walter West expressed the opinion that 'it is quite possible to produce a thrilling film ... without resorting to the usual form of thrill-getting ... the plot of Dead Certainty contains no deaths, murders, thefts, fires or accidents.'[91] If such was the case, his leading male players, Stewart Rome and Gregory Scott, were unlikely to have been offered the kind of parts which would have provided them with the opportunity to be heroic, and it is, therefore, not surprising that their portrayals should be regarded as rather colourless. In *The Penniless Millionaire* (1921), with Stewart Rome playing the lead, there was 'nothing very convincing' in the characterization,[92] and the farcical

nature of some elements of *Snow in the Desert* (1919) made both Rome
and a pre-Hollywood Ronald Colman 'look ridiculous'.[93]

Gerald Ames was typical of the kind of British actor who failed to
find an economy of style suited to the numerous roles he played. In
Sheba (1919), based on a 'Rita' novel of operatic bigamy, Ames was said
to be 'less stagey than usual',[94] and in *Possession* (1919) – a tale of Russian
illegitimacy – he played the hero 'somewhat colourlessly'.[95] The morbidity
of *Sunken Rocks* (1919) – a doctor murders a drunkard in order to marry
the inebriant's widow – was said to prevent him from 'doing particularly
good work [and] there were cries of "pussyfoot" at the trade show'.[96]
Ames was university-educated and something of a sportsman; he listed
his recreations as riding, motoring and fencing and had been the only
Englishman to reach the fencing semi-finals at the Stockholm Olympic
Games before the war. He cut a rather dashing figure on stage, fighting
'thrilling duels with Henry Ainley in *The Prisoner of Zenda*', and was said
be 'an especial favourite amongst British screen leads, either as a hero
or villain'.[97] His acting in *The Nature of the Beast* (1919) was said to be
'admirable' but the reviewer wrote for *Cinema Chat*, which appears to
have been a one-publication publicity machine for the Hepworth Company. Ames was nearing forty when he attempted to swashbuckle his
way through many of the Hepworth films and like his duelling opponent
in *Possession*, Henry Edwards, he turned his hand to directing; he was
quoted as preparing a screen treatment of a comedy called *Great Snakes*
(1920), and he shared directing duties with Gaston Quiribet on *Once
Aboard the Lugger* (1920), which was described as 'a really good British
comedy, well acted and a first-class light entertainment for any public'.[98]
Ames was featured in nearly thirty British films of the period, most of
which were ostensibly starring vehicles, but his popularity was limited,
and it is difficult to assess, without a substantial record of his work,
why he did not command a greater following. He was, like many other
British actors, essentially stage-bound, and the roles he played on screen
may well have reflected that to such a degree that it precluded his
adoption of a credible screen persona.

Henry Edwards was a co-partner in the Hepworth Company and
made more than a dozen films with Chrissie White, who became his
wife in 1922. He was fifteen years on the legitimate stage and had
toured America and England with a series of sketches he had written.
He was a cultured man, listing music, painting and photography as his
hobbies.[99] *Pictures* wrote of him: 'he has given the public numbers of

fine features which bring something more than mere entertainment with them. In these productions are touches of sheer beauty and cultured appeal which bespeak a man of ideals.'[100] In advertisements he was referred to as 'England's foremost producer and actor' and was accorded equal status with Betty Balfour as one of only two artists who had 'kept the movies moving', even though he returned to the stage after the collapse of Hepworth's Company.[101] He was more than forty years old when he played the hero to his wife's heroine in a series of mainly rural melodramas in the early 1920s, but was still capable of rousing the lyrical passions of his fans:

> A handsome hero of the Screen
> Is he who haunts me when I dream,
> For Henry Edwards is the one
> I lavish my affections on,
> His pictures I rejoice to see,
> They make the dull world Heaven for me.
> He simply thrills me through and through,
> He looks so brave, so strong, so true.[102]

Edwards was responsible for adapting, producing, and playing the leading role in a number of films; of *A Temporary Vagabond* (1920), the title character played by Edwards was said to be endowed 'with the sheer force of his personality, his debonair good fellowship, his whimsical charm, that have so endeared him to thousands who appreciate his genius'.[103] *The City of Beautiful Nonsense* (1919) was said to demonstrate Edwards's 'technical dexterity and originality', but the chief acting honours went to Henry Vibart and Gwynne Herbert rather than Edwards and his co-star, Chrissie White.[104] Another reviewer claimed that the film 'proves once and for all, without danger of contradiction, that, given the story, the players, and the producer, Britain can turn out pictures that reach the highest standard'.[105] *The Kinsman* (1919) was said to be 'a beautiful play, beautifully produced ... and for once we get away from the "stage set" appearance of the interiors, a defect too frequent in British productions'. The plot of the film was a light confection centred on heirs, impostors, doubles and the like – scarcely modern in theme.[106] The same could be said of *The Lunatic at Large* (1921), with its plot about rich and eccentric members of British high society. Exhibitors were advised to advertise the film along the lines of 'visitors will be able to see Henry Edwards as a rich man who has fits of madness', 'Henry Edwards in a fine British comedy', so it must be assumed that if the selling point of the film was thought to be the name of Henry Edwards, he must have had some drawing power, both as a director and actor.[107] As an actor this was later demonstrable on 'his welcome and triumphant return to the screen in The Flag Lieutenant', in 1926.[108] His reputation as a director of note and an actor of some style is not in dispute; however, he was hardly of an age which would entitle him to anything other than an outsider's odds in 'the race for the hero championship'.[109]

The Trade Show Critic Annual announced with its tongue firmly in its cheek that 'an amazing incident happened in 1920 – a cinema journal one week actually went to press without a photograph of Guy Newall'.[110] What is, perhaps, surprising, is that Guy Newall was far from an attractive actor, looking rather like a 'spiv', with an expression that suggested that if he had been a cat, the cream he had just eaten would have been on the turn. Rachael Low's description of him as possessing an 'ugly and even misleadingly coarse appearance' is apposite, and it is somewhat surprising that he played the hero in so many films.[111] Newall was often involved in the writing and production of films as well as acting in them, usually in tandem with his wife Ivy Duke, and he appears to have been particularly fond of light comedy-dramas which almost inevitably had him playing either an aristocrat or a hero whose woman had done him wrong. In The Lure of Crooning Water (1920) and Fox Farm (1922) his roles were similar; in both he played a farmer betrayed by women who were more interested in high life than rural life. The plot of Fox Farm had Newall's character deserted by his wife after he had been blinded in an accident; the character was 'much given to lighting his pipe, slumping in a chair and arguing that it's no use pushing against fate'.[112] In The Lure of Crooning Water Newall played a farmer whose emotions were toyed with by an actress, with temptation resisted in the final reel; it was said to be a production that 'can safely be shown on any screen'.[113] A similar propriety was noted of What the Butler Saw (1924), a farce filmed in Berlin, featuring a particularly vicious parrot. Reviewers congratulated Newall for creating a film in which 'there is nothing to offend the most fastidious' and which in other hands 'might have been vulgar and suggestive'.[114] The Bigamist (1921) was provocatively titled but the substance of the film fell far short of its title. Newall directed the film and played the hero who 'conquers his own passion' and becomes a 'faithful watch-dog'; bigamy, in this instance, was a sexless affair, with

Newall's character selflessly maintaining 'a self-sacrificing role ... to the end'. Giving 'his usual portrayal of the immaculately dressed, perfectly mannered Englishman', Newall rather daringly avoided a happy ending – bigamy? – and one critic expressed the opinion that 'we very much doubt whether the bulk of picture-goers, trained as they are to having all obstacles cleared away in the last two hundred feet and the uniting of the hero and heroine will quite appreciate this state of affairs'. Despite impressive booming the film was said to have lost money – happy endings were, for better or worse, *de rigueur*.[115] So much for self-sacrifice and fatalistic metaphors! Marketed under the Lucky Cat emblem, Newall made some comedy films which were quite well received: *I Will* has been discussed at length in Chapter 1, and Newall, as was often the case, played a young aristocrat ('as the hero, Mr Newall is a find of importance').[116] Newell wrote *The March Hare* (1919) for his wife, Ivy Duke, but the film's best performance was said to have been by 'Betty, a remarkably clever terrier', which seems to be an early indication of the validity of the adage about acting with animals and children.[117] *Wings of the Turf*, which appears to be the American title of *Boy Woodburn* (1922), was said to be a typical 'English melodramatic affair, with the racecourse as a background ... like most English productions, it does not try to hold particularly to continuity'. Newall directed the film as well as playing the lead male part and the review went on to suggest that he 'ought to confine himself to one or the other; in this production he didn't cut much ice in either capacity'.[118] In film stills he looks nothing like a hero – more like the George Cole character in the *St Trinians* films – and it must have been a combination of talent, enthusiasm and commitment to a medium for which he undoubtedly had a flair that kept him active throughout a period when many other talented performers were denied the opportunity to accomplish anything like his degree of success.

The screen performances of many British actors induced one commentator to claim to have identified the reason for Britain's lack of success in the international film market. Quoting French sources, the film critic of the *Morning Post* told his readers:

A French film critic, writing in the *Excelsior*, thinks he has discovered the reason why the British cinema industry lags behind the American, the French, the German, and even the Italian. It is due purely to British temperament. There is no race in the world to whom showing their sentiments is so repugnant, he says. The spirit behind the cinema is the very opposite of the characteristic British spirit. When there are no words the face has to interpret the emotions, he continues, but with the exception of Betty Balfour, the features of English cinema actors and actresses remain perfectly wooden. At times it is even painful to see them struggling to put a little bit of life into a scene. He goes on to say that the British industry should concentrate on the strong and silent type of man ... parts requiring extreme reserve.[119]

This may well have been a French journalist simply exercising his traditional right to decry all things English, but it should be noted that the strong and silent type of man is a stereotype much beloved of English writers, a stereotype that has currency in most forms of popular entertainment. Its importance, as a type, in British films, is especially relevant when it is seen in conjunction with the matinée-idol style of acting; what appears to have been the case is that British actors found it especially difficult to find the middle ground between the florid mannerisms of West End theatricalism and the painfully rigid, wooden style referred to by the French journalist. It could be argued that those who discovered that middle ground, whether by chance or design, were those who naturally gravitated to Hollywood.

Critics were not slow to recognize the kind of persona and the style of acting which were suited to film; they would contrast, for instance, the 'ultra-theatricalism of the male protagonists' in *The Usurper* (1919), Stephen Ewart and Geoffrey Kerr, with the natural screen presence of its female lead, the American actress Gertrude McCoy.[120] This criticism may well have contributed to the practice of importing American stars to appear in British productions. Reviewing *Knocknagow* (1918), from the Film Company of Ireland, a critic commented: 'seldom if ever, have so many perfect men and women been gathered together into one cast; this applies more to the men, who look like men, and are not like the doll-like creatures we are so used to in heroic parts'.[121] Significantly, the film was a success in the United States, where it took more money in one week in Boston than Griffith's *Birth of a Nation*. Reviews of the film itself in London were mixed, with some complaining that it was little more than propaganda;[122] it was evidently not to the taste of those who found George Pearson's tale of Irish horse racing, *Garryowen* (1920), such an attractive proposition: 'It inspires a real love of Ireland and all things Irish. It brings Ireland and England closer together. Parliament might sit for ten sessions without doing as much.'[123]

The comment about 'real men' portrayed in *Knocknagow* reappears in a review of a French film, *Uncle Bernac*, starring the English actor Rex Davis. In Britain Davis was featured in *Won by a Head* (1920), one of the ubiquitous racing-set pictures, a couple of boxing dramas – *The Knockout* (1923) and *The Pride of the Fancy* (1920) (of the latter a critic wrote that it was 'a melodramatic sporting picture with not much detail … suitable for uncritical audiences')[124] – and little else of note. His promise was clear to those who saw *A Couple of Down-and-Outs* (1923); the film was 'a sentimental tale of the shameful trade in worn-out horses', and Davis was said to be a 'fine manly hero'.[125] Of his appearance in *Uncle Bernac* it was said:

> Davis is the ideal hero, and enjoys a rough-house as thoroughly as do his audiences. He is manly and sincere, and can play the hero without effeminacy or the aid of highly burnished 'Marcelle' waved hair, affectations which ninety-nine out of a hundred of our film stars apparently cannot do without, no matter what type of part they are attempting to play. He can act, and it is a matter of some regret that so few opportunities are found for him at home.[126]

Opportunities, in abundance, were found for British actors with far less screen presence than Rex Davis, and it must have been frustrating to someone with undoubted star potential to be ignored. It is more than a matter of conjecture that the British film industry's reliance on stock types from the London stage, and film stories which accommodated such types, hindered the development of stars with anything approaching universal appeal.

With the power of the predatory American industry, with its cheque-book seductions of potential and demonstrable European talent, it is, perhaps, understandable that so few male actors working solely in the British industry in the 1920s were able to imprint their personalities and image on film. It was with an attitude approaching fatalism that *Cinema Chat* told its readers, 'It is almost ironical reflecting that many American film stars are either British or of British parentage', but given the American penetration of world markets and the failure of the British industry to compete, even in its home market, it would appear that any actor with ambition would turn to Hollywood in much the same way as any young stage aspirant would seek to conquer the West End of London to validate his professional status.[127] With the British film industry commanding only nominal support from those whose opinions defined culture, acceptability and achievement, it was, perhaps, inevitable that British actors with a commitment to the cinema and their own financial and professional status should make the journey to Hollywood, and it is principally in the films those actors made for the American industry that film-goers and historians are reminded of the wastage and the squandering of talent for which the apparent ineptitude and limited vision of the British film industry must be held responsible.

4

The Audience Votes: 'Far from the Promised Land of Public Esteem'[1]

B y the mid-twenties the British film industry was in a state of confusion:

> a ramshackle affair, characterised by self-pity and self-delusion, lacking ordinary commercial vision, and not seldom ordinary commercial honesty, having no real policy and but a few ideals, pleading poverty and craving charity, neither understanding nor wishing to understand the meaning of patriotic impulse; shrieking for what it calls encouragement when what it needs is resurrection.[2]

The most obvious reason for the industry's parlous state was economic; with too many pictures – most of them imports – chasing too few cinemas, the public was able to maximize its power to choose the kind of films it wished to see. The situation for British producers was further exacerbated by the rental sector of the industry, which bowed to the block-booking practices of the American producing concerns, consistently resisting any regulation of their industry and consequently excluding British films from equal access to the marketplace. But this is not the whole story. Stoll's output of films was guaranteed exhibition in the company's own cinemas, but failed to sustain enough audience interest or product loyalty to make its producing arm viable. British audiences apparently made a conscious decision to boycott British films, but why exactly did that happen? Why, for instance, did *The Wonderful Story* (1922) empty every cinema in which it was shown?[3] Why did the public stay away in droves if a film was advertised outside a cinema as British-made?[4] With the benefit (or burden) of hindsight, J. Arthur Rank's publicity manager recalled 'the time when cinemagoers would not have wanted to cross the street to see a British film'.[5] Given the choice between British and American product, British audiences over-whelmingly chose American.[6]

In asking 'Is there a Slump?', a journalist reported that some managers, especially in the Lancashire region, 'had received a direct hint that much of their present fare is not highly esteemed by their patrons'; this was said to be linked to the 'stupidity of future booking' which did not allow cinema managers to meet the changing public tastes, so the comment may well have applied to foreign as well as home product.[7] Less than charitable was Basil Dean, who succinctly pointed out that 'the public refused to accept an inferior article'.[8] But what was inferior about the product? Were British producers so inept, both technically and artistically, that the public was justified in showing contempt for an obviously inferior product? Film reviews do not entirely support either a totally negative view of British product or an overtly optimistic scenario. For every review noting technical deficiencies there were other reviews citing the excellence of particular productions. *Sunken Rocks* (1919) was said to 'overcome, once and for all, any accusation that was made against our photography',[9] and *The City of Beautiful Nonsense* (1919) was described as 'a magnificent feature, absolutely faultless', demonstrating that 'Britain can turn out pictures that reach the highest standard'.[10] *The Lady Clare* (1919) was 'a triumph. It is right round the course and back to the winning post while most of its rivals are gripping the cords',[11] and *The Usurper* (1919) was regarded as superior to more than 90 per cent of American films in 'photography, production and casting'.[12]

Such reviews, though, may be misleading. *Sunken Rocks* may well have contained excellent photography but it was also described as morbid.[13] Similarly, 'few better examples of production' were to be found than *Testimony* (1920); the 'art direction is perfect and the acting exceptionally good', but the production was said to have been spoiled by 'the weakness of the story'.[14] *The Edge of Youth* (1920) was 'a practically faultless production', according to one review, but the film was derided for exhibiting 'sentimentality of the most hackneyed type'.[15] The problem of choosing film subjects was accurately pin-pointed by one commentator who wrote: 'You can't feed an audience of several millions daily with the cream of the world's imaginative literature without shortly resorting to skimmed milk.'[16] Reviewing *God's Clay* (1919), a critic commented: 'In the early days of the business, hundreds ... of first rate stories were spoiled by bad production, indifferent acting and poor photography. Nowadays it is the more common practice to waste a good cast on a bad story. God's Clay is an instance ... the story is a very injudicious or unfortunate choice.' From a lurid novel by Alice and Claude Askew, the film told the story of a paralysed wife who murdered her seducer and escaped detection by making it look as though the crime was committed by his mistress.[17] Producers evidently failed to note the 'unfortunate choice' of story matter as the novel was filmed again in 1928 by Graham Cutts.

More than almost any other criticism, the one which deals with film subject matter is the most noticeable in reviews of the period. It has already been noted that film-makers exhibited particular tendencies as far as choice of subjects was concerned; what is also noticeable is the reliance on and, therefore, the built-in references to, published material. Cecil Hepworth, Britain's foremost producer of the time, wrote:

> The onset of the first World War corresponded in time with the coming into fashion of film pictures made from well-known stage plays or from recently published books. Whether it was an understandable desire to cash in on popularity already acquired or only a result of the paucity of original material suitable for the purpose, I cannot be sure; probably it was a little of both.[18]

The apotheosis of this liaison between literary popularity and film may be found in *The Story of the Rosary* (1920). A reviewer reminded potential bookers that the film was taken from a play, a novel and a song, and continued, 'it does not very much matter if the photo-play be well or ill done' – its original popularity, in previous literary incarnations, supposedly gave the film a built-in popularity factor. The review went on to note that the film was not very well done, that it followed the 'play precisely with the usual incoherent result'.[19]

There may be more to British producers' reliance on literary sources, and literary popularity, than is at first apparent, although there is nothing particularly endemic to the British industry in publicizing a film such as *The Edge o' Beyond* (1919) by using the prior success of Gertrude Page's novel – exhibitors were urged to sell the film on the basis of 'over a

million copies [of the novel] sold'.[20] Some of the most popular writers
of the time were courted not only by British producers but by their
American counterparts as well. *Cinema Chat* reported that Jesse Lasky,
of Famous Players-Lasky, was in Britain negotiating contracts with Sir
James Barrie, Arnold Bennett, Robert Hichens, H. G. Wells and a number
of other successful playwrights and authors. What was significant about
Lasky's negotiations was that they were for 'original stories written
specifically for the screen, with special consideration for [its] require-
ments', not for previously published material.[21] It has already been noted
that the medium of entertainment involved a complex process of cross-
fertilization, with the published word occupying the principal position
of power and influence. *The Great Gay Road* (1920), from the Walter
West stable, aptly demonstrates that process. When the novel of the
same name was published, the *Daily Telegraph* noted that it contained
'rich material for a play', and, subsequently, the novel was adapted for
the stage, and then, much later, for the cinema.[22] The cinema, it would
appear, was the last in line when it came to access to suitable stories for
exploitation in its particular medium. It could also be argued that the
self-confidence of the British industry was so lacking, because of its
inferior position *vis-à-vis* the reputation of its competitors, that it chose
to use established criteria of excellence, and/or popularity, to gain a
modicum of vicarious esteem. There were commentators who still saw
the industry as 'an outcast and a wanderer in the wilderness, far from
the Promised Land of public esteem';[23] there were those who remembered that film production had been, in the first instance, the
province of 'ex-stage supers or ex-clowns ... To have "bin on the 'alls"
was often considered such a fine and sufficient qualification for film
work'.[24] Even directors with academic qualifications, such as the ex-
schoolmaster George Pearson, were subject to derision by those who
saw the industry as somehow lacking in respectability. When Pearson
wanted to enlarge his studio in Winchmore Hill the local residents 'rose
in opposition ... since they felt it would lower the cultural standard of
their neighbourhood'.[25] Would they have acted in a similar manner if a
publishing house had been involved, or a play-house offering the best
in theatrical entertainment? It is, perhaps, understandable that those in
the industry with pretensions to respectability, in an artistic as well as
social sense, would seek to use whatever means available to introduce
an element of legitimacy into their chosen profession.

The most obvious attempt to forge a cinematic identity through literary connotation was Stoll's policy of producing films based on the works of 'Eminent British Authors', using the name of the author as the selling point of the film. The first film to be released under this banner was *The Amateur Gentleman* (1920), from a novel by Jeffrey Farnol, and this was followed by a series of films culled from the works of A. E. W. Mason, Olive Wadsley, 'Rita', Baroness Orczy, Rafael Sabatini and others; the favoured Stoll author was Ethel M. Dell and some fourteen of her novels were used in the series.[26] The literary 'eminence' of writers such as Dell and 'Rita' was lampooned in the novel *Scarlet Kiss*, which was filmed by Fred Goodwins in 1920; Gertrude de St Wentworth-Jones noted that 'any woman who can afford to buy a penny exercise book, a penny pen and a penny bottle of ink can make herself eligible for admission into a literary club',[27] and reading some of Dell's works raises the question of Stoll's interpretation of eminence – certainly the novels sold well, but their wearisome litany of middle-class prejudices, and their devastating silliness, do appear to be at odds with many other popular novels of the time, both in style and content.[28] *Scarlet Kiss*, for example, is a sprightly and often acerbic commentary on middle-class morality without the mock-Russian convolutions which characterize many of Dell's novels.

The problem of adapting popular novels was noted in a review of Henry Edwards's adaptation of Olive Wadsley's novel *Possession* (1919); the film was an 'excellent production' but the problem was the weakness of the story: 'it is presumed that the adapting of the story from a popular novel is the cause in so much as the adaptor is under the necessity of adhering to the original story.'[29] Many so-called popular novels did not translate successfully to the screen: of *Knave of Diamonds* (1921), from a Dell novel 'of the usual order', it was said that the material was inferior to the handling.[30] 'Of the usual order' implied the author's customary excursion into the ranks of the 'higher orders', with characters 'bearing the unmistakable stamp of high breeding in every delicate movement' – 'pure Tatler', as Dell's biographer appositely noted. The story was concerned with a self-sacrificing widow of a drunken Baronet who marries her lover's sick brother in order to save his life.[31] *Woman of His Dreams* (1921) also featured a drunken spouse; the plot had the long-suffering wife deserting her husband and being redeemed by friendship when a long-time male friend rescues her from a shipwreck. Although one reviewer admitted that 'the author's name will ensure success at any cinema', it was noted that 'the story is insipid [and] gets tedious towards the end'.[32] The sea also played a major role in *The Tidal Wave* (1920) which again had near-drowning as the means of causing a rescued artist, 'Columbine', to be wooed by a humble fisherman; the adaptation was hardly successful although, as previously noted, its visual appeal was stressed.[33] Even when technical expertise was apparent in the adaptation of one of Dell's novels, as with *A Question of Trust* (1920), the results were less than satisfactory: 'excellent photography and delightful backgrounds are wasted on a ridiculously unconvincing story ... the general effect of the film is depressing.'[34]

Films based on novels by other popular writers met with similar criticism. The chief appeal of *At the Mercy of Tiberius* (1920) was said to be the novel, by Augusta Wilson, on which it was based.[35] *The Iron Stair* (1920) was 'founded on a great novel by Rita',[36] but the film was 'perilously thin melodrama ... the exceedingly stilted subtitles and the conventional melodramatics discount the punch of the Dartmoor scenes'.[37] *Calvary* (1920), from another novel by 'Rita', was, supposedly, a 'melodramatic story of a man's love for a woman above him in station', but the novel reads like a treatise on religion, and employs the Archangel Michael as a character who bestows visions on the unfortunate terrestrial hero. The purpose of the book was briefly outlined by the author: 'This book embodies the subject of many years' anxious thought and study of religious systems. They demanded written expression ... I feel that those who have known the soul's struggle for TRUTH will understand my meaning.'[38] Both Dell and 'Rita' appear to have written out of particular obsessions, out of a futile desire to hold back the passage of time, to return society to a period in which manners, behaviour and morality were more to their liking. The reviews of films adapted from their novels generate a sense of disbelief, a bewilderment at why those novels were chosen as film properties.

Charles Garvice was another writer whose obsession with the upper orders of society makes him almost unreadable today. The adaptation of *Nance* (1920) posited a situation in which a village girl refuses the worthy advances of a 'gentleman', accepting instead the status of his mistress until such time as it is discovered that she also is of 'gentle' birth. The film was said to be 'trashy and badly presented, with much too liberal a supply of lengthy subtitles'.[39] Another Garvice adaptation, *With All Her Heart* (1920), was said to end with more questions raised about what had happened in the film than had been answered.[40] Reviewing *God's Good Man* (1919), it was stated that 'of plot there is none', despite the fact that it was based on one of Marie Corelli's lengthy sagas; the preponderance of langorous sub-titles was also noted, the example given being: 'Even if I have to die and leave you soon, I shall know all is well with my soul for you have made it beautiful with love.'[41]

The titling of *Night Riders* (1920), a western, made in Hollywood by the Samuelson Company, also came in for some criticism: 'the sub-titles are as bad as in most British films'.[42] *The Woman with the Fan* (1921), based on a Robert Hichens novel, contained 'too much subtitling ... and wants reviewing before exhibition to the public',[43] while the sub-titling in another adaptation, *Aunt Rachel* (1920), was dismissed as preposterous. In the original novel the country people speak in a strange dialect which, if reproduced on the screen, would undoubtedly have appeared preposterous:

'Theers a look of summat stirrin' i' the place, gaffer.'
'Wy, yis, Mr Eld, theer is that sort of air about the plaais to-day.'[44]

Numerous screenplays, whatever their origins or subject matter, were subject to similar criticism: *Castles in Spain* (1920) 'is not well adapted to screen presentation ... and the use of an unnecessarily large number of long sub-titles does not make it more acceptable'[45] and the sub-titling of *The Black Spider* (1920) was said to be 'extremely stagey', despite its 'original' subject matter.[46] It would appear that film producers were unable to create a product that did not obviously reflect other literary forms and that in creating new forms of expression, alternative methods of story-telling, they lagged behind their American competitors.

While the use, or misuse, of the mechanism of titling may well have added to the problems of British producers, it is not as prevalent a criticism as that of story choice. *The Bigamist* (1921), another literary adaptation, was 'a lavish production applied to an unworthy story' which, even after cutting, was deemed 'tiresome'.[47] The plot of *Queen's Evidence* (1919) was said to be 'far fetched',[48] and *Inheritance* (1920), which was 'well-produced, for the most part, with excellent photography and backgrounds', was spoiled by the 'weakness' of the story. The plot was a convoluted affair about a junior member of the squirearchy who weds the fisher-girl who has saved his life and because of the watery connection finds himself a dockers' leader. He is released from the double misfortune of labour and class alienation by the death of his wife, which leaves him free to re-enter 'proper society' by means of wedding 'a lady'.[49] 'Improbable' would appear to be a word better suited to the plot than 'weakness'. Another film which 'technically can give points to most of the American work' was *Duke's Son* (1920) but it was regarded as failing because of its 'highly artificial and rather unconvincing story' about card-sharping dukes and would-be adulterous millionaires.[50] *Cherry Ripe* (1921), from Helen Mather's novel, was 'unconvincing' and contained 'several scenes which will create laughter instead of tears'. The film was recommended only for audiences who were easily pleased, those who could find entertainment in a story about a lawyer who evicts an orphaned gipsy girl, subsequently marries the orphan's sister and then sees the error of his harsh ways after killing a squire whom he suspects of harbouring evil thoughts about his gipsy wife.[51] According to Broadwest's scenario editor, Patrick Mannock, there was a 'glut of screen stories dealing with gipsies and old violins', none of which was suitable for filming, and it does appear that a high proportion of films were set in some never-never land, a long way from Credibility Crescent.[52] The director Reginald Denham titled the section of his autobiography dealing with his experience in the film industry 'Concerning a Glimpse of the Nether Regions', and while many British films did not quite sink to that level they certainly eschewed any reference to the common-place, to the world with which their audience was familiar.[53]

The House on the Marsh (1920), another story by a woman novelist, was about a feisty governess unmasking her employer as the leader of a gang of thieves, and a review of the film was quick to point out that 'a clever cast, technical ability, inventive ingenuity and such well-studied settings have been lavished on a cheap sort of story ... the producers have decided to play down to the popular taste'.[54] The question of public taste was also broached in a review of *The Winding Road* (1920): 'the big public go for this sort of stuff'. The bulk of the film's action takes place in a prison where a cashiered major is incarcerated; his subsequent release is afforded by his rescue of a brutal warder from rioting convicts. It is a matter for conjecture as to whose side the audience was on; the choice between a brutal warder and, presumably, equally brutal convicts seems like no choice at all. Perhaps audiences were expected to enjoy the riot, as the usual British fare was noticeably lacking in action other than that which took place in a boxing ring or at the race track,[55] as was the case with *Silver Lining* (1919); it had 'scenes which hold one sport or another', the 'story lacked originality', and 'the producer found it necessary to insert a large amount of padding' to link the sporting scenes together.[56] The story of *A Sportsman's Wife* (1921) was 'not very strong, but the race scenes are as well done as ever',[57] as were similar scenes in *The Gentleman Rider* (1919), although the 'character sketches may be based rather on novelette standards'.[58] *The Way of the World* (1920), which was praised for providing 'a picture of the life of the British people', was said to have 'no plot in the ordinary sense', but was loaded with 'good race course and boxing scenes to provide variety'. What plot did exist concerned a carter adopting a sick child and beating the child's father in a boxing match. It is, perhaps, a rather interesting picture of the life of the British people, in which boxing and racing, as well as child neglect, are seen as features particular to that life.[59]

If reviewers found the subject matter of British films difficult to swallow, and audiences palpably thought along similar lines, some producers failed to understand that the medium in which they were working demanded a particular kind of scenario. In answer to a request from a reader about where to send scenarios, the editor of *Cinema Chat* replied that an agency he had previously recommended as being interested in original screen stories had told him 'there is practically no opening in England, except for novels'.[60] A film critic expressed the opinion that 'I almost believe that some [British producers] would have preferred adaptations of the Telephone Directory to the first original work, by an unknown author, that could have been offered them',[61] and the managing director of one British production company was quoted as saying: 'If all the film dramatists and scenario hacks were to die or go on strike, or join the army in a body, we should still be able to rig up a few million very tolerable screen dramas from the wealth of resources to be found simply in the fiction of the day.'[62] Despite such confidence in the power of borrowed source material, questions were asked about its suitability, questions which suggest that some commentators, some members of the British film-making community, realized that something was wrong with the way in which British films were developed:

Can it be that British film producers are lacking in ideas? I only ask the question because during the past few months I have seen so few absolutely original home-produced pictures shown. Most of the all-British films, to my mind, seem to rely too much on popular novels and successful stage-plays ... I make one suggestion, for what it's worth – that the British producer ceases trying to bring budding film actresses to the fore, and directs his attention to discovering a few more authors with brains and imagination who can write a good scenario. Unless something is done, the majority of the new British stars of the shadow stage will be out of work.[63]

In 'Can We Beat the Yank?', the journalist Louis Dagmar wrote: 'Little encouragement has in the past been given to scenario writers so far as England is concerned, so that it is little wonder that writers for the film have sent their scripts to America.'[64] There certainly was some insight into the way in which a lack of purpose-written material acted against the development of the British film industry. The novelist Hall Caine was aware of the need for writers to be involved in film production. He drafted a document which he sent to British authors 'younger and stronger than myself, showing that this is a very necessary and worthy thing to attempt to do'.[65] Newspapers and periodicals offered prizes for original scenarios, a few directors and producers were quoted as being aware of the need for new material, new ideas, but did anything come from this apparent realization that British films need an injection of original talent? Very little, it would appear. In 1919, 166 feature films were produced in Britain; of these, 135, (81 per cent) were based on either published novels or plays. Given the problems of the film industry, given the level of debate in the trade and general press as to the need for new material, it is, therefore, not surprising to find that in 1924, when production had slumped to fifty-five films in that year, the proportion of films based on novels and plays had fallen to thirty-four, or 65 per cent.[66]

A caveat must be entered with regard to these calculations; a number of anomalies may well skew the figures. For instance, there were films based on popular songs, on comic-strip characters, on newspaper serials; there were also several instances of the chicken and the egg syndrome, such as *Unmarried* which was published in book form to coincide with the release of the film.[67] What the figures demonstrate is the dependence of the British film industry on secondary sources, with the industry apparently seeing itself as part of literary Britain. Those ties were further encouraged by the magazines which served the cinema-going public; not only did the publications encourage the visual demands of their readers, by providing photographs of popular players, but they also published film stories and invited readers to contribute to the magazines either by writing poems or by passing judgement on the anachronisms and other assorted idiocies to be found in the latest releases, as in the 'Let George Do It' column in *Pictures*. The assumption to be made, therefore, is that far from presuming that the picture-going audience was an ignorant audience, as some commentators implied, magazines treated their readers, the film-going public, in such a way as to suggest an implicit literary awareness – why else would *The Children of Gibeon* (1920) be advertised in terms of 'slowly but surely the best novels of our best writers [Walter Besant] are finding their way to the screen', or, in the case of *Edge o' Beyond* (1919), 'You have read the book – you will want to see the film'?[68] The popularity of Charles Garvice's novels was sufficient reason to recommend *With All Her Heart* (1920) and in a number of reviews of the period there is an assumption that the cinema-going public was also a reading public.[69]

In an attempt to isolate any further trends occurring over the same period, and to note the kind of source material producers thought suitable for adaptation, it is necessary to examine the social milieu in which British films were set. Given that so many of the films from the early 1920s have been lost or destroyed, the cast and character lists in Denis Gifford's *British Film Catalogue*, as well as reviews and plot summaries from magazines of the period, have been used as the basis for calculation. Where there is doubt as to the social setting of the film, I have consulted the original novels or plays. The arbitrary category 'lifestyles of the rich and privileged' is used to determine the class setting of a film, with the intention of gaining a clearer vision of producer preference. The criteria used to locate films within 'lifestyles of the rich and privileged' take account of the social status of characters, whether they were titled, whether they were described as landowners or employers, whether their residences were staffed, and their named professions. Location is also used to assess status, with that popular territory 'Ruritania' signifying a particular kind of privilege. As stated, the category proposed is entirely arbitrary. The findings are significant in so far as they relate to previously cited evidence concerning the mass audience's rejection of British films and their consequent preference for American product. British cinema-goers were offered a menu of films from which to choose and they chose American films. If equality of production values is allowed – and evidence has been cited to verify such an assumption – the question arises, again: why was such a choice made?

This assessment process is not entirely without difficulty. For instance, *The Fordington Twins* (1920) is described in *The British Film Catalogue* as follows: 'Fishmongers inherit and are blackmailed by their tutor who pretends their uncle is still alive.' In basic outline the précis is correct.

Two brothers who run a Bethnal Green fried fish shop do inherit a considerable fortune from a landowning relative. The dialogue between the men is a litany of dropped and additional 'h's' (as with 'Hexellent idea') and they are described as 'absolute outsiders'. It would, therefore, be possible to classify the novel, and film, as situated in a working-class milieu. However, much of the story takes place in a country town where the lawyer who plans to rob the twins of their legacy is embroiled in a personal attempt to woo a socially superior young woman, become master of the local hunt and take possession of the land and country house of the deceased. The fish-fryers' legacy appears to be little more than a plot device on which to hang a Home Counties melodrama with the Eastenders providing comic relief; because the writer decided that his comic creations were not entitled to virtuous old money, he allowed them to get relatively rich, in their own right, by the purchase of shares in Red Gulch Oil, an American oil company. What the novel implies is that it is more acceptable for working-class characters to be enriched by new money than to inherit old money, and land. On the basis of a closer examination of the plot, therefore, the film not only fits into the appropriate designation because it features a lawyer but because the milieu in which much of the novel is set is County England, in which social relations are cast in an agrarian glow.[70]

Of the ninety-eight novels used as the basis for feature films in 1920, ninety-four may be considered set in the middle to upper reaches of British society. If the figures suggest anything – and it must be remembered that these were the films British audiences crossed the road to avoid – they should be contrasted first with the equivalent sources in 1924, by which time some recognition of the changes in post-war society should have been apparent in the product, and second, with the original material used for films. Using the same criteria, all the feature films produced in 1924 could be classed as dealing with 'lifestyles of the rich and privileged'. Once again there are films which are difficult to classify; *Decameron Nights*, after all, is simply a medieval fantasy, but the principal characters are undoubtedly members of the ruling classes of the society in which the film is set and so, in one sense, it fulfils the 'lifestyles' criteria. *Owd Bob*, directed by Henry Edwards, was 'a simple country story of shepherds and their dogs', but the social formation included a squire and the film, therefore, framed events within the static setting of idealized class relations.[71]

Nets of Destiny, another 1924 production, was based on a novel entitled

The Salving of a Derelict which had won a £100 literary competition in pre-war days. The novel's title appears to offer a rare morsel of social commentary, but such is not the case; the central character is a lawyer whose father's suicide leaves him in less than secure financial circumstances; he temporarily becomes a deck-hand on a ship, at which time 'his breeding, his gentle upbringing, fell from him like a garment', but all ends well when he is able to recompense his lover's family for the fortune his father has misappropriated. The novel clearly portrays the difference between the innately noble hero and the brutish sailors with whom he has to contend. Their language, as in the case of most novels attempting to give voice to characters from the 'lower orders', is, at times, almost incomprehensible.[72] Just as many novels of the time which set all or part of their story in Europe sought to give the plot some validity by including stray phrases of schoolboy French, so many middle-class novelists used their own notions of how other people spoke to identify the differences between classes, with language often linked to morality, and, more often than not, working-class characters functioning as a kind of metaphor for all that was foreign or threatening, all that was alien to English middle-class values.

British producers favoured a particular genre of novel or play and apparently replicated that preference when using original sources. Of the films with original scenarios in 1920, 87 per cent fall into the category 'lifestyles of the rich and privileged'. In 1924 that proportion falls to 83 per cent, but given that there were only nineteen feature films based on original scenarios in 1924 the presence of, for instance, the war reconstruction film *Zeebrugge* is sufficient to obscure the fact that there was virtually no difference between the subject preferences of producers in the separate years. This suggests that original scenarios were far from innovative as far as subject matter was concerned. If this was so, why was it thought necessary to create original scenarios if they did not differ in any significant way from pre-published sources? The industry was aware of the problem of finding new source material. American producers were avidly wooing British writers – note Lasky's negotiations with British authors for original screenplays – while British producers continued to film the same kind of material whether it was suitable to their medium or not. Those producers whose wares were rejected by the public had examples before them of the financial benefits to be reaped from using original material as well as advice from fellow producers on how to tackle audience apathy. George Pearson's reputation as a leading British producer and director was based on scenarios written specially for the screen, and he was adamant that film must find its own way of telling its stories, that the new medium called for a new approach to story-telling. Pearson wrote in the programme notes for the trade show of *Nothing Else Matters* that the 'adaptation of the printed tale designed for the individual reader must inevitably pass … the universality of the film must eventually breed the film tale-teller, just as the printed word bred the novelist'.[73]

And yet, despite Pearson's spectacular success, which, for some years, outstripped his British competitors by a long way, the staple diet of the majority of British film producers continued to be adaptations of novels or plays. These were novels of which the 'chattering classes' talked, plays which had enjoyed successful West End runs; questions, therefore, must be raised regarding their intrinsic merit. In some cases reviewers appear to question the taste of London audiences and this suggests that such plays may have had only a limited regional and/or class appeal. What should be, and should have been, understood is that the audiences for film and drama were different. When Ivor Novello and Gladys Cooper were filming *Bonnie Prince Charlie* in Scotland, Cooper, although no stranger to adulation, was shocked by the overt displays of attention directed at Novello by his fans. Further proof of the less than genteel idolatry exhibited by film fans was on display when Novello and Cooper starred together in London in one of Novello's less successful plays, *Enter Kiki*. The fans who turned out every night to catch a glimpse of Novello presumed to call both the star and Gladys Cooper by their first names, and did so with much vocal abandon. This pleased neither Cooper nor her coterie of stage-door aficionados, who wrote to *their* favourite explaining that 'reluctantly they had come to the conclusion that the rival fans were cheapening the atmosphere around the Play House'. Such was their fear of contamination by Novello's fans that they decided to withdraw from the theatre and wait nearby for Miss Cooper to appear, so that their mutual admiration could be conducted away from the common gaiety of 'the profile's' admirers.[74]

What British producers failed to do was turn theatre into film. Of *The Glad Eye* (1920) – an adaptation of a French farce – a reviewer regretted the fact that the story 'has lost most of its point in being transferred to the screen', but could it have been otherwise?[75] The theatre was (and is), primarily, a medium for text, a vehicle for the spoken word. West End theatre was, especially, based on a performance-led tradition, dependent on outstanding personalities.[76] The way in which film tried to deal with this was to rely, in the first instance, on those actors whose theatrical reputations were thought to be transferable assets, and, in the second instance, to employ a plethora of sub-titles. But as the director and actor Henry Edwards noted: 'Too many sub-titles are merely a confession that the scenario writer or director, or both, could not visualise a thought in a given time ... or that they could not visualise a thought at all.'[77] British producers may not have understood the need for visual narrative, but they must have been aware of the criticisms of their work.[78] More often than not the hybrid offspring of theatre and film simply did not work; *The Twelve Pound Look* (1920), from a J. M. Barrie play, was 'much less convincing, both in story and acting, than the play' and, patently, the majority of audiences were similarly unconvinced.[79]

The journalist and critic Norman Lee entered the film industry in a slightly later period, by which time the custom for stage adaptations was even more entrenched; he described his introduction to directing as follows: 'In order to "play safe" I followed the theatre technique. I selected established plays, engaged artistes who had played in them and shot scene by scene as they reeled it off. The result, of course, was stagey and restricted production.'[80] 'Playing safe', presumably, meant buying up stage successes at inflated prices; in 1923 Simon Rowson paid £20,000 for the Brandon Thomas farce, *Charley's Aunt*, which had been performed regularly on stage since 1896;[81] for an original screen story he was prepared to pay £500 to £600.[82] Walter West offered £500 to 'any author who can supply him with an original story suited to his requirements for filming', but he was said to be disappointed in the material sent to him.[83] It may well have been that Broadwest's strategy had more to do with publicity than a genuine desire to find new stories. There were instances when the unusual circumstances surrounding the acquisition of a story were used for publicity purposes; *The Castle of Dreams* (1919) was written by an eighteen-year-old, Audrey Oliver, who, it was reported, 'had never been in a studio before visiting Wilfred Noy', the director. Some idea of the kind of plots in which producers were interested may be gauged from Oliver's story, which stretches credulity to breaking point; a rich girl is prevented from eloping with her father by the arrival of a surprise guest with prior knowledge of the somewhat tangled familial relationships on show.[84] Scenario competitions usually offered prizes of about £200, as did Ideal, which was looking for 'a screen contribution to the solution of reconstruction problems'.

The contest was won by S. Trevor Jones with 'a story of Love and Labour' entitled *Build Thy House*.[85]

Just as so many propagandists had promised that British films would conquer the world, so the promises of exultant politicians at the end of the war failed to materialize. Few desperately needed new houses were built compared to the orgy of commissions for war memorials from 'regiments, schools, corporations, parish councils, colleges, railway stations and every hamlet, village, town and city in the country'.[86] Downing Street was, of course, refurbished, but, as the 1921 census showed, there were still 750,000 more families than houses in Britain.[87] The political somnambulism of those in power, who seem to have briefly addressed the issues then, like Pontius Pilate, to have washed their hands of the situation, appears to have been based on an arrogant reliance on class stereotypes:

> The mark of the worker is his modesty. He never claims the full measure of his power. He measures himself against his kind; but he has never in bulk made any protest against the class judgement that makes him an oaf ... He has never made any protest against the way he is pilloried in literature ... But the picture cannot continue much longer. It was part of the old understanding that people who were clever, who had money, who had brains, would run the world.[88]

The post-war circumstances put considerable pressure on that 'old understanding'; the personal experiences of hundreds of thousands of men to whom promises had been made were at variance with the presumptions inherent in that understanding.

There was a growing awareness that 'old philosophies and old governments will not give them a chance', that 'millions refuse to accept the comfortable doctrines propounded by the possessing classes that riches and poverty are ordained by God, and that in His House are many mansions, which the poor will enjoy after a life-time spent in the midst of penury and want'.[89] Perhaps the most intensive fragmentation of personal expectations occurred to those who had to confront the fact that there was nothing sacrosanct about heroism; one month ex-servicemen were war heroes, the next they were 'temporary gentleman' living on hand-outs, good-for-nothings living on public charity, traitors if they took part in railway stoppages, revolutionaries if they were policemen striking for a better deal.[90] The experience of many such demobbed men was summed up by Will Oxley, whose descent from war hero to work-house inmate provides a discordant counterpoint to the anthem, 'A Land Fit for Heroes':

> I was a hero for four years once, but the War stopped. They gave me a gratuity and sent me home. The gratuity I spent like a hero … but hero-worship quickly dwindled. There are plenty of heroes in the economic field; they get battered by big guns constantly and nobody says, 'Brave man'. I became a mere unit in the unemployment scheme and as the months went by the blessings of peace fell thick upon me. The mere inflation of being physically safe shrank to nothing … the job which seemed so easy to get when I came out of the army began to look as far away as first prize in the Irish sweep.[91]

If politicians failed to find a blueprint for a new society, or, more importantly, the means to finance minimal elements of that hypothetical blueprint, the film industry attempted to provide images of stability, and, sometimes, hope. *Build Thy House* (1920), the Ideal company's reconstruction scenario, offered hope in the form of a Labour Member of Parliament, but significantly fudged its message by that old plot device of 'lost memory', with its implication that the padre who becomes a campaigning MP does so by accident. Ideal was anxious to distance the film from government policy, announcing that the film 'has nothing to do with Dr Addison's Housing Scheme' – Addison being the government minister detailed to implement the 1919 Housing and Town Planning Act.[92] One review of *Build Thy House* described it in the following terms: 'as a film with a message it is a joke, and the preliminary sub-titles ought to be eliminated, when it will become a quite usable, though not brilliant, war melodrama turning upon lost memory.'[93] Another review stated: 'It handles the pressing problem in a restrained and, above all constructive spirit, not preaching fire and slaughter, but endeavouring to show the way to a happier time in which labour shall enjoy a better life, without violence or injustice to other sections of the people.'[94] In opting for a Laodicean solution to the pressing problems of unemployment and lack of adequate housing, the reviewer echoed the fears expressed in much of the popular and conservative press about the Labour Party's supposed support for all manner of industrial action.[95] The same attitude is to be found in *Topical Budget*, the British newsreel of the period; its ambivalent attitude to industrial action, demonstrated during the transport strike of 1919, had hardened by 1921 when it announced that the 'Coal War' was 'The Greatest Menace We Have Ever Known'.[96]

Not only did organized labour's perceived support for class action threaten the industrial status quo, it demonstrably sought to influence cultural givens; the Arts Guild, set up by the Independent Labour Party, proposed involving communities in the provision of their own entertainment; the Labour Publishing Company brought novels such as Mrs Holdsworth's *This Slavery*, with its Marxist heroine participating in a strike in a manufacturing town, to the attention of the public.[97] One reading of the review of *Build Thy House* cited above suggests that labour's own actions – specifically strike action – were instrumental in bringing 'violence or injustice to other sections of the people', and that the film is, simply, a reiteration of anti-labour sentiment, although the fact that a Labour Member of Parliament, played by the redoubtable Henry Ainley, was the central character must have signified a realization that organized labour was entitled to a voice in the running of the country. The desire for change was demonstrated in the 1923 general election, when Labour replaced the Liberals as the political voice of the organized working classes, taking 191 seats against the Liberals' 158 seats. *Housing* (1920), a short comedy by Walter Forde and Fred Goodwins, dealing with 'the troubles of poor John Citizen when seeking to find a house', was probably far more acceptable to those whose values were dependent on the restoration of a mythical pre-war idyll in so far as it presented the problem in terms of slapstick, although audiences to which the problem was relevant may well have had a deeper reaction to its presentation.[98]

If such a reliance on traditional forms of preserving social equanimity can be said to be indicative of a failure to recognize new realities, new responsibilities, a similar attitude to Britain's literary heritage was evident in some of the more populist film magazines of the period. There appears to have been a certainty about the future success of the British film industry because of its access to 'the best material possible' in the English language.[99] However 'famous' or 'eminent' the authors of the works on which British films were based, the result appears to have been depressingly similar. Butcher's may have advertised their distribution of Stoll's films 'by famous authors' with the emblem of a Union Jack and the slogan 'Be British ... keep a date for a British film every week during 1923', but exhibitors and audiences failed to respond to the message.[100] Perhaps the war had sapped the British public of its patriotic resources; perhaps its expectations of peace, of entertainment, of a new era did not accord with those who sought to control public policy and popular entertainment. There certainly appears to have been a breakdown in the interface between those who sought to control and modify traditional forms of popular entertainment and those who were its principal consumers. The decline in the popularity of the music hall was accompanied by the extension of the cinema network, but the British product which replaced the music hall was substantively different in nature, in class origin, from that of the music hall. Only rarely do music-hall stars appear in British feature films of the period and it would appear that those in control of the industry were bent on replacing what they regarded as the vulgarity of the extant working-class vernacular with a middle-class film version of accepted behaviour and acceptable entertainment.

The slump that saw every British film studio shut in November 1924 was not simply a matter of economics, not only a perceived failure of taste on the part of British audiences. There were British audiences for some British films. In the midst of failure, success was demonstrable. The films featuring Betty Balfour were making their star and her producer, George Pearson, very rich indeed. And where were Balfour's theatrical roots? The Fred Karno troupe, which had spawned Charlie Chaplin, had also featured Syd Chaplin and Betty Balfour on the same bill. Balfour was the only British world-class star of the period, and her background was not in drawing-room comedies, it was in variety, in music hall, and the characters who formed the basis of her relationship with British audiences were defiantly working-class, blatantly fixed within a social milieu which eschewed the decorous, ignored the languid mannerisms of good taste and mocked, with spirit and verve, the threadbare artifice which underpinned so much British product.[101]

It is not unreasonable to suggest that working-class audiences rejected British films and turned to the American product because it had more in common with the music hall than did British films. There was a brashness, a vulgarity, an espousal of familiar values, to which audiences could relate in American films and which was absent from the home-made product. Although the stories took place across the Atlantic, the types were familiar and therefore more accessible to the British working-class audiences who provided the bulk of the market for film in Britain. The transition of material, of artists, from music hall to film was part of a visible process in American films; a similar process did not take place in Britain, at least not on a comparable scale. Commentators then, and since, castigated any signs of slapstick in British films, treating it as if it was a species of irritating insect to be eradicated by a swift, sharp dose of middle-class disdain. There was little or no attempt to bridge the divide which was based specifically on class division, class-specific forms and tastes in entertainment. The heroes of British films were so because of class entitlement rather than for reasons of plot; the individualistic performers of the music hall were displaced by 'types' embodying class values, and acted within a range of expression particular to that class. There was no equivalent in British films to the cowboy, 'the heroic free man'; there was no appearance in the majority of British films, in British literature of the period, of the great slabs of urban life, peopled by urban man, urban woman.[102] British producers, in denying the vitality of the music hall, in refusing to avail themselves of that vitality, reiterated the lack of understanding that was a feature of class relations.

There must, therefore, be at least a suspicion that the choice of subjects by British producers was linked to a completely different range of ideas, to a social and cultural rationale which excluded many of the themes present in American films. That British producers sought some kind of social and cultural acceptance is understandable, and their employment of extant theatrical and literary prestige undoubtedly was a strategy by which they sought approval. The industry was accorded few compliments outside the trade papers; its prestige was minimal and whatever status it sought for itself, by appealing to what could be termed middle-class antecedents, appears to have been solicited in terms reflecting the values of its supposedly more acceptable allies, rather than on the basis that existing forms of popular entertainment, into which it sought to integrate itself and from which it could have drawn performers and material, possessed powerful and legitimate cultural identities in their own right. The failure of the British industry at that time may well have been due to a lack of respect for its natural audience – mirroring the lack of respect accorded the industry itself by the cultural establishment – a lack of respect for the tastes of that audience and a failure to appreciate that same audience's class-specific forms of entertainment. By refusing to look beyond the boundaries of conformist source material the British film industry denied itself the participation, the appeal, the identification with, and therefore support of, an audience which could have secured its popularity and financial stability.

Part II

Screening Britain

5

Responses to the Slump: 'Reclaiming the Stolen Soul of England'

The British Film Weeks movement gave British producers the opportunity to display their product within a nationalistic context while
risking a further erosion of their already tenuous hold on the hearts and
purses of British audiences. The events had been scheduled for November 1923 but were postponed until February 1924 due to a mixture of
lack of interest and adverse economic conditions.[1] The weeks were
promoted with the banner 'British Films for British People' and the
reasons why British films were special were listed:

> Because British films are good British films.
> Because British films are upholders of British traditions.
> Because British films mean British labour.
> And because British films are the sheet anchor of The British
>   exhibitor.[2]

The assertion that 'British films are good British films' is subject to
debate; there is ample evidence, from critics and audiences alike, that
the opposite was the case. British exhibitors and renters could take
issue with the 'sheet anchor' argument; they were showing upwards of
85 per cent American films. And what were the British traditions it was

important to uphold? The overt message of the British Film League was patriotism. One film given considerable publicity and wide release was British Instructional's *Armageddon*, a reconstruction of incidents in Allenby's Palestine campaign. The film was shown at the New Gallery cinema in Regent Street, supported by civic dignitaries and full cere-monial dress, and in other cinemas across London those who had served in Palestine took to the stage and vouched for its validity.[3] Advertise-ments for the film read 'don't miss it if you are a patriot', a rallying call expressing the fact that 'of all peoples we English are possibly the most purely patriotic'.[4] The manager of the Great Hall cinema in Tunbridge Wells was well pleased by his patrons' reactions; they were 'most patriotic in their comments'.[5] The Prince of Wales may have given an exemplary speech at the inauguration of British Film Weeks but 'neither luncheons nor speeches can, in themselves and by themselves, effect very much unless translated into action'.[6] Most regions certainly found time for wining and dining but the promotion of British films was decidedly patchy.

A Film League survey claimed 70 per cent of participating cinema managers 'strongly appreciated' the events; 18 per cent of managers claimed business had been 'normal' while 12 per cent registered a decrease in takings.[7] An overview claimed some suburban cinemas 'did a little better than usual but the majority of houses secured average attendances'.[8] There were, however, problems with both the publicity and the films themselves. Hull exhibitors suspended their attempts to 'boom' the weeks when copies of the films arrived in such poor con-dition that they could not be shown.[9] Very little promotional work was attempted in Leeds and exhibitors in the Midlands blamed 'prolonged unemployment in the region' for poor attendances. In Lancashire there was 'a loss of patronage' in cinemas where British films were shown, and although 200 cinemas in South Wales showed at least one British film during the weeks very little was done 'in the way of focusing public attention upon this Week'.[10]

The nature of the films on show may be gauged by assessing two films trade-shown during British Film Weeks: *Lieutenant Daring R.N. and the Water Rats* and *Eugene Aram*. Very little is to be said for the former; the names of its producers and director are unfamiliar and one review claimed the film was 'utterly divorced from reality and crudely developed [with] production values varying from fair to poor'.[11] *Eugene Aram*'s pedigree was more substantial. Based on a novel by Lord Lytton, it had been a successful starring vehicle for Sir Henry Irving, and was produced by the established firm of Granger-Davidson and directed by Arthur Rooke, who had been on stage for many years. Rooke's output was varied, with a number of rural romances, notably *The Lure of Crooning Water* (1920), and numerous sporting films. He made several films with the 'perfect English couple', Guy Newall and Ivy Duke, and directed the American star Gertrude McCoy in an adaptation of an Edgar Wallace story, *The Diamond Man* (1924). With *Eugene Aram*, Rooke was in classic English territory; the film was about squires, dashing captains, murder, sacrifice and heroism. Publicity for the film was unequivocal: 'Eugene Aram will become known as Britain's greatest picture.'[12] Ultimately the film's credibility was compromised by the flamboyant mummery of its leading man, Arthur Wontner, and a cast of hundreds who had little to do but decorate the space behind the star turn.[13]

Another prestige production given extensive 'booming' was *Becket*, directed by George Ridgwell. Ridgwell had gained valuable experience in America with the Vitagraph company. Returning to England he adapted a number of novels by the ubiquitous Ethel M. Dell and the equally fantastic E. Phillips Oppenheim, whose novels were said to provide a sardonic commentary on post-war Britain. Films made from his stories were regarded as impenetrable by American audiences and his 'absurdity in story-telling methods' was also noted.[14] Ridgwell directed thirty two-reelers based on Conan Doyle stories, featuring Eille Norwood as Holmes, and an adaptation of Edgar Wallace's novel *The Four Just Men* (1921) which was said to be well produced but little more than an episode.[15] *Becket*, made for Stoll, featured the footlights luminary Sir Frank Benson in the name role and was, apparently, little more than a record of Benson's stage performance, bravura even at the age of sixty-five. Some attempt had been made to open up the play by filming part of it at Canterbury Cathedral but, like Stoll's other historical subjects, *Guy Fawkes* (1923) and *Dick Turpin's Ride to York* (1922), the film was slow, with bad sub-titles.[16] Attempts to sell the Stoll product in the United States were met with indifference; the magic of English history meant nothing to American audiences.[17]

In print Sir Oswald Stoll — an Australian by birth — was forthright in his appraisal of the state of the British film industry: 'We are placed in the position of a defeated people, conquered by America, and forced to pay a yearly tribute for many years to come.'[18] Stoll's film-making policy did little to alter that position; his *modus operandi* was to film plays which drew West End audiences and novels that were talked of, featuring as many West End thespians in them as possible, then show them in a Stoll theatre. It was, unfortunately, this theatre-based policy which led another Australian, the newspaper proprietor and theatrical entrepreneur Hugh McIntosh, to complain about how Englishmen were portrayed: 'The Average Englishman shown in pictures is an idiot with an eyeglass. He doesn't exist!'[19] Such characters did exist, especially on West End stages. Such characters gained further exposure in British films but there appears to be little evidence to suggest British audiences appreciated them. On the contrary, during British Film Weeks *Bonnie Prince Charlie*, featuring Ivor Novello, was the one film featuring a British male star gathering plaudits.[20]

As always, the spectre of the theatre and its representation of masculinity was present in the references to Novello. That he was Britain's premier male star cannot be doubted; railway companies ran special excursion trains to Culloden Moor so that the public could watch the filming of *Bonnie Prince Charlie* and during British Film Weeks his popularity matched that of Betty Balfour.[21] In a letter to *Cinema World* a reader from Eltham questioned Novello's abilities: 'What is the attraction of this artiste? Is it the way he does his hair, or has the Flappers' Guild insisted on his continual appearance?'[22] On a different level, D. H. Lawrence mocked the 'softness' of contemporary Englishmen and derided the 'luscious filmy imagination' which responded to the sensual charms of actors such as Novello and Rudolph Valentino.[23] Novello's film *The White Rose* and a Balcon and Saville production for which Alfred Hitchcock wrote the scenario, *Woman to Woman*, featuring a far from 'masculine' performance from Clive Brook, were singled out, during Film Weeks, for criticism by the BBC, which was subsequently accused of broadcasting anti-British propaganda, although *The White Rose* was a D. W. Griffith production.[24] Such performers, or performances, may not have appealed to those with fixed views on British masculinity but this by no means altered the way in which principal roles were written for the cinema and the stage. As one commentator wrote in the following decade: 'it is possible there are so few female roles in plays and films in England for the reason that it is a man-minded country and the authors find it more profitable to write parts for men.'[25]

Part of the problem was, undoubtedly, the film industry's link with the West End of London. If those with the interests of film paramount in their minds are to be believed, cinematic popularity was seen, by many, as no more than a stop-over on the way to Shaftesbury Avenue: 'We have so few really first-class actors and actresses that we can ill afford for them to desert the studio. Yet most of our artistes, having made for themselves a name and gained popular opinion on the screen, seem to turn their attention to the legitimate stage.'[26]

With the development of film-making in California the differences between British films and American imports may well have been compounded. Hollywood was separated geographically from the cultural centres of the eastern seaboard; it created its own culture, its own perverse reality. George Bernard Shaw noted: 'I do not concern myself with Hollywood. I write for America, a quite different country.'[27] Hollywood's cultural roots were diverse – many of its leading producers had entered the cinema industry without first serving a theatrical apprenticeship, and the diversity of personnel and backgrounds, a mirror for the polyglot nation, enabled writers, directors and producers to draw on an extraordinary variety of plots, types and characters.[28] Conversely, the British industry paid allegiance to the West End tradition of the great actor-managers: 'the Garricks and Irvings would carry about with them in private the impress of great Individuals of the Imagination – separated by all the arts of the formal stage-play from that everyday nature of Everyman, which is the particular province of Film-photography.'[29] The London bias undoubtedly influenced the kind of films produced and the kind of male performances transferred to the screen. The virtual reproduction of stage hits, starring theatrical gentlemen, many of an uncertain age for playing heroic roles, was commonplace; no wonder the brooding beauty of Novello touched so many hearts.

While the *Bystander* trumpeted the beauty of London's theatrical players, and *Pictures* assured its readers that such beauty, in itself, was sufficient to ensure Britain's cinematic success, a few dissident voices suggested the unthinkable:[30]

> If the industry is to be saved, it will be saved by a man possessed of a morsel of commonsense and a modicum of understanding. He will seek his players behind the bars of public-houses and the counters of shops and in factories and work-shops. He will nurse his findings and train them to act before the camera ... had that been done ten years ago, there would have been no need for a week during which to tell the public how very bad are our pictures.[31]

Such advice was generally ignored. The majority of producers continued to favour the 'West End Adonis of the crimped hair and knife-edge trousers' and the stage beauties who were given 'very little to do but look charmingly pretty'[32] in roles which appeared to have been designed, rather than written, 'for the garden ... Muslin and picture hats and a blank stare'.[33]

It was also clear that whatever advantages Britain possessed in the way of scenery or the physical beauty of its players, it lacked a monopoly on its own subject matter. The American Bryant Washburn filmed *The Road to London* (1921), claiming that he had to teach English cameramen how to photograph their own countryside,[34] and a German, Ernst Lubitsch, breathed life into Anne Boleyn, an affront remedied by banning the film.[35] Sarah Bernhardt impersonated Queen Elizabeth I, the Danish actress Asta Nielsen brought *Hamlet* to the screen and Douglas Fairbanks *was* Robin Hood.[36] D. W. Griffith was certain that he 'could make as good pictures here [in England]' as he could in America, but those would have been Griffith films first and foremost.[37] If non-British directors could make films in Britain, if directors and producers from all over the world could translate English literature and British history into box-office success, what was left for the British film industry to do? What was the point of asserting, as did the director George Dewhurst, 'I am going to specialize in British scenery', if visiting directors could use the identical scenery to better effect, or could construct equally effective sets on Hollywood back-lots?[38]

The most prolific British film producer of the early 1920s was Walter West. For British Film Weeks, Butcher's, with whom West had a financing deal, included seven films from the West stable among its programme of twelve productions. The only West production not to be directly concerned with sporting events was *Hornet's Nest*, adapted from a novel by Andrew Soutar whose literary preoccupations were also sporting, but who had a penchant for spicing his plots with illegitimacy. In *Hornet's Nest* a lowly damsel commits suicide because a squire's son, who has fathered her child, is not allowed to marry her.[39] West had first-hand experience of the financial difficulties endemic to the British film industry; his production company had gone into receivership as early as 1921, but he survived, with backing from his wife, the popular American-born star Violet Hopson, and guaranteed release from Butcher's.[40] By 1926 West was bankrupt again and in 1927 it was reported that his wife had set up a studio at Hove to train extras for the film industry.[41] British

Film Weeks did little for West's reputation; he made a series of short racing dramas with the champion jockey Steve Donoghue in 1925, which were backed by Gainsborough Films, and delved deep into the grab-bag of British melodrama for *Maria Marten* and *Sweeney Todd*. *Maria Marten* (1928) was said to lack suspense, speed and punch 'and the direction is so respectable that the atmosphere is lost ... the theme and direction are without grip or interest', and *Sweeney Todd* (1928) was not recommended for those who liked modern entertainment.[42] Although the quota legislation gave West's career a temporary fillip he was already, by 1924, a spent force as a producer.[43]

Other producers and directors fared as badly: Kenelm Foss – actor, writer, director, a man who spoke and wrote with enthusiasm of the medium's potential – left the industry; by 1929 he was managing a string of 'Sandy's All-British Sandwich Bars' in central London.[44] A. E. Coleby, 'a patient, sincere, hard-working' director, with a considerable string of mediocre films to his credit, died a disappointed man, according to Victor McLaglen, who starred in *The Call of the Road* (1920) for him. McLaglen noted that Coleby 'had gone out of fashion' before his time.[45] The same could be said for Hugh Croise; he had directed for the London Film Company before its demise and was a founding member of the British Association of Film Directors; he directed a variation on *Three Men in a Boat*, *Four Men in a Van* (1922), and persuaded the illustrious thespian Sir Seymour Hicks to remake *Always Tell Your Wife* (1923) which Hicks had first filmed before the Great War. Alfred Hitchcock was credited with continuing production after Croise fell ill.[46] There were a number of other directors of the same professional status as Croise, veterans of the industry, producing competent but uncompelling films, who appear to fit the description of a character in the actor Miles Mander's novel, *Gentleman by Birth*: 'Mr Timms had a very long experience of film production and during that time had produced sixty-seven dull pictures.'[47]

In the British Film Weeks edition of *Pictures and Picturegoer* it was declared that British producers had failed their public because they had 'allowed Douglas Fairbanks to snatch from us a legacy that is the very soul of England'.[48] The film referred to was *Robin Hood* and if that historical episode, re-created in Hollywood, defined 'the very soul of England', what exactly had been stolen? On the most immediate level the character played by Fairbanks was a romantic hero, a man of daring, guile and not a little energy. In real life Fairbanks also cut a dashing figure and one of the complaints made by British film-goers was that there were few Fairbanks-like heroes in British films. A letter from a male film fan outlined that complaint: 'The British Isles are full of romantic history and legend, and romance walks hand in hand with beauty; why then, do our film companies give us ugly or even plain heroes ... surely all the handsome men with brains are not on the other side of the Atlantic?'[49] Given the adage concerning 'the eye of the beholder' it would be, perhaps, carping to complain of the 'looks' of British actors, although stills from the period, as well as some of the extant performances, tend to substantiate the writer's opinion.

There were leading actors such as like Guy Newall whose features were harshly treated by the camera but who was, as previously noted, one half of what was regarded as an exemplary English couple. Actors such as Jameson Thomas, and ranks of matinee look-a-likes, sparked minimal screen magic but regularly played leading men. Thomas may well have been 'too shy, too gentle and unassuming in the pushful world of celluloid' but that did not stop him going to Hollywood; neither did it add anything to his performances.[50] In one of the last memorable silent films made in Britain, *Piccadilly* (1929), Thomas' acting opposite Anna May Wong's casual, but professional, performance, is hideously mannered, and in later films, such as *Night Birds* (1930), sound on film does not appear to have altered his style in any way. Thomas, and many other lesser actors, played leads in British films; roles which their lack of charisma and often inadequate film technique failed to fill with conviction. But if these were the men, the heroes, charged with personifying 'the soul of England', what hope was there for England and for its film industry?

That there was, and is, a fundamental difference in the way heroism is portrayed in British and American films is borne out by viewing retrospective assessments of screen heroism. The segment about screen heroism in the television series *The Best of British* commences with Sir John Mills reading the following: 'From Tom Brown to Bulldog Drummond, from Biggles to Bader, the British Hero has been represented as schoolboy, sleuth, soldier, sailor, sky-pilot and spy.'[51] The narrative designates Kenneth More as personifying 'all the finest qualities of heroism', citing his performances in *North West Frontier*, *A Night to Remember* and *Reach for the Sky* as evidence. The excerpt from *North West Frontier* shows More telling Herbert Lom that there would have been no native rebellion if the region had been adequately policed by the British, a fictional variation on the view of the British film pioneer Lieutenant Colonel Bromhead that an Anglo-Saxon alliance between the American and British film industries would shape the future of the world.[52] A diversion by way of North Africa to show the self-sacrificing heroism of John Gregson is immediately followed by a scene from *The Malta Story* featuring Jack Hawkins, in uniform, 'in the kind of part that made him the archetypal British hero'. In approximately 23 minutes of film there are in the region of 20 minutes of images of British servicemen, plus the Canadian actor Douglass Montgomery, in uniform, sacrificing his life for the benefit of an English village. Even when Jack Hawkins appears in 'civvies', in *The League of Gentlemen*, his character is an ex-serviceman. Apart from a clip from a Gainsborough bodice-ripper showing Stewart Granger and James Mason fighting, there is no visual evidence to support the notion that someone engaged in everyday pursuits was, or is, capable of heroism.

A line of dialogue from *In Harm's Way*, demonstrative of John Wayne's status as an American Hero, seems apt: 'Old battles are fought by tired men who'd rather be someplace else.' British heroism often appears defined by notions of another age, by old men fortified by mannerisms of a past they have themselves disfigured by reducing it to propaganda. Too often, British films have been accomplices to notions of achievement and heroism that depend for sustenance on the dubious etiquette of *déjà vu*.[53] Perhaps the President of the Trade Union Congress of 1924 also noticed the class bias in British films. Margaret Bondfield called for producers to tell the 'real story of the British people and their struggle towards liberty and culture, that would not be a story of Kings and Queens'; she suggested setting films in the period of Chartist agitation, in the years of the Enclosure Acts; she wanted films to tell the story of the Luddites, of Wat Tyler, of the 'heroic endurance on the part of the masses of unknown people with here and there a leader appearing in a most dramatic way', but, with few exceptions, British film-makers scorned the commonplace, the real-life dramas of the masses or stories of a hero driven by exclusion or injustice to seek solutions, restitution.[54] From Hollywood, so long accused of debasing the tastes of British audiences, would come the stories of Everyman which were ignored by the British industry.

In another television series, *Hollywood Chronicles*, the veteran actor Jackie Coogan asserts: 'the kind of people we choose as our heroes says a lot about the people we are.' American heroes were described as having 'a touch of the rebel about them ... striking individuals ... most of them rising up from the common man ... they also have a self-effacing sense of humour that lets us know they're human after all.' The Everyman qualities of Will Rogers, John Wayne, James Stewart and Spencer Tracy are examined before moving on to the anti-heroes of Montgomery Clift, Marlon Brando and James Dean. The gentle homespun philosophy of the slow-talking, quick-witted cowboy Will Rogers was said to provide the benchmark against which the ideal American hero was judged. Gary Cooper was said to be 'at his best when called upon to play the common man'. James Stewart exemplified the notion that 'good guys can finish first' and Spencer Tracy was regarded as a 'soft-spoken hero' whose screen persona was characterized by 'the power of integrity and belief in our fellow man'.[55] Were there *ever* such heroes in British films? Where then did England's soul reside if not in Everyman?

In a rare juxtaposition of popular culture and high art, W. H. Auden called on a number of British heroes to help explain the contradictions of the age and his own personal frustration; among others he invoked *The Four Just Men*, from Edgar Wallace's novel about murder for the sake of national survival:

> Remember not what we thought during the frost, what we said in the small hours, what we did in the desert. Spare us, lest of our own volition we draw down the avalanche of your danger; lest we suffer the tragic fate of insects.
> O Four Just Men, spare us.

Auden begged Bulldog Drummond to save him

> From all nervous excitements and follies of the will; from the postponed guilt and the deferred pain; from the oppression of noon and from the terror of night

and summoned up the greatest detective of all to clarify the state of flux into which he felt he, and society as a whole, had fallen:

> In the moment of vision; in the hour of applause; in the place of defeat; and in the hour of desertion,
> O Holmes, deliver us.[56]

These British heroes, and other notable fictional creations such as Raffles, may shed some light on who exactly were the custodians of England's soul. Sherlock Holmes and Raffles were pre-war creations;

they were both educated men, both principal components of a male double-act with a Freudian sub-text; Holmes and Watson, Raffles with his adoring chum from public school, Bunny. These male double-acts reached cinematic fruition with the pairing of Charters and Caldicott in *The Lady Vanishes*, *Night Train to Munich* and *Millions Like Us* (among others) in which a gilding of comedy cannot conceal the fact that their shared educational background offers some protection against contemporary reality and isolates them from any engagement with the here and now except when cricket is concerned. They share with Raffles and Holmes a general immunity to women – rarely, but sometimes inexplicably, broached – and a distrust of femininity which is not primarily misogynistic but rather a celebration of maleness, of the world of the all-male club in which, as Kipling said, the loveliest sound in the world could be heard: 'deep-voiced men laughing together over dinner'.[57]

Raffles is a more socially complex character, a gentleman, an Old Harrovian who, from his rooms in Albany, operates as an amateur cracksman, not primarily for pecuniary reasons but for the thrill of the game. Both Holmes and Raffles have no identifiable profession other than gentleman, with Holmes being an amateur sleuth and Raffles an amateur cricketer. That they were gentlemen allowed their creators and illuminators to exploit the idea that is best expressed by Chesterton: 'The romance of the gentleman has been the religion of the Englishman.'[58] Being both gentlemen and amateurs Holmes and Raffles were clearly designated heroic; they were above 'the awful fight for money', which was said to 'hurt our good nature more than we can bear'. Those whose social and financial status allowed them to escape the debasing experience of gainful employment were, by extension, able to retain more of the qualities which were deemed important to identity.[59] A 1923 series of Conan Doyle adaptations did little for the screen careers of Eille Norwood who played Holmes and his Watson, played by Hubert Willis.

Another important ingredient of the heroic English identity was the threat, usually in the shape of a foreigner or outsider of some kind. Throughout the Holmes *oeuvre* there is a sense that the cases he solves, the violin-playing, the cocaine addiction, are carefully constructed anticlimaxes, anticipating the ultimate encounter with Moriarty, a traitor to his class and intellect. In the first West End production of *Raffles*, in 1906, the tension in the play was sustained by the conflict between Raffles and a famous American detective. Despite suspect morality,

Raffles is 'one of us' and therefore excluded from the judgements of normal justice; playing the game is the thing. The morality of the game is not a matter for debate when it is played with a straight and entertaining bat by 'one of our own'. A stage portrayal of a sympathetic character with obviously flawed notions of morality was tolerated, but two film versions using the same character appear to have skewed the stories so as to protect audiences from any socially suspect presumptions as to Raffles's true nature. In *Mr Justice Raffles* (1921), from the Hepworth company, Raffles tackles an evil Jewish moneylender, thus pre-empting any discussion of the morality of the title character; if he was ranged against so familiar a stereotype he was undoubtedly on the side of good. When Raffles returned in 1932 he was a 'reformed burglar' fighting to clear his name and reputation, which had been besmirched by yet another dastardly foreigner.[60]

The ennui cloaking Holmes as closely as London fog and the thirst for danger motivating Raffles were echoed in Bulldog Drummond's first foray into the nation's dramatic consciousness; he places an advertisement in *The Times* which reads: 'Demobilized officer, finding peace incredibly tedious, would welcome diversion.' What better diversion than a trip down Jingo Avenue: all foreigners are 'bloody', all are suitable cases for treatment with fist or gun. From his flat in Mayfair, Drummond saw off 'heathen Chinese, mysterious Russians, ugly men of vague Scandinavian extraction or, worst of all, Germans, and into the bargain, Jewish'.[61] National honour was vindicated by a hero whose disdain for everything non-British was the ultimate expression of national identity; a hero whose brainpower was 'more often used to confirm prejudices than to dispel them';[62] prejudices that were most aptly enunciated by the villainous Englishman in Wilkie Collins' *The Woman in White* – 'You foreigners are all alike!'[63] The 1925 production *Bulldog Drummond's Third Round*, with the dapper Jack Buchanan, and an earlier feature, *Bulldog Drummond* (1923), filmed in Holland with the fading American matinée idol Carlyle Blackwell as Drummond, both employed the expected stereotypes of vicious foreigners at odds with the stout-hearted British hero. To a lesser or greater degree the characters created by Kipling, Buchan, and even Edgar Wallace, exhibited the same kind of insularity: the 'Englishman with a smile on his clean-shaven lips, engaged in admiring himself and ignoring the rest of the world'; or putting it right.[64]

The pattern for British heroes was well-used, and only those cut from a certain cloth were capable of protecting British reputations, British national identity: 'members of Parliament and members of the Athenaeum, lawyers and barristers, business men and minor peers ... each character carries round with him his school, his regiment, his religion, often touched with calvinism; memories of grouse-shooting and deer-stalking, of sport at Eton, debates in the House.'[65] Graham Greene was referring specifically to John Buchan's novels, but, as noted previously, British film producers appeared to be obsessed with stories about life among the upper classes. Perhaps a glimpse of such lives, such places, may well have matched the flickering dreams of cinema audiences, but by conflating privilege and heroism, by making heroism class-specific, British producers were offering pictorial validation of Wyndham Lewis's comments on British society: 'It is by Snobbery, in fact, that a community is ruled.'[66]

What, though, of Robin Hood? How does he fit into the national equation? Sherwood Forest was his address, not Mayfair; he may have been high-born but among his friends, his fellow outlaws, were society's rejects; and he fought the rich on behalf of the poor. The British film industry was quick to subvert a character which crossed class barriers. In a modern-dress version of the Robin Hood story, *Crackerjack* (1938), the central character was re-named Drake – another name synonymous with national identity – and his mission was to steal from the rich in order to endow hospitals and carry out similar good deeds. Modern dress compelled the actor in the role, Tom Walls, to feature evening suits and a jaunty monocle as the uniform of heroism, however comedic.[67] Reel and real life overlapped when one reviewer was surprised to find the actor's character residing in a Bayswater hotel in one of his films; London W2 was a foreign country, Belgravia his usual habitat.[68] And if Walls' film could be said to exemplify the English confidence in 'nonsense as the only way of settling their social and political problems', both his technique and the character he portrayed were subject to adverse scrutiny by commentators who questioned their continuing relevance.[69]

The Englishman, according to Hilaire Belloc, left government, the organization of society 'to his betters, the American acknowledges none'; in so doing the Americans, and the film industry which catered to that notional equality, reinforced attitudes which were inimical to Britain where all members of society supposedly admired the wealth and superiority of the privileged, with no evidence of envy or class antipathy

– 'Full unity marks the whole nation'.[70] The British social paradigm was rigid compared to the theory, and in some instances the practice, of American society. There was a different spirit motivating social relations in the United States: 'we [in England] have the forms of democracy and not the spirit and I fear the forms without that essential idea that goes with them are dangerous.'[71] In England past triumphs were used to validate the mistakes of the present; there was a particular kind of arrogance which alluded to a period in which 'the Englishman was … in the nineteenth century the richest man in the world; we might even say the only rich man in the world', and for the rich there was no need for mediation, for negotiation.[72] To admit that custom was the arch-enemy of understanding was tantamount to recognizing that the challenges of a new age were not responsive to tradition, and that the dysfunctional elements in society needed to be addressed with at least a modified set of values; instead of the past illuminating the present it seemed to cast a shadow over it.[73] In the face of social fragmentation, of reactions against the horrors of war, the urbane indifference of complacent politicians and the deadening weight of poverty and disablement, not only the ruling classes dealt their cards from an antique pack; a significant proportion of those whose lives were directly influenced by the failure to come to terms with post-war economic and social change reverted to history, calling up images of a time when every workman was his own boss, when personal industry was a hedge against the world at large.[74] The more radical wing of the Labour movement saw the countryside as a promised land, a panacea for unemployment and industrial blight, but as one commentator noted: 'All political parties carry around with them, as a sort of talisman, a land programme which is little more than a vote trap.'[75] In the 1923 election Stanley Baldwin sought to project an image of himself which was calculated to convince the public that he stood for 'the personal', the 'human touch', for 'the old bluff Master-and-Man, parish-pump relationship'. His campaign slogan was 'honesty' and he promised a return to the old decencies, the Old England. The cultural, political and social dichotomy of Baldwin's reactionary stance was personalized within his own family, with his son becoming a socialist Member of Parliament and bitterly defying almost everything for which his father stood.[76] Chesterton may have proclaimed in *The New Jerusalem* the absolute necessity of 'going back to the old even to find the new' but the fact remains that history, the distortion of history, may be a shared and illusory fortress against change, and, in a more divisive sense, a justification for ignoring evidence which signals necessary change.[77] There is a danger to any society when atrophy is preferred to adaptation, and while there were elements within British society which pulled, in different directions, against the deification of an *ancien regime*, there is a sense within the period that the overwhelming reaction to the anthem 'The Anglo-Saxon race is in danger' was one of retrospection:

> We cannot dance upon the table
> Now we're old as souvenirs,
> Yet as long as we are able
> We will remember bygone years.[78]

In the years immediately following the Great War the paternalist solution may have seemed attractive to those who sought to nullify the disruption of established class mores fuelled by conditions at home and events in Europe. The Irish problem refused to go away, refused to be tempered by four years of war. The British campaign in Northern Russia, against a proclaimed workers' state, was hugely unpopular, and if the Labour Party was 'meekened by the spectacle of communism triumphant', members of the other two parties were horrified at the possible penetration of foreign ideas into Britain.[79] It was said that Churchill willingly spent £100 million 'trying to put the clock back in Russia to his own feudal date, which is about the middle of the fourteenth century', but the class and interests he represented were unwilling to spend a similar amount on the social well-being of a deprived section of their own society.[80] It was foreign ideas at fault if the values of the paternalists were questioned: 'Away with their filthy books which corrupt our innocent sons and daughters, English justice, English morals, England for the English.'[81] And away with American films!

If American screen images were threatening, and they were thought to be so especially to the inhabitants of places like Shoreditch and Wigan 'who do not understand the King's English' and who were 'quite uneducated, absolutely unintelligent, and obsessed by a sadistic love of violence and brutality' fostered by American films, the morality of the film-makers and stars was even more dangerous.[82] For some, that was the attraction of American films and American stars: 'We like to imagine them as reckless and dissipated creatures defying the conventions, outraging the dull respectabilities. We like to think of Hollywood as a glorious sink of iniquity, full of drink and dope and illicit love, scarlet nights and unrepentant mornings, fortunes flung away to satisfy a whim.'[83] It was disingenuous of those who proclaimed a higher moral code, a distaste for the barbarism of Hollywood, simultaneously to feast on the antics of the Bright Young Things disporting themselves in Belgravia and environs, and reported with maximum prurience by Fleet Street for 'the middle-class readers of the newspapers as an outrage against ... common decency'.[84] There was no need to look to Hollywood to find people who drank, took drugs and stole each other's men or women; the press was full of stories about the self-proclaimed 'People of the Aftermath' whose reaction to the war, and against the drive towards the re-establishment of pre-war insouciance, was a dereliction of propriety, an embracing of largely American forms of culture and entertainment: 'There's negro music in our ears, the world is one huge dancing floor.'[85]

The fundamental problems in Britain – unemployment, lack of housing – could not be disguised or glossed by any number of rural romances. If there was no rebellion, there was bitter disappointment, not the least because the sacrifices of so many young lives appeared to be squandered in a nihilistic orgy.[86] Those with the means engaged in a reckless and high-profile exhibition of nonchalance in the face of the disequilibrium around them. The working classes were counselled not to display behaviour which would undermine their respectability, a key ingredient in the paternalist equation; they were urged to wait, to be patient, and if the building of Jerusalem seemed a long way off, it would be built, one day:

> There's a good time coming, boys
> A good time coming;
> The pen shall supersede the sword,
> And right, not might shall be the lord,
> In the good time coming,
> Worth, not birth, shall rule mankind,
> And be acknowledged stronger,
> The proper impulse has been given –
> Wait a little longer.[87]

With a show of some impatience, and, perhaps, misplaced optimism, the working classes elected a Labour government, but if they thought a representative government would be more inclined, more able, to meet their demands, they were soon disillusioned. The extent of the Labour Party's vision in opposition, or in government, was minimal; its

Utopian dreams were limited to conjecture about a society in which 'all the arduous and dirty work would be passed on to machines, while the citizen only did enough to justify working-class complacency; with gymnastics for all, and a great Army of University Extension lecturers to keep up the intellectual tone',[88] – or as D. H. Lawrence gently lampooned:

> We've got a change of government
> if you know what I mean.
> Auntie Maud has come to keep house
> instead of Aunt Gwendoline,
> They say that Auntie Maud, you know
> is rather common; she's not
> so well brought up as Gwendoline is,
> so perhaps she'll be more on the spot.[89]

Being on the spot may have required more than the minimal vision displayed by the Labour government; in office the Labour Party simply went through the administrative motions like a pianola operator playing 'Greensleeves', with no clear policies for tackling the housing and industrial crises.

The film industry, always a bastion of conservative Toryism, gave a cautious welcome to the Labour government: 'The view of the present Labour Government, it is understood, is that the cinema should provide a cheap and innocent relaxation to the people after the daily labour is over. Hence the hopes of the film trade.'[90] While Ramsay MacDonald was auditioning for the role of premier, *Film Renter and Moving Picture News* published 'A New Year's Message from the Future Prime Minister' which was as bland as it was complacent: 'I shall always be glad to do anything I possibly can to assist those who are fighting so splendidly for British films ... we have reservoirs of nature, ideas and life, as well as artistic taste and sensibilities which are an inexhaustible reservoir for film production.'[91] Another article reminded readers that MacDonald 'has publicly declared' that he was 'sick and tired of the foreign film'. With foresight the article concluded that MacDonald's antipathy towards foreign films may be a temporary malaise, readily 'cured by his accession to office and his removal from the Opposition'.[92] Such was the case; in office Labour was as radical as one of Hepworth's languid rural romances, although, in truth, with Labour only sustained in power by the Liberals, it was as radical as it was allowed to be. The mainstream of the Labour Party had elected to participate in the running of a capitalist society, of an imperial power, and its acceptance of the written and unwritten rules of the British power game precluded it from sanctioning class war or social revolution.[93]

Furthermore, if the eloquence of Ramsay MacDonald is to be given credence, he was as fervent in his participation in the mythology of Old England as were his fellow statesmen from the Liberal and Conservative parties. The image MacDonald portrayed, and endorsed in print, was that of a countryman, a romantic but high-minded squire, rather than the outsider with a penchant for London Society and titled ladies:[94] 'The Premier is a distinctly outdoor type ... no one is more stirred by the beauties of the landscape; for in him there is the spirit of the poet, too, as anyone who has heard him read "When lilacs last in the door-yard bloom'd" can attest.'[95] This evocation of the rural myth, the mythology of squire and subject, nature and man in harmony, was synonymous with both the anti-industrialism of poets like D. H. Lawrence and W. H. Auden –

> They invited them into a squalid town,
> They put them in factories and did them down
> Then they ruined each other for they didn't know how
> They were making the conditions that are killing
>   Them now.[96]

– and 'the very soul of England' appropriated by Douglas Fairbanks in *Robin Hood*.

British film-makers favoured a similar template: 'we have wonderful scenery, the type of scenery which will be welcomed in all parts of the world, representing as it does, a quiet, orderly beauty amid which humanity may blossom in its highest form.'[97] But what was that highest form of blossoming humanity? It was the negotiation between the dispossessed – 'a robber band has seized the land and we are exiles here' – and those beneficiaries of often accidental acts of history which gave them possession of vast tracts of the British countryside. *This* was the English speciality served up as representative of British national identity.[98] For the sake of national identity everyone was led to believe an ancestor had sat for Gainsborough or Reynolds, that the country house and thatched cottage were the only architectural sureties and that it was an entirely functional activity for thousands of people to desecrate the rural environment by gathering lilacs down whatever English lane they could locate in advance of the constantly recruited batallions of suburban soldiers intent on arcadian plunder – weekends only.

There may well be some truth in Coward's assertion that the period was 'without a style of its own, but with full liberty to borrow from any wardrobe of the past', but such was the selectivity of the images purloined that the collection of relics given prominence, the aura of authenticity which validated everything from Shell Oil advertisements to the vogue for country dancing, served to alienate urban Britain from its habitat.[99] The trustees of Britain's national identity decreed that suburbia was heaven, that the true British way of life only began at the end of the Metropolitan Line: 'The Happy Homestead to which Hubby smilingly gave Wifie the key, that little corner of a loving heart that is forever Metroland.'[100] Similarly, the films marked truly, deeply British were those which British Film Weeks scored with traditional tunes. *Beside the Briar Bush*, first released in 1921, was, according to reviews, what British and Empire audiences wanted to see: Scotland, lairds and castles, happy peasants finding love amid the heather.[101] *Brenda of the Barge* was applauded for being 'typically English': 'we float lazily through the locks and quiet waterways that are to be found nowhere else in the world.' A lack of knowledge of European waterways and inordinate praise given to a film which was unsuccessful on its initial release in 1920 hardly suggests a balanced review, or an appreciation of film as a property in its own right, rather than an expression of national identity.[102]

If anyone could be trusted to portray the rural myth on screen it was Cecil Hepworth: his films were regarded as being 'representative of English thought, deeds and character, without any imitation of other countries whatsoever'.[103] Hepworth was represented during British Film Weeks by five productions, with the remake of *Comin' thro' the Rye* the centrepiece. With ill-judged optimism Hepworth showed an incomplete version of the film accompanied by a mimed tableau on stage to piece together the missing reels. Its presentation, with multiple dissolves bridging scenes in which 'LIVING actors [went] silently through their parts' on stage between completed scenes, may well have been 'a remarkable precedent', but it did very little for Hepworth's finances.[104] Hepworth was a veteran film-maker, and in many ways a visionary figure within the British industry; before the war he had experimented with the reproduction of sound for film – the vivaphone – although the way he constructed his films in the post-war years was said to be outmoded; Ernest Betts described the process as building up stories in 'chunks –

generally of pineapple or Hepworth rock'.[105] What appears self-evident is that his integrity and vision coalesced to produce films redolent of an England of the past, portraying a vision which was, for many British critics, enough to negate any criticism of the films as entertainment: 'No American film contains such beautiful pictures as Comin' thro' the Rye.'[106]

This is not to say that Hepworth was not aware of the demands of the age, of the British film industry itself; he answered the call of the British Film League to 'Capture America' by opening offices in the Loew State Theatre in New York and was confident of placing eighteen films in the American market.[107] Such optimism flew in the face of reality. According to one report, only seven British films had been sold to the United States during 1922 and 1923 and the American exhibitor, Samuel Rothapfel, who controlled one of the premier New York venues, the Capitol Theatre, was equally certain that American audiences would not respond to the old-fashioned kind of films Hepworth made, which were 'too slow in their tempo, their sub-titling is very bad ... [they] are in need of dramatic overhauling'.[108] The rural myth which permeated much of Hepworth's output was far from applicable to the American experience. American popular culture fed off and into a myth which was primarily optimistic, forward-looking, embracing the art of the possible, the possibility, the probability of self-advancement; it was ever ready to superimpose a sunrise on a sunset, laughter upon tears, riches in place of poverty; it did not trade in the social or economic verities which were integral to the stories Hepworth filmed.

Winston Churchill clearly understood the schematic differences in the British and American situations; writing of the opportunities exploited by Chaplin he noted:

> Life was more fluid than in England ... its forms had not set ... personalities were more important than convention ... Class distinction mattered very little when the assistant of today was so often the employer of tomorrow. Even poverty wore a different face in America ... it was not the bitter, grinding destitution Charlie had encountered in the London slums ... it was not imposed from without.[109]

Churchill's key phrase concerns the poverty 'imposed from without'. A particular class of British society was thought to be born to poverty: poverty imposed as part of an inalienable social formation, class and poverty feeding off and reinforcing each other. A statement such as 'personalities were more important than convention' was antithetical to the British situation, where convention was more important than almost anything else. That is why advertisements in a whole range of magazines differed so markedly in America; film magazines such as *Picture-Play Magazine* included not only the usual kind of invitations to write or act for the movies but also more general advertisements for home-based education, for courses of various kinds, to teach skills which were useful both in terms of employment and enhancement of the quality of life.[110] *Fame and Fortune*, a men's magazine, was suffused with a spirit mirroring Churchill's statement that 'the assistant of today is so often the employer of tomorrow'. The magazine ran for at least twenty-five years, promoting a devotion to the work ethic and personal enterprise which it summed up in a poem entitled 'A Success Secret':

> Though some inherit lands and gold,
> And fortunate are they,
> They still must work the wealth to hold
> Or it will get away,
> Bad luck or good luck never found
> Those talents buried in the ground,
> The fish are caught within the sea
> And never on the shore,
> A poor man he will always be
> Who never tries for more,
> The truth exists and always will;
> One gets nowhere by standing still.[111]

The validity of the American Dream is, of course, a subject for debate, for argument, and yet its power was sufficient to imbue the American film industry with a particular view of democratic practices; in film the treatment of labour relations, of racial relations, owed more to the dream than to reality, but in doing so it portrayed the possibilities inherent in a system which reduced the essential elements of its dream to a Jack the Giant-Killer fairy tale where the erstwhile outsider could find his or her way inside.[112] On the contrary, the enduring power of the class system in Britain determined how society was presented on screen. The treatment of poverty on screen, the arrangement of social types, the portrayal of heroes, of heroic acts, lacked democratic credibility compared to American films. The proportion of films set within a particular social milieu takes on significance because it excludes whole sections of society from a range of personal qualities which, in turn, denies access to, and identification with, national identity. The myth of a contented and unchanging society – of sections of that society happily subservient, content with poverty – was transformed by British film-makers into images as remote and entrenched as the privileged smiles in portraits hung in county seats and Belgravian town houses.

In stills from Hepworth's films one sees in his heroine's faces a sense of refined suffering, purity under threat, stifled happiness, and, at times, a hint of sexual hysteria – a sense that the roles were the cinematic equivalent of the work of the Pre-Raphaelite Brotherhood, a revisionist order motivated by a distaste for the contemporary lack of sincerity and fervour. Alma Taylor could have posed for Rossetti's *Found* or Holman Hunt's *The Awakening Conscience*, and Hepworth's pictorial sense, his rural absorption, set her against a vista in which her presence acted as a conduit for a way of life which had ceased to exist on its own terms, which survived on a life-support system of metropolitan money, anti-materialism and nostalgia.[113] It may be stretching the imagination to suggest that Hepworth and D. H. Lawrence were an artistic alliance pre-empted by the censor, but the figure of Constance Chatterley in Lawrence's novel of 'the rape of the countryside by industry after World War I' embodied what Lawrence regarded as the rightful nature of English man/woman's relationship with each other and with the land, and the same kind of retrospective idealization is evident in Lawrence's deification of the game-keeper and his life-style as Hepworth exhibited in his choice of subject matter. Lawrence's novel begins, 'Ours is essentially a tragic age, so we refuse to take it seriously' – so too British audiences refused to take Hepworth's plangent vision seriously.[114]

As Hepworth's images fine-tuned the rural idyll, so Lawrence's poetry employed negative contemporary imagery – 'Oh, over the factory cities there seems to hover a doom so large, so dark, the mind is lost in it'[115] – to attack the failure of modern society to deal with man's unhealthy separation from his agrarian roots. While titles flickered on the screen – 'Oh God, put back thy universe and give me yesterday'[116] – the images appearing in so many British films were of a timeless England, with elegiac depictions of an unruffled social order and gracious paternalism, with little but the changing seasons, and fraught but muted sensibilities, to disturb the progressive anaemia of a moribund vision. There were minimal excursions into the cities – 'with byres of poverty down to the river's edge, the cathedral, the engines, the dogs'[117] – where 'the dead tread heavily through the muddy air, through the mire of fumes heavily, stepping weary on our hearts', and where dark corners and disordered geometry contained threats and temptation.[118]

The 'hideous carnival of brutalising passion' present in the great cities of England, and in American films, was poison to most British film-makers.[119] But it was an urban, working-class audience which largely sustained the film industry – 80 per cent of tickets sold were in the lower price brackets, less than ninepence a seat – and it was to their tastes, and their preferences, that British producers should have been directing their product.[120] Instead, the audience's tastes were mocked: these crass film fans were said to 'consider that no picture of modern life is complete without a cabaret scene, or better still, a limited ballet on a dining-room table'.[121] These same audiences, this body of film-goers mostly ignored by British film-makers, were those to whom a few pence meant escape, for they relished, most of all, American sunshine; they dreamed, for minutes, sometimes hours, of far-off places, far-off dreams – always the safest – in halls raked back to back with factories and slums. Cosseted against the fog and the cold, thrilled by the exploits of Tom Mix and Buck Jones, they laughed at the antics of Chaplin and Keaton with ebullient, raucous laugher; threatening laughter which destroyed, in an instant of spontaneous release, the myth of the graceful submission of the working classes to natural order and social mortification.[122] How incredulous must have been the reaction to Chaplin's announcement that he wanted to make films in the slums of England and not in some saffron-dappled vale where he could have donned the red of hunting squires and dined on the Roast Beef of Old England.[123]

One producer's appetite for particular British recognition was showcased during British Film Weeks. J. S. Blackton had far more than roast beef and cabbage in mind when he returned from America. Blackton had once been at the forefront of the American film industry but his star was waning. His declining Hollywood career was punctuated by reviews which noted a flagging technique and a growing tendency to film melodramas which were 'rather poor melodramas, too English for the American taste'.[124] Blackton's imagination, and his return to England, were inspired by a conversation on Sir Thomas Lipton's yacht, Shamrock: if Lipton could be knighted for selling tea, Lever for selling soap, and Dewar for selling whisky, why couldn't Blackton be honoured for his pioneering work in the film industry?[125] There was a legitimate case to be made for Blackton presuming that a peerage would be forthcoming.

The awarding, more accurately the buying and selling, of titles had fallen into some disrepute, a process archly commented on by one contemporary writer: 'In these days when someone for whom we have no respect receives a knighthood or a title, we may at least console ourselves with the reflection that he may not have done anything to deserve it.'[126]

Blackton's last great adventure, in search of a peerage, was transformed into *The Glorious Adventure* (1922), featuring the exquisite society beauty Lady Diana Manners; the film – 'Old Englishe' at its most stately – was a failure both in England and America.[127] In England Blackton moved in all the right circles, he photographed the right places, he employed the right performers, but he evidently made the wrong films. It may have appealed to those whose notion of culture was a flick through the pages of Burke's Peerage, and Blackton ensured the cream of British society turned out for the première of his epic, but his technique and vision had not moved with the times. Blackton's selection of subject matter may be read as an homage to those with whom he wished to ingratiate himself, those whose history, whose lineage, gave them social precedence and in whose grace and favour his future social status rested. Blackton's contribution to the British Film Weeks was another piece of moth-balled history. From an overblown novel entitled *My Lady April*, *The Gipsy Cavalier* (1922) featured the boxer Georges Carpentier as a fop posing as a gipsy; the plot was set in the gipsy valleys of a never-never England with a villainous King of the Gipsies and a titled character played by a titled actor – Sir Simeon Stuart. Like his only other British-made film, *The Virgin Queen* (1923), it was slow and decorous, and less than favourably received by British audiences. Blackton's period in England was notable primarily because of his capacity for self-advertisement and it would appear that his reputation remains dependent on his position as a pioneer of the industry rather than as a director of individual flair and imagination.[128]

The British Film Weeks failed to revive the careers of a number of important figures in the industry; reputation counted for nothing with a public openly expressing a preference for American product. Exhibitors and renters understood their audiences far better than did producers: 'Show in your theatres British films, whenever they are good enough to show; but show a film no matter what the country of origin, that is good entertainment, and one that the public will be interested in.'[129] It remains a matter for debate whether or not it was a lack of the necessary

George Pearson and Betty Balfour were at the forefront of popular entertainment in the early 1920s

ALMA TAYLOR

The 'First Lady' of British films in Post-war Britain

Ivor Novello outraged defenders of British masculinity but appealed to movie fans everywhere

A wry comment on the state of British Cinema in the 1920s

No. 908. Vol. LVIII.

March 6, 1924

The

BIOSCOPE

PRICE
6d.

Copyright

Registered at the G.P.O. as a newspaper and for postage to Canada at magazine rate

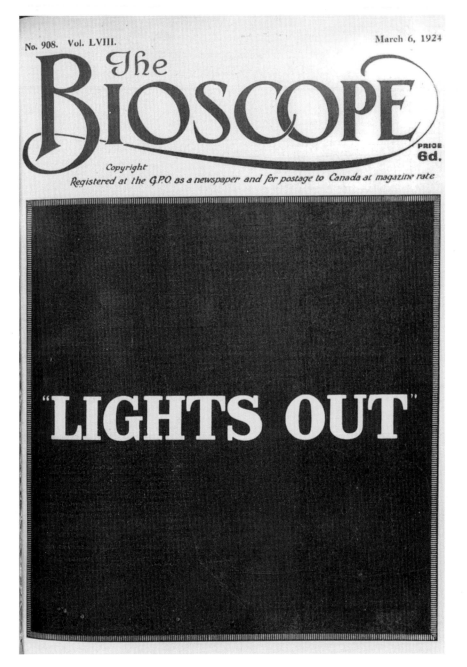

"LIGHTS OUT"

The British film industry signals its own demise

THE
KINEMATOGRAPH
WEEKLY
Registered at the G.P.O. as a Newspaper.

NOV - 8 -
No 863
VOL. 81 Pri
30/ PER
POST

ARMAGEDDON
The most noteworthy Film of the Year
PASSED & APPROVED BY
HIS MAJESTY'S ARMY COUNCIL
WILL COMMENCE A SEASON AT
THE NEW TIVOLI, STRAND, LONDON
ON MONDAY 12TH NOVEMBER, 1923
NEW ERA FILMS LTD
26/27 D'ARBLAY ST WARDOUR ST W.I.
NE: REGENT 5319   GRAMS: NURAFILM

The British Essentials

Betty Balfour

Back to basics in Quotaland

personal and creative attributes which led to so many actors, directors, personnel of all kinds, failing to engage British audiences; it is as likely that the industry itself failed to realize, to nurture, the potential of those on whom its future depended. The exceptions to the rule were few; the Pearson and Balfour films did a roaring trade during British Films Weeks although most of them had been seen before.[130] *Southern Love*, an early Herbert Wilcox production filmed in Vienna with the American star Betty Blythe, was another raging success in Britain and was sold, at its trade show in January 1924, to North America for £63,000.[131] What was common to Wilcox's exotic melodrama (based on Longfellow's poem *The Spanish Student*), Ivor Novello vehicles and Betty Balfour's impersonations of Cockney spirit, was that they dealt in familiar cinematic clichés; they were first, and only, designed as entertainment, rather than expressions of English superiority or art.

If the soul of England was compromised in any way, it surely was by the failure of the industry to recognize its role as a provider of entertainment; in perpetuating a series of stereotypes, in forcing its creative personnel to work within a self-imposed range of material, the British industry not only curtailed creative possibilities but denied the experience of a mass audience ready and willing to respond to the wider consciousness, the more elastic imaginations, at work in Europe and North America. While commentators, and industry personnel alike, announced that 'British was Best', the exhibiting and rental sectors of the industry knew otherwise. Booking practices may well have distorted the situation but there was an audience willing to respond to a particular kind of British film. Reviewing the events of British Film Weeks it was clear that lessons had to be learned:

> It is useless expending thousands of pounds on stories the themes of which leave a nasty taste in the mouth; it is useless attempting to make photoplays that will not have a general appeal ... It is no use having Film Weeks and telling Kinema patrons that big things are to follow if the productions they embark on are merely stupid pictures, badly acted without any sense of direction.[132]

Apparently too few producers and directors were willing, or able, to recognize what it was that British audiences wanted to see. With the British industry about to self-destruct it was only the strong, the original, the producers who saw in film the most important global entertainment medium of the century, who would survive.

6

Government Intervention: Legislating the Intangible

I n opening the debate in the House of Commons on the second reading of the Cinematograph Films Bill, on 16 March 1927, the President of the Board of Trade argued that the premise of the Bill, the reason why legislative measures had been contemplated in support of the British film industry, was a sentiment 'prevalent in the House and the country and throughout the Empire'. That sentiment was defined as 'a realisation that the cinema is today the most universal means through which national ideas and national atmosphere can be spread, and even if those be intangible things, surely they are amongst the most important influences in civilisation'.[1] What became clear, in the debates, was that the British definition of civilization, of morality, of 'intangible things' was superior to American versions of the same and once again it was 'the perverse public' who had to be persuaded of the supremacy of Britishness.[2] The *Daily Express* clearly outlined the British public's apathy to the home product, which, it argued, was a by-product of British audience's exposure to American films:

> From begining to end of these quota negotiations, not one word has been said about producing the kind of film which the British public wishes to see, but the ordinary man will be disposed to think that should be the keystone to the whole discussion. The

plain truth about the film situation is that the bulk of our picture-goers are Americanized to an extent that makes them regard a British film as a foreign film, and an interesting but more frequently an irritating interlude in their favourite entertainment. They go to see American stars; they have been brought up on American publicity. We have several million people, mostly women, who to all intent and purposes, are temporary American citizens.[3]

This Americanization of the British general public had led, it was claimed, to the 'lowering of the standards of British taste and even British morals' but, as a number of members argued, a quota, of whatever per cent – starting at 5 per cent in 1929 and rising to 20 per cent by 1938, for exhibitors – left British audiences open to American influences for the rest of the time. Were audiences meant to be so morally uplifted, so assured of Britian's right to arbitrate taste and define civility, by a fraction of the time they spent in the cinema that they would be immune to the contrary propaganda contained in American films?[4] The British audience's apparent preferences were, according to one commentator, based on a false premise:

It is false to assume that the public prefer American films. The present generation, grown up within the last seventeen years, were either infants or barely adolescent, when they first ventured into a place of entertainment [and] they were confronted with the American picture. At that time they were a generation without a past. The War created a psychological hiatus, hence they never became acquainted with British drama, with its comedies, humour and all that accompanies it, as it existed before the War.[5]

This analysis allied itself with the British industry's obsession with the historical and literary pedigrees of source material: 'I cannot believe that in a country, which since the days of Shakespeare, in practically every century and almost every decade, has produced literary genius which has commanded the attention and admiration of the world, will fail today in producing a scenario which is comparable with that produced by other literary genius.'[6] It was almost as if the British film industry was charged with re-imposing the lost history of the nation on those whose cultural and cinematic eduction had been obtained by sitting in cinemas watching Hollywood movies. The twin planks of the British film-makers' re-educational plan were the rural melodrama and the West

End success – celluloid scenes from the lives of the privileged staged for the benefit of society columnists, with the country house and Mayfair as alternating locations. This narrow vision, this assumption that in Britain there resided some inherent superiority, peppers the parliamentary debates on the future of the industry: 'Is there any reason why we cannot produce good films? ... After all, we have the advantage of scenery. Take Haddon Hall, for instance – where would you find a finer example of an English house? – or some of the old Dorsetshire manor houses, with green lawns and beautiful trees as a setting for a film. We have advantages which America has not got.'[7]

Consciously, or unconsciously, British producers and directors attempted to appropriate the most significant form of twentieth-century working-class culture, attempted to wash British screens clean of the comparatively classless images of Hollywood. In doing so, according to the critic C. A. Lejeune, companies such as Gaumont produced particular kinds of films with a specific creative and cultural rationale ('you can take your eldest aunt or your youngest sister to a Gaumont-British film and know that there will not be a single line or situation to bring the blush of shame to the cheek of modesty')[8], and at Elstree, E. M. Forster opined, 'British Ladies and Gentleman turn the movies into Stickies'.[9] The fact that cinema was 'a complete drawing-room and backyard of the world's manners' was anathema to those whose identity and cultural legitimacy were defined in terms of a rigid set of manners and customs which separated them from, placed them above, the rest of society.[10]

If it is legitimate to suggest that at least some knowledge – however inaccurate – of how people in another country live and behave may be gained from watching that country's films, the clearest evidence of how British film-makers portrayed Britain may come from the United States. If Americans regarded England as 'a refuge from an egalitarian society', on what evidence did they base that opinion?[11] Did British films lead them to imagine England to be 'a glorified park, studded with thatched cottages, preserved rustics and ringed with hotels, for the delectation of her retired or travelling rich'?[12] These images of Britain, these class-pocked reels portraying man's insularity from his fellow man, were what the British industry produced. Is it any wonder that a sizeable proportion of the British population rejected them in favour of the ersatz democratic images from Hollywood? Would a death-row prisoner be inclined to spend his waking hours watching films in which, reel after reel, the central character was executed? Would British audiences, among them men and women fighting for a living wage, women whose defiance led them, for the first time, to the ballot box, and widows and the wounded and disabled desperate to salvage something from a victory gained at far too high a personal cost, wish always to be told that victory was conditional, that solace awaited them only in death and that although the sun might never set on the British Empire, darkening skies and chained ambition were the only birthright they possessed?

Writing in the 1930s, Stephen Spender argued that the working classes 'exist, as never before in history, as part of the general consciousness' and if the British film industry wanted success it had to address that wider consciousness.[13] If the cinema was 'a candle to tempt night moths' then its flames had to be attractive to as many cinema-goers as possible.[14] Failure to do so would condemn it to the periphery of popular culture. Film was a competitive industry. To bemoan the fact that Hollywood had all but colonized the British market was to ignore evidence suggesting that it did so because it supplied what the public wanted. It was the somewhat dubious, but successful, flexibility of Hollywood which enabled it to function so adroitly across the globe: 'Hollywood's ambition is to suit the world ... any outpost that possesses a screen and a projector. Her God is the box office. Art must go overboard if the public want hokum! If they tire of hokum, give them art. Hollywood is capable of producing both with efficiency.'[15]

Hollywood was synonymous with film culture; the stars of Hollywood films were as familiar as any of the more important British social or political figures of the time. The principal extant British audience surveys are from the 1930s, when the quota legislation had ensured the British film industry's survival, and what the surveys show is the continuing influence of American ideas and fashions, the American way of life, on British audiences. In Mass Observation's 'May the Twelfth Survey', conducted during King George VI's coronation celebrations, the way in which American popular culture had become entrenched in the lives of ordinary British people manifested itself in many forms: the Coronation itself was described as 'a good show, in the way a good Disney is a good show'.[16] Another correspondent likened the procession through London to scenes from *Ben-Hur*.[17] The sights and people of the day were conjured up in images which related specifically to the American cinema: exuberant crowds sang songs from the Astaire and Rogers musical *Follow the Fleet*,[18] a card-trick seller in St Martin's Lane provoked

Chaplinesque comparisons, as did the way in which other young men behaved.[19] A hat-seller was said to have some of the aplomb of Maurice Chevalier, two sailors at the Edgware Road underground station were reminiscent of Popeye, and one fortunate fellow danced with a girl who was said to resemble Jean Harlow.[20] One diarist awoke on Coronation Day thinking of Ginger Rogers[21] while another received a letter from a Hollywood star on that same morning, which she read to her friend on the bus as they travelled to see the procession.[22] One less than committed monarchist was far from thrilled by the seried ranks of the privileged on special view: 'If I was Al Capone I'd bump some of these off.'[23]

How could the British film industry compete with such a juggernaut of ideas and images? Hollywood appealed to that most basic of wants, the desire to be amused, but the British film industry, apparently more attuned to Victorian ethics, consistently failed to provide amusement. British films did not appeal to the mass taste, neither did they satisfy popular expectations. There were, of course, successful British films, but as one reviewer noted, the clamour greeting some home productions had more to do with nationalism than any objective appreciation of film, as did the often hostile reception given to invading product: 'The phrase "Britain rules the waves" is always in those film fans' minds, and knowing quite well that, though it may rule the waves, it certainly doesn't rule the motion picture industry, they find fault in American pictures which they would have been blind to in a British one – Brittanicus sum.'[24] It was all very well, as Victor Saville pointed out, to make pictures 'telling the story of how we built a great Empire and made ourselves the richest nation in the world ... but they only dealt with certain groups of historical personages and did not greatly add to the knowledge of the ordinary British character'.[25] The audience for such pro-British cinema was said to be more likely to be found in the suburbs surrounding London,[26] where, according to John Betjeman, the past provided a refuge from present danger: 'A love of the ancient has bitten into most of us. I suppose everyone who feels afraid, as most of us do ... prefers looking back.'[27]

If British directors did look back, if they imagined themselves on some kind of recherché mission, they appear to have been caught between two contrary ideas. To be successful they had to appeal to the public, but in being successful they risked their reputations. Michael Balcon complained of being forced to make films which were 'no more than entertainment opium for the masses'[28] and Basil Dean 'found little satisfaction in the knowledge that crowded audiences were saving us from shipwreck.'[29] Dean may have appreciated the appearance of members of the Royal Academy of Music, the Guildhall School and the Royal Philharmonic Society at the première of his overblown Mozart tribute *Whom the Gods Love* but it was George Formby who filled the company's coffers.[30] It would appear that British producers and directors, Dean and Balcon among them, disagreed with the opinion that 'In no other field of human activity has it ever been suggested that it is less honourable – morally, artistically or commercially – to gain the adherence of a multitude than to win the applause of a clique.'[31]

This schizophrenic approach to film-making was mirrored in the movie-going public. A similar kind of ambivalence was to be found at the first-run cinemas of London's West End where 'temporary American citizens' displayed their preferences: 'that awful smart-Alec, pseudo carbon-copy of cheap American comes west for his entertainment at weekends.'[32] To the distaste of the great and the good, this was evidence of corruption because the films 'deliberately inculcate false values. Virtue for them has no rewards but wealth and kisses – the two things which in this world it has most to do without. Envy is neither sinful nor foolish when it is directed by poverty towards luxury; no one is ever beautiful who pays ultimately for her folly; the cherry orchards of the studios are always saved.'[33] The implication of such criticism, a refusal to countenance envy, for instance, as a legitimate response, echoes all the way back to Tom Paine, who railed against societies, governments, which treat 'the people as hereditary property' and deny them the right even to question their economic and civil disenfranchisement. In this instance it was cultural disenfranchisement – a denial of taste, a denigration of audience preference.[34]

The American images deemed socially, and morally, undesirable were those which undercut a value system which deplored change, which refused to acknowledge an alternative social vision. American films contained images which were at variance with what the British establishment wished the general populace to see: the images questioned authority, made heroes of anti-establishment characters and were laced with the culture of the crowd.[35] It was said that the British film industry did not understand the psychology of characterization: 'Why isn't there a villain in British films?'[36] Were British producers convinced of the innate purity of the class whose members they portrayed? Were there no miscreants in Grosvenor Square? Was the English countryside a haven for the godly and the chaste? In seeking to interpret 'the spirit and the heart of England' it was legitimate to suggest that 'it is a heart that has a very gentle beat' but surely the plethora of war and spy films contained characters whose pulses were far from steady?[37] With the influx of actors from Europe in the 1930s, British films found a ready-made cast of villains – Peter Lorre, Paul Henreid, Oscar Homolka and, for a time, Conrad Veidt, for example – whose roles sanctioned the view of those who refused to countenance a threatening screen character who was British.

Such attitudes were not confined to the eminent and quotable; *Justice for Sale* was regarded as 'not quite the right theme to entertain the British public';[38] as it dealt with 'corruption in American law courts' it obviously came within the remit of the British Board of Censors which rejected portrayals of 'the constituted Authorities and Administrators of the Law' suggesting they were 'unjust or harsh, incompetent or riduclous', even if they were American.[39] Certain audiences, the suburban respectables, also rejected these images: they did not go to see gangster pictures,[40], turned their noses up at Marlene Dietrich because she wasn't 'a real lady'[41] and would not tolerate James Cagney's lack of refinement.[42] What they wanted were 'films that show the true spirit of our Fighting Forces, or the glory of our Royal Family and Empire ... they will come out in thousands'.[43] They also, apparently, jettisoned part of their own reality, claiming a right to that marginalized, though trenchant, national identity which was defined by accent: here was an aping of upper-class accents which 'becomes so refined that at times they are hardly under-standable'.[44] And British film-makers pandered to this suburban diaspora, this wilful self-deception, producing 'an awful vista of old bound *Punch*'s dwindling down the dark shades of a country-house library'[45] and film sets 'furnished in the higher suburban manner with accents and behavior to match'.[46]

Further evidence of the difference in mentality between the British and American audiences may be found in the advertising of films. In North America, *The Iron Duke* was reviewed under the slogan, 'Duke's name is cleared in scandal with titled beauty'; a mock headline an-nounced Hollywood's celebration of the British Empire, *Clive of India*, with the caption 'English clerk captures India';[47] and the 1935 British production *Drake of England* became *Drake the Pirate* in America, where it was advertised as 'Disowned by his country, outlawed by the world, he shaped the destiny of an Empire'.[48] It is difficult to imagine the British industry marketing a film with such individualistic publicity. Individualism, the cult of the heroic outsider, was scarcely on the intellectual agenda in Britain, because, by nature, by birth, the British hero was an insider. Hollywood specialized in heroes at odds with society, with nature, with the world at large. From cowboys to gangsters, from homesteaders to rustlers, from mechanics to cooks, the American cinema thrived on the rebel; even the screwball comedies of the 1930s featured society figures whose actions were generally at odds with what was expected of characters of their social status. Perhaps this cinematic toppling of the assurance of the refined and privileged was disturbing to some British audiences; their refinement, and their so-called respectability, was a form of cultural and moral parasitism which, if those on whom they depended for legitimacy were ridiculed, so, by extension, were they.[49]

The irony in such a situation, in the debate about American influences, is that all classes of British society were subject to the same threat. Was it simply intellectual and class condescension which presumed American films to be detrimental to the British psyche? Was British society threatened because the earliest film memories of a significant proportion of the privileged classes were of Charlie Chaplin, of American heroes? Was the judgement of the arbiters of what was acceptable, socially and culturally, undermined by their exposure to Buster Keaton or Rudolph Valentino? There would be no suggestion that Lord Killanin was unsuited to high office, or social influence, because he went to the cinema at least once a week and that he particularly liked westerns and comedies; that his earliest film memories were of *The Iron Horse* and *The Covered Wagon*. Was Baron Moyne's ability to function in the House of Lords undermined by a liking for Buster Keaton, or did the Earl of Lanesborough lose credibility because he was fond of westerns and musicals – films with 'good music, good stories and happy endings'?[50] For a class, or classes, to be presumed at risk – and it was only one class so threatened – intimates a propensity to be influenced, a situation lacking fundamental stability. Was this the risk in Americanization? What was the disease, the irritable taste syndrome 'these masses are suffering from that demands this form of dope'?[51]

The manual working classes went to the cinema more than any other section of society:[52]

> Brothers, who when the sirens roar
> From office, shop and factory pour
>   'neath evening sky;
> By cops directed to a fug
> Of talkie-houses for a drug ... [53]

and they were 'sufficently tainted with dislike for their conditions and mistrust of those who seemed responsible to witness appreciatively a person or group who acts in opposition to accepted norms'.[54] Such 'a person or group' was excluded from British films; not so from American movies. Perhaps this was the true reason for distrusting the America cinema. There were too many films which, within a set formula which included retribution as a sop to the moral guardians of the age, glorified the 'honest Joe' tilting at windmills, the misfit created by social conditions, the Dostoevskian 'idiot' whose accidental guile was harnessed to a seemingly impossible mission. In Britain there was a growing awareness, and an expression of that awareness, that the fate of the unemployed, the economically disenfranchised, was determined by 'the wishes and whims of "the master class"', that 'the policy which governs England is not a policy which has its source in the masses' and the examples of heroes in American films who refused to accept the opinions and decisions of 'the master race', who were prepared to redress the imbalance in their own lives by committing anti-social acts, may have been the reason why Americanization was defined as threatening.[55]

The General Strike of 1926 demonstrates how a narrow view of national identity may be used to alienate a section of society, rather than harness shared experiences for the common good. If a significant proportion of the population lived as proxy American citizens, as suggested by the *Daily Express*, then those with access to the media, and therefore public opinion, further distanced this same group of people from involvement in a shared national identity. The General Strike was 'us' versus 'them', with the press orchestrating a version of the industrial conflict using the same themes it had used in the Great War, with 'strikers' and 'revolutionaries' replacing 'hun' as the enemy. If 'The Pistol at the Nation's Head' was a call to arms, reveille was 'For King and Country'. Baldwin's newsreel message to the nation, 'STEADY', may well have sounded a reassuring note but the press were more adamant in summoning up the spectre of an England under threat.[56] The *Daily*

Mail recycled Wordsworth for the benefit of those who failed to grasp that a revolution was in progress:

> We must be free or die, who speak the tongue
> That Shakespeare spake; the faith and morals hold
> Which Milton held.[57]

But if the organized working classes staged a strike, the government waged a war, with detailed strategies to deal with the disruption to transport and contingency plans to feed 'the people'. Just as the conduct of war – visually represented in innumerable films by game-playing, with flags and symbols on a board, like chess or draughts – was the prerogative of those who were educated in the finer points of such games, those same people, from that same class, had no other recourse but to define the terms in which the conflict was conducted because to recognize demands, to undertake realistic negotiations, would have undermined their view of the way society operated. Oliver Twist's plea for 'more' was an act which threatened order; to those to whom the request was made, the issue of hunger was immaterial, it was the act itself which breached the rules, and the same mentality – 'the schoolboy silliness and bluff'[58] – governed the 'respectable' reaction to the General Strike.

When the strike was broken, 'The Triumph of the People' was a victory for those whose values were consistent with a view of society which could not, and would not, countenance legitimate class grievance. Consensus was imposed, and the British way of dealing with threats to internal peace was to be seen in the future with long lines of hunger-marchers appealing 'with cool dignity and dramatic stoicism' to the paternal consensus for relief.[59] To underscore the achievements of 'the people' – those who had broken the strike – the BBC broadcast *Jerusalem* following Baldwin's announcement of the end of the strike.[60] And if there was any doubt as to who 'the people' were and, conversely, which section of society was excluded from that short-hand code for national identity, newspapers published photographs of such notables as Lady Mary Ashley-Cooper and Lady Carmichael-Anstruther peeling potatoes in Hyde Park. The *Illustrated London News* commented:

> We feel that the heart of England must be sound ... when we
> read that Mr C. E. Pitman, the Oxford stroke, is driving a train
> on the Great Western Railway from Bristol to Gloucester, the

Headmaster of Eton (Dr Alington) and about fifty of his assistant masters have enrolled as special constables ... Lord Chesham is driving a train and the Hon. Lionel Tennyson is a 'special'.[61]

It could not be clearer who 'the people' were. It is obvious where the 'heart of England' lodged, and if that heart was untouched by the brief rebellion of those who should have known better, the pleasures particular to the sensibilites of those in whose trust the nation's heart was kept were untouched by the strike. Edgar Wallace's play *The Ring* opened and continued to play to packed houses throughout the strike; the narrow streets around Covent Garden were packed with limousines from which silk-hatted gentlemen and women wearing diamonds with gratuitous ease emerged for the opening night of *The Marriage of Figaro*.[62]

If there was a failure to address the issue at the time – and the issue concerned a section of society, obviously not 'the people' who were marginalized by economic failure – the restaging of events for the purposes of celebrating an important element of national identity showed a similar lack of understanding of the pain and frustration felt by those for whom the General Strike marked a seminal political and social experience. *Royal Cavalcade* was made to celebrate King George V's Silver Jubilee in 1935. The film daringly includes a brief exposition of the General Strike, linking documentary footage of strikers and policemen playing football together with a fictional episode in which a striking ticket-collector is seen travelling on the same vehicle his industrial action should have kept off the road. When an upper-class volunteer ticket-collector asks for the striker's fare, a situation of potential conflict is diffused by a swift and entirely incredible leap into war reminiscence. This cinematic fragment suggests that its makers could conceive of no contemporary solution to the issues raised by the strike, that the past – a period when the whole nation was threatened – was the only reference point between the two characters embodying a different form of conflict. The cinematic message seems to be that the only way to create consensus, and to keep that consensus safe from the present and secure for the future, was to invoke the ghosts of the class of 1914–18.[63]

And so it was with British films. The British speciality was war, and, as the House of Commons was told, British exhibitors had done their bit for King and Country: 'They have loyally shown and done so since 1914 every film of a patriotic nature.'[64] It was also noted, 'it is a pity so much of the production ... which goes on should only be in the direction of war films',[65] something mentioned by *Variety* in its review of *The Luck of the Navy* (1927): the film was, it opined, yet another version of 'pass the flags and raise the headstones'.[66] War may be 'an absorbing subject' but surely there were other topics which would please the British public?[67] During the course of the debate a list of British films was offered to illustrate British excellence; these were *Hindle Wakes*, *The Triumph of the Rat*, *The Lodger*, *Palaver*, *The Chinese Bungalow*, *Second to None*, *Mons*, *Mademoiselle from Armentieres* and *The Flag Lieutenant*.[68] Of the films, *Mons* (1926) was a reconstruction of the famous battle and retreat, *Mademoiselle from Armentieres* (1926), *Second to None* (1926) and *The Flag Lieutenant* (1926) were set in wartime, and *Palaver* (1926) was an Empire drama about tribal conflict. The producer of *Second to None*, Dinah Shurey, also produced an anti-socialist tract, *The Last Post* (1929), set against the General Strike, and *Carry On!* (1927), a tale of war and spies which was singled out for savage criticism: 'the scenarist has furnished a script which would have been torpedoed in 1918, but now makes the film appear like a diehard's attempt to sing a hymn of hate six months after everybody's kissed and made up.'[69]

Mumsie, *The Guns of Loos*, *Land of Hope and Glory*, *Roses of Picardy*, *Blighty*, *The Luck of the Navy*, *Victory* – the list of war dramas is almost endless; most of them were praised by British reviewers for their patriotic content and sincerity.[70] *Mademoiselle from Armentieres* may have convinced *Bioscope* that it was a 'convincing and realistic picture of trench warfare',[71] but its content did not exactly please one Member of Parliament: 'I went to see the British reply to The Big Parade and when I saw the spectacle of French peasant girls running about the British front line during a bombardment, I realised that for mawkish and ridiculous sentimentality there was nothing to touch [it].'[72] *Victory* (1928) was said to be 'a farrago of the war fever period of Germans and their behaviour. Nothing is left out; comic paper Germans, musical comedy cockney soldiers, humour concerned with decayed fish and wounds in the pants.'[73] It was also claimed, 'already the fans are writing to the newspapers asking producers to let up on the flag-waving stuff and make some straight movies'.[74]

This 'crude and commercial flag waving, screaming to the gallery for applause'[75] which was, it seems, the film industry's attempt to assure its audience that 'an English passport is itself a title of nobility',[76] was intended to guide a committee determining whether or not pre-quota films could be registered as suitable for exhibition. Because registration was to depend on whether a film was 'adequately patriotic', this, for one commentator, conjured up images of committee members 'chasing the heroines who run up and down the trenches' and determining, for the sake of patriotism, whether they were French or British.[77] This was, it was argued, a means by which 'the wreckage of the past' could be recycled and in answer to the question whether films like *Roses of Picardy* (1927) should be allowed a second chance because of their patriotic subject matter, a dissenting voice was unequivocal: 'I should say "not on your life".'[78] American war films were, apparently, no better. Colonel Applin, the Member for Enfield, was appalled by *What Price Glory*: '... in the three campaigns in which I have been engaged I never saw a British officer or a British sergeant behaving in the way these people in the American film were alleged to have behaved.'[79] Worse still was *The Big Parade*: 'not one mention was made of the English [sic] army.'[80]

A number of the non-war films noted above were among the productions of men and companies which would provide the British industry with future prestige and economic rewards, and, it could be argued, did not need a quota, be it 2.5 or 20 per cent, to gain success. The same producers, whom other writers have dealt with at length, may have been responsible for war films but their vision was essentially that of show-men, men with entertainment in mind.[81] If there was a stirring in the dry bones of the British film industry, some producers were prepared to shake those bones until, by some act of celluloid alchemy, they turned into living, breathing performances which garnered popularity and profit. *The Triumph of the Rat* (1926) and *The Lodger* (1926) had very little to do with film as an expression of national identity; the former reprised Ivor Novello's smouldering 'apache' and *The Lodger* was a variation on 'Jack the Ripper'. Both films were produced by Michael Balcon for Gains-borough and exploited the market for Britain's only genuine 'heart-throb'. *The Lodger*, directed by Hitchcock, was said to be equal to the best Britain had ever produced, 'the most imaginative picture yet made',[82] and *The Triumph of the Rat* used a mobile camera further to enhance Novello's status as a film-friendly actor.[83]

The Chinese Bungalow (1926) was a melodrama of the most basic sort: infidelity, revenge, attempted murder and Matheson Lang in Chinese make-up. There was nothing to distinguish the film as innately British, apart from its English heroine, and it was 'a strong drama', 'humane and vigorous'.[84] Given that there was a worldwide vogue for films starring the Japanese actor Sessue Hayakawa, the film was probably an opportunistic venture on the part of its producers, Stoll. *Hindle Wakes* (1927) was very British, the story of a defiant Lancashire working-class girl, but the film moves and is shot like a dream with a roller-coaster pace that could not help but please. It was 'an outstanding British film', although 'somewhat sombre and pessimistic', but a 'splendid box-office attraction everywhere'.[85] So working-class stories could be good box-office! Perhaps it wasn't simply the milieu in which the tale was told. The film's star was Estelle Brody and she, like a number of other North American female stars, was lured to England to add popular appeal to the home product. The sale of *Nell Gwyn* (1926), starring Dorothy Gish, provided Herbert Wilcox with the cash to buy land on which Elstree Studios were built,[86] and he also used Betty Blythe and Mae Marsh, among others, to give his films universal appeal. *Southern Love*, a steamy Spanish drama featuring Betty Blythe, was one of the big successes of British Film Weeks, if, as it appears, the main point of the film was 'the exploitation of Betty Blythe's ample physical charms'.[87] Wilcox trawled predominantly British waters for his subject matter, especially with his later 'Way of a Neagle' series,[88] but, for almost three decades, he understood what audiences wanted. American reviews of his films may not always have been positive but even a carping comment does not conceal how well Wilcox understood the basic tenets of movie business: 'it simply goes to prove that the English have grasped the idea of sexy stuff and have proceeded to undress their players – or at least some of their women players.'[89]

In later years Wilcox was accused of making films confined to an area 'encompassed by the three or four square miles of central London owned by the Duke of Westminster', offering that staple dish on the British menu, romance among the rich and privileged.[90] Initially British audiences reacted favourably, especially as the principal star of these later films, Anna Neagle, was one of the few female home-grown stars to forge a lasting and affectionate relationship with her fans. Neagle could carry a film on her own and often her chorus-girl spark compensates for Wilcox's increasingly pedestrian productions. An American review of Neagle's performance in the second Wilcox production of *Nell Gwyn* reveals her true potential: 'Anna Neagle paints an honest and dazzling picture in the title tole, touching it up with a bar-room lustiness that most of our stars wouldn't dare attempt.'[91] After the Second World War, in a different cultural and political epoch, British audiences rejected

Wilcox's more gentrified productions, but, ever the showman, he turned sensational bankruptcy hearings into a best-seller in which he cast himself as hero of a less than accurate history of the British film industry.

Michael Balcon cannot have failed to notice that when Mae Marsh arrived from Hollywood to star in *Flames of Passion* (1922) for Herbert Wilcox, 100,000 people turned out to see her at Waterloo Station.[92] Such was Marsh's success that the film was advertised as 'sold in every county on the globe'.[93] Balcon also engaged a Hollywood star, Betty Compson, for the huge sum of £1,000 a week to work on *Woman to Woman* (1923), a war film, which was then sold through Selznick Pictures to America. *Variety* gave the film a glowing review:

> there seems to be no evident reason for the continual apathy expressed towards British-made films, as this assuredly must be an example of the better grade of work over there. It is un-questionably equal to the vast majority of releases viewed in first run houses over here and vastly superior to those witnessed in our daily change theatres.[94]

It would appear that when competent British producers and directors, those with a genuine love of the medium, worked with expert per-formers, the result was film entertainment rather than the false trappings of national identity grafted on to celluloid.

Neither did such films, nor their producers and directors, attempt to answer Ramsay MacDonald's plea for film-makers to 'uphold to foreign nations a better conception of the moral conduct and social habits of a people who profess to belong to the leading nations of the world'.[95] *The White Shadow* (1924), from Balcon and Saville, was set in Paris, with Betty Compson again helping the film into North American cinemas.[96] Gainsborough's Betty Balfour vehicle *Sea Urchin* (1926) was also set in Paris, as was Ivor Novello's *Rat* series, and while geography may not have been of primary importance – audiences were interested in stories, not geography, it was often said[97] – exotic locations and popular stars were obviously attractive to film fans. The whole argument about British films ('quite English, you know') was, and is, undermined by Hollywood's capacity to make the 'Best of British': *Robin Hood, Cavalcade, The Barretts of Wimpole Street, Mrs Miniver* and scores of other British subjects were treated to a process as intangible as the concept of national identity – the making of popular entertainment.

If British films were expected to exhibit 'the very ideas which have been wrought into our national character which might in some way be embodied in our national life', those 'very ideas' were difficult to process. The Bishop of Southwark tried but failed to outline them.[98] The fallacy of attempting to define British films in terms of 'our own typical civilisation and our own standards' was that it implied a rejection of film's universal terms of reference.[99] Cecil B. de Mille could not understand why British producers and directors didn't simply look at Hollywood's success and attempt to inculcate the same values, the same bottom line – 'the only test is that of pleasing the American audience' – into their own productions. He asked, 'What would you say to a man of commerce who proposed to commence manufacturing steel but refused to study the methods employed by the biggest and most success-ful manufacturers?'[100] The answer was obvious: 'There was no reason why a British film, because it was British, would be of a higher or better character than an American film.'[101] As George Pearson noted, 'No British director can make a worse film for having seen Hollywood, and the chances are that he will make a better one.'[102]

The imposition of a quota of British films on renters and exhibitors had consequences, good and bad. Protecting the industry undoubtedly saved jobs and the small firms supplying films to meet quota require-ments provided basic training for entrants to the industry. But perhaps the most negative result of the quota was that one particular kind of 'typically English' film was given a new lease on life. There were dozens of films which were, essentially, photographed plays, featuring theatre casts with no pretensions to subtlety, directed with a total absence of cinematic finesse. As one participant in the 1927 debate concerning the quota said, 'I have seen ... many films from many different countries, and, apart from the absolutely low class American pictures, which no respectable picture house is exhibiting now, the most deplorable films I have seen for tawdry tale and bad photography are British films, which are rushed through in a hurry in order to meet an artificially created market.'[103] These were the films which, in the first half of the decade, had been among those declared 'British and Best' on the grounds that were written by someone with a St Martin's Lane reputation and featured players who dined at the Café de Paris or Romano's. These British films were rejected by the mass audience in the early 1920s and, once resurrected courtesy of government patronage, were hissed again off the nation's screens.

National identity on film strays into nationalism. *An Englishman's Home* becomes not so much a celebration of identity as a cultural and political assault on other nations, other cultures. The subtleties of character, personal and national, give way to caricature when drafted to some ultra-cinematic purpose. Draped in the Union flag, and posed with British bulldogs, British lions, John Bull's ghost forever charging glasses to the Empire, film producers may have heard their audience, 'Give us a chance to see ourselves. We will be interested,'[104] but who defined 'ourselves' and who retained the copyright on Britishness? The language of the cinema was new, it could not simply reproduce on screen stage dialogue or lengthy paragraphs from novels; this was the past acting against present and future success. But such was the nation's literary reputation that the British industry fell upon plays and novels with 'immense rapacity, and to the moment largely subsists upon the body of its unfortunate victim ... While all the other arts were born naked, the youngest has been born fully clothed.'[105]

The majority of British films of the 1920s were too polite to undress in public. They kept their stays and their prudery, their proofs of purchase for the second-hand. While Hollywood played art and commerce on the universal *tabula rasa*, the British industry presumed to barter for the nation's soul, its tears, its laughter and its pounds and pence, with classic topiary and country house charades. If, as Hilaire Belloc wrote, England was 'on all sides pretence at odds with reality', then British film-makers played their part in that deception.[106] What they failed to do was lie convincingly. In the film magazines of the time the artless presumption of entertainment displayed in posters of grouped dowagers and honorable gentlemen contrasts bizarrely with the vibrant advertising for films from studios concerned with entertainment, not with pedigree, and the British successes of the period only serve to underscore the failure of the industry as a whole to connect with its natural audience.

That failure to connect may have been an inability, or a refusal, to communicate with the mass audience, a failure to incorporate a generosity of spirit, a willingness to listen as well as to be seen and heard, within that most democratic form of mass communication, film. There can be no doubt as to where the following advertising copy originates. It defines a particular spirit, an ability, a desire, a compulsion even, to connect with an audience:

Some pictures can make you relive every moment of your life, substituting episodes from your own life for those identical episodes you see on screen. The only difference will be the faces of the characters, and you'll enjoy the picture a hundred times more because it has been so true, so honest, so vivid ... You can't get away from it – it's your story too.[107]

The British film industry, and those who defined suitable cases for filming, were not in the business of filming 'your story too'. But this was an industry which, for its survival, had to meet and greet potential backers on their terms or risk rejection. Whether or not the British film industry ever truly learned to listen to its audience, or to trust its audience, is another question. What can be answered, without fear of contradiction, is that in the 1920s the majority of British film-makers would have regarded 'your story too' as irrelevant: 'on all sides pretence at odds with reality' was the nature of 'British and Best'.

7

The Betty Balfour Connection:
'Ain't we sisters'

2 9 *Acacia Avenue*: somewhere in Metroland, the home of the Robinson family. The plot: bright, and not so bright, young things fall foul of their own lack of sophistication. The precious young things, among them Jimmy Hanley and Dinah Sheridan, betray the film's stage origins. Although the plot decrees that young Mr Robinson suffer the attentions of a married flirt and that his sister, Pepper, be terribly modern and venture a trial marriage, the performances suggest the most risqué thing the characters could do was say 'No' when a someone stepped through French windows asking 'Anyone for tennis?' In 1945 the film was advertised with the slogan 'Old enough to know better, young enough not to care', and through the harmless commentary on suburban manners two veterans show exactly what it is they do best. Gordon Harker, as Pa Robinson, had specialized in the comic, and the sometimes sinister, Cockney for years, both on the stage and in films. Betty Balfour, as Mrs Robinson, had been in some of the best and worst British films since 1920. Both stars inhabit *29 Acacia Avenue* as real characters, with an economy of style which is at odds with the forced gaiety and juvenile theatrics of almost every other actor, and if the film has any lasting merit it is as a record of the ease with which Betty Balfour inhabited screenland.[1]

Balfour understood the special needs of the screen very early in her career: the flamboyant mannerisms, still evident among some of the actors in *29 Acacia Avenue*, had to be controlled; what was appropriate on stage simply did not work in front of the camera.[2] In newspaper and magazine articles she called for studios to train actors for the screen, not to rely on the reputations of stage performers.[3] Balfour had a special gift, of 'making an audience believe she was going through a certain emotion', and it was this ability, and the sensitivity of George Pearson's direction, which impressed even American audiences.[4] The owner of New York's Capital Theatre thought *Love, Life and Laughter* (1923) 'could not be bettered, both as regards story, entertainment, and production values'.[5]

The ingredients of the *Squibs* series of films with which Balfour made her name were those which, potentially, make any film, British or otherwise, successful; they were about good and evil, albeit addressed in a light-hearted manner, and set in familiar territory. Squibs' policeman boyfriend is sensible and trustworthy, her father a working-class rogue, with a fondness for beer and gambling, while Squibs is, in the words of an admirer, 'the quintessence of sprightliness and sparkling humour'.[6] Pearson described the plot of *Squibs Wins the Calcutta Sweep* (1922): '[It] opened straight away with a murder, moved in a perfectly reasonable way into the wildest comedy, and came back to the murder solution in hectic Paris, where Squibs had gone to spend some of her winnings from the Calcutta.' With hindsight Pearson claimed Rupert Brooke as inspiration: 'Tragedy and Comedy will not leave the world while two things stay in it – Death and Fools.'[7]

The film retains an energy which shows Pearson's mastery of the medium. There are aerial shots of Piccadilly, street scenes taken in Paris and close-ups of Balfour which exploit a range of emotions from sheer delight, in a scene where her boyfriend Charlie gives her an engagement ring, to a mixture of sorrow and joy when she rescues her sister from a murderous husband: the two sisters are seen in tears, embracing, followed by the end caption, 'Ain't we sisters'. Before the dramatic dénouement Squibs shares her good fortune with her neighbours and friends, amusingly falls foul of modern plumbing, regularly trips, or is ill-at-ease in finery and furs and, perhaps most importantly of all, exhibits, in her portrayal, an appreciation and understanding of one of the most enduring of stereotypes, the hard-boiled working-class girl with a heart of gold.[8] The film also respects various aspects of working-class life; it allows audiences to share, however vicariously, in a sense of release from difficult circumstances, a familiar working-class scenario of which the popularity of sweeps, football pools and prize crossword puzzles was an integral part.[9]

Like *Squibs Wins the Calcutta Sweep*, *Mord Em'ly* was also released in 1922. This time Balfour played the daughter of a char whose father is away, staying as a guest of His Majesty in Dartmoor Prison. Although the film is ostensibly about the capacity of a working-class girl to find a silver lining no matter how dark the storm, it had something to say about the conditions in which many film-goers lived. The opening scene of *Mord Em'ly* is one in which 'gently swaying poplars framed a landscape of extraordinary beauty' with a title superimposed – 'God Made the Country'. The scene fades to reveal 'a picture of hideous roof-tops, a sea of slum dwellings' over which was written 'And Man Made the Town'.[10] Pearson's staunchly middle-class background, and income, allowed him the luxury of pastoral indulgence – it was the cosy familiarity of a semi-rural existence he missed when working in Hollywood[11] – which was denied the characters in his films as well as the greater proportion of his audience.

What is, perhaps, significant about *Squibs* and the other working-class-centred films made by Pearson is that while demonstrating his cinematic obsession with capturing 'just a bit of life' they rely on 'Betty's laughter-making flair' to convey an admiration for the indomitable spirit of the working classes.[12] This attitude was, in many ways, just as spurious as that of other producers who peppered their films with working-class caricatures simply for comic relief, but at least Balfour's characters were not condemned, in the last reel, to return to spilling the contents of basement larders for comic relief. Cockney comedy proved popular with the public and very good business for the Welsh-Pearson Company. Pearson noted that the proceeds from films about working-class characters enabled him to buy his son a place at Oxford.[13]

Squibs MP (1923) was part farce, part wish fulfilment; it may have been 'just a bit of life', but Pearson's focus was clear. Women of thirty had recently been enfranchised and because Balfour's character was only twenty it was necessary to create a device by which she was eligible to stand for election to Parliament. The comic reason given was that she had been 'up the pole' for ten years after a bout of measles during which time she had been in a trance.[14] In much the same way as Jeffrey Richards has argued that Gracie Fields was used to personify and cement a class consensus in the following decade, Betty Balfour's performance in *Squibs MP* was used, by Pearson, to delineate his views on society, on war and women more particularly.[15] The speech Squibs delivers to Parliament is indicative not only of the anti-war feeling of the time but of the debate about women's emancipation:

> And the most important matter to the British Empire is babies and I rise to represent babies. Is there any member present who will look me in the face and tell me that he prefers battleships to babies? Here I stand with a battleship in one hand and a baby in the other, and I say blast, in the best sense, all battleships. Let us have brighter babies. We don't want lumps of iron over water but lumps of life on earth, and I propose a babies base at Southend and not building a naval base at Singapore.[16]

When the film was shown during British Film Weeks one of the Members of Parliament present was Mabel Philipson, formerly Mabel Russell, the Gaiety Girl who had featured in the original Squibs sketch on stage.[17]

With *Squibs' Honeymoon* (1923) the series ended; Squibs marries her policeman; her father, too old for scurrying down alleys making illicit wagers, settles down to help run the dairy business she has bought with her sweeps winnings. As one cinema-goer was heard to comment: 'Well, that Betty Balfour aint 'arf a nib. Fancy startin' out in the Walworth Road and then winnin' all that money and becomin' an MP! And now she's married a copper and settled down – so I reckon that's about finished her.'[18] The opening titles of the film convey not only the inevitability of the end of the series, but also the attitude of almost all film-makers to women, and, more specifically, to the 'natural' place of working-class women: 'SQUIBS, whose escapades as Flower Girl, Calcutta-Sweep Winner, Milk Vendor and Member of Parliament had astonished even herself, felt that after all the simple Life was best ... '[19] Like so many other working-class characters in films, success was applicable only if temporary.[20] The *Squibs* films were made before organized Labour had raised its voice at Westminster, before the Depression had severely punctured middle-class notions about the inevitability, the deservedness, of poverty; even a star of the magnitude of Betty Balfour was denied a role in which class frontiers were permanently breached. The 'simple life' was within one's own class. Balfour's *Squibs* films were comparable to *The Perils of Pauline* serials, with the perils, in Balfour's case, irrevocably rooted in a class tautology which compressed and ultimately denied the possibility of escape.

The final films of note Betty Balfour made in the early 1920s were *Love, Life and Laughter* – a title later used for a Gracie Fields film – *Wee MacGregor's Sweetheart* (1922) and *Reveille* (1924). *Wee MacGregor's Sweetheart* was a simple tale of a girl wishing to marry her young man against the wishes of a snobbish aunt and was popular at home as well as in the Empire.[21] The central plot device – an unsuitable match – was also featured in the *Squibs* series. There is an amusing scene in *Squibs Wins the Calcutta Sweep* where she parades her swish new clothes and jewels in front of her fiancé's mother, who has always treated her badly because she disapproves of Squibs' family. Apparently taking delight in mocking her future mother-in-law's lack of enthusiasm for their marriage plans, Squibs affects a haughty demeanour, refusing even to acknowledge the presence of the glum harridan. Suddenly Squibs leaves the room, returning in a trice, dressed in her usual plain garb; a title reads: 'Cheer up! Laugh you chumps! I was just playing at being the Lady, but it ain't me ... I'm just old Squibs of Piccadilly.' Evidently a Piccadilly flower-seller with £60,000 was enough to placate her future in-laws. The scene concludes with the caption: 'Stop thinking my money'll make a difference ... it won't.'

For British cinema-goers, especially the young women who voted Betty Balfour their favourite screen heroine, films in which an escape from poverty was plotted as possible may well have been motivational. *Love, Life and Laughter* certainly was a rags-to-riches tale in the best tradition. The film was a standard back-stage melodrama, giving one reviewer the chance to 'study the squalor of a London doss-house'.[22] The story concerned a struggling chorus girl and a pessimistic young writer, with the inevitable parting and reconciliation. Balfour's character became a star as well as the saving grace of the would-be playwright, and for its time it was unusual in so far as its ending was equivocal – the audience was left to judge whether or not the ending would bring happiness.[23] Perhaps caught up in the hype of British Film Weeks, one journalist wrote: 'It is the most convincing Photoplay one could possibly witness, made out of a commonplace story ... The genius screen star gives in this picture a performance which ... outshines Mary Pickford at her best.'[24]

Betty Balfour was said to portray 'boundless ambition ... rather than the pessimism one might have expected her to exhibit', given the slum conditions to which the early reels of film condemned her, and she, 'as usual, bubbles over the charm and high spirits ... her appearance at a gala night before the Prince has all the colour and realism of an actual royal performance, yet the way in which she preserved her balance ... amid all her success is nobly feminine and makes her all the more lovable.'[25] The 'noble femininity' of working-class women was also subject to stereotyping by sympathetic observers: Pett Ridge, whose novel formed the basis for *Mord Em'ly* (1922), commented that 'For resolute industry in good undertakings, women can exhibit a self-sacrifice that is at times almost painful to witness.'[26] One of the film's notable features was said to be the way in which it showed 'that happiness does not necessarily go hand-in-hand with opulence' and it seems the moral of the film was presented in predeterministic mode, with Balfour's character sacrificing personal success for personal happiness in the final reel. One smitten critic claimed Balfour 'has never done anything better than Love, Life and Laughter' and on its reissue in 1928 the film was said to exemplify 'the success of England's Sweetheart' and to provide further evidence of why her 'captivating smile and bright eyes captivated millions'.[27]

Reveille was an entirely different kind of film altogether.

> 'September, 1918! The Great War is nearing to its close, and London is a whirlpool of hectic, artificial gaiety. The World is going to pieces; laugh while there is yet time ... Happy laughter, wild laughter, hollow laughter. Any laughter rather than the laughter of guns spitting death in Flanders ... But above all the laughter of the flappers, who live for one end only, one burning passionate conviction ... The Boys who are back on a few days leave ... Give them a good time!'[28]

Pearson said the film was 'a scrapbook of pictures of life caught in the living, no hero, no villain, no plot, no tying up of loose threads' but there is a hero and a heroine.[29] Stewart Rome played a soldier, a 'working man, but a thinker and idealist; convinced that he is fighting on the side of righteousness in a crusade to end war; and who after the war passes bitterly into the Valley of Disillusion and Hate'. What Rome's character, Nutty, found in the 'Valley of Disillusion and Hate' was socialism and it was left to Balfour's character to rescue him from that ideology's divisive clutches. If Rome's character owed something to Pearson's fondness for Rupert Brooke, the Balfour character was a cipher through whom Pearson reasserted his conservative values, his belief in the equity of the status quo, and the role of women as guardians of the nation's morality. *Cinema World* praised the film – 'this most wonderful of productions ... a film that literally set a nation talking' – and it reflects on Balfour's talent that she could make something of a thumbnail sketch of a reactionary angel.[30] Such was Pearson's reputation, and perhaps the mood of the country itself, that the Prince of Wales attended a special presentation of *Reveille*.[31]

Few of Balfour's films remain from this period – a copy of *Squibs Wins the Calcutta Sweep*, a few snippets from other films – and it is therefore difficult to evaluate how important they were and how much of an impact Betty Balfour made on the British public. What remains is a record of achievement noted in newspapers and magazines; Balfour topped the polls for the most popular British star from 1924 to 1927 and was featured as late as 1929 on the cover of *Picture Show Annual*. In a *Girl's Cinema* poll to find the magazine's favourite heroine, Balfour topped the list, above Mary Pickford, Dorothy and Lillian Gish, Gloria Swanson, Pola Negri, and half a dozen other American stars.[32] If the endorsement of products is indicative of popularity, even the most cursory examination of contemporary sources shows a wide and varied range of products attached to her name: Grossmith's Oriental Face Powders and Creams, Kia-Ora Squash, Lux Soap, Odol toothpaste, Optrex eye-drops, Pond's Vanishing and Cold Cream, Symington's soups and many others. There was a Betty Balfour Club, run by James Lawson from his home in Tyldesley, Lancashire, which had members in America, Australia, India, New Zealand and South Africa who clubbed together to buy a commemorative cup to present to the club's patron in recognition of her work.[33] Balfour was said to receive, on average, 5,000 letters a year from all over the world and she delighted in the fact that she was regarded as 'everybody's pal'.[34] The *Picture Show Annual* of 1928, in an article headed 'They Kept the Movies Moving', wrote: 'Betty Balfour is a comedienne who is second to none, and had she been an American star she would have had world-wide recognition. As it is she kept the flag flying in the dark days of stagnation in the British film industry.'[35]

When Balfour's contract with George Pearson lapsed she was paid £500 a week at British International Pictures and whenever she sneezed, presented an award or attended the cinema her name was featured in the newspapers.[36] *The Times* noted that she was 'probably the most popular British girl on the screen to-day',[37] and when it became known that only £100 had been spent, over three years, on publicity for Balfour's films, *Film Weekly* commented that an American firm 'had offered to spend four times that amount on publicity for one picture if she would accept their contract'.[38] She received offers from Famous Players-Lasky, Paramount and other American companies but refused their contracts. Although the 'national humiliation' of the British film industry forced her to work in Germany and France, she was adamant that she would reject all Hollywood offers and it is likely that her patriotic stance endeared her even more to her fans.[39]

The films with which Balfour completed her contract with Pearson were indicative of much of what was positive about their relationship, while showing the cracks that were widening between them. A competition was organized in the *Referee* newspaper to find suitable material for a new film.[40] What Pearson found, however, was a novel by H. de Vere Stacpoole called *Satan*, which he rewrote to feature Balfour in the girl-dressed-as-a-boy role of Jude. Pearson and Balfour are cited as co-producers and filming took place in Jamaica. Many British films were produced overseas at the time, in the South of France, Italy and Germany; Stewart Rome, a regular in British films, toured the world in 1926 filming backgrounds for five different movies.[41] Pearson embroidered the plot of *Satan's Sister* (1925) so heavily that the picture became 'a romantic fantasy rather than a realistic adventure melodrama or farce'. The story was lightweight nonsense about pirates and treasure; it was said to have been lushly photographed, and Balfour's performance was praised.[42]

Returning to London, Pearson obtained the rights to a facile Oliver Sandys novel: 'a melodramatic mixture of love, crooks, dupes, dopers, pubs and palaces, calamity and courage.' *Blinkeyes* (1926) was about an East End dancing girl escaping her humble origins. She does so by marrying into the peerage, thus acting out another familiar urban myth: that a chorus-girl could become a duchess.[43] The *Daily Telegraph* was far from impressed with the slum backgrounds and the character's 'anti-toff' sentiments, but, inevitably, the film ended in a chaste orgy of romantic capitulation.[44] *Bioscope* noted that 'Pearson has an unconvincing story upon which to work, and it cannot be said he has overcome the difficulty ... the story is confused and continuity jumpy.'[45] It may well have been 'a vivid picture of London life' but Pearson was tiring of that locality and perhaps it showed.[46] Balfour had been understudy to the musical comedy star Ada Reeve when *Nothing Else Matters* catapulted her to screen stardom; Pearson had recognized qualities in the actress which were to bear considerable reward in her portrayal of the brash and sometimes irascible character of Squibs and it comes as something of a surprise to find Pearson transforming her into a proxy member of the aristocracy.[47] Pearson expressed regret that the film was unworthy of Balfour's talents.[48]

If Balfour's later films continued to demonstrate that 'You can wear out the shoes of the working girl, but you cannot wear out her spirit', it was to Balfour's flair for footwork that producers next looked for inspiration;[49] in *A Little Bit of Fluff* (1928) and *Sea Urchin* (1926) she was cast as a dancer. *Sea Urchin* was made for the fledgling Gainsborough Company and directed by Graham Cutts. Balfour's character dances in a Paris nightclub until rescued, in the last reel, from her dubious occupation; happiness, inevitably, awaits her in England.[50] *A Little Bit of Fluff* reunited Balfour with Sydney Chaplin, with whom she had shared billing at the Wood Green Empire when they had both been on a Fred Karno bill.[51] There were adverse comments in the press even before the film was completed, with *Cinema* questioning the process of filming: 'For a Little Bit of Fluff the scenes are being made in sequence ... I don't remember a film made this way before [and] the producer is working without a script. That seems all wrong.'[52] The film was based on a play that had been popular during the Great War: 'What a War! It must have been,' commented one journalist on seeing the film, implying that audiences must have been readily amused in times of crisis.[53] The film was directed by the American Jess Robins and the *Daily Mirror* concluded it was about 'a stage star who is spoiled by Press agents and peroxide'.[54] Ben Travers was partly responsible for the titles, and that may explain why the film was described as 'purely farce, bordering on slapstick'.[55] At £80,000 *A Little Bit of Fluff* was a substantial property, but it appears to have been primarily a vehicle for Chaplin: Betty Balfour 'hasn't a fat part';[56] she has 'nothing to do but "feed" Chaplin'.[57]

Balfour's roles in *Paradise* (1928) and *Cinders* (1926) were familiar: in *Paradise* she was a milliner and in *Cinders*, the familiar drudge in a London boarding-house. *Paradise* was England. Kitty Cranston, Balfour's character, wins a crossword competition and with her winnings (£500) goes to the South of France in search of romance and excitement.[58] Gambling scenes were filmed in the Prince of Monaco's palace and the film's extras included the comedian Leslie Henson, American actor Ernest Truex, directors Basil Dean and Graham Cutts and two writers of popular fiction, E. Phillips Oppenheim and Cosmo Hamilton.[59] Directed by the American Denison Clift, whose technique was said to be 'ir-reproachable', the film was 'well acted, lavishly mounted, beautifully photographed'. Clift was praised for possessing 'a genuine conception of the true abilities of Betty Balfour' and her performance was regarded as her best, in 'her most attractive film to date'.[60] The *Sunday Graphic* called the film 'worthy' and the comment may well have applied to the sentiments inscribed in the film's dénouement: Kitty Cranston's deserted fiancé arrives in Monte Carlo, deliberately parts her from her small fortune in order to reduce her appeal to an unscrupulous gigolo played by the Franco-Spanish actor Alexander D'Arcy, whose Valentinoesque aspirations were met with almost total indifference by the public, and convinces her that 'true Paradise awaits her in England'.[61]

Balfour was hugely popular in France; even in small towns La March-ande des Fleurs de Piccadilly was a familiar character.[62] Episodes in the *Squibs* series were filmed in France and in 1925 Balfour had co-starred with the former American matinée idol, Carlyle Blackwell, in *Monte-Carlo*, directed by Louis Mercanton.[63] Mercanton and the actor Fred Wright devised a vehicle for Balfour which had much in common with *Squibs*. Balfour's character in *La Petite Bonne du Palace*, released in Britain as *Cinders* (1926), was a maid in a London boarding-house, persecuted by a harsh proprietor and selfish guests. With a convoluted plot about the possession of a hotel in Nice being determined by the presence of someone, anyone, in the Embankment Gardens at a specific time, the film transported Balfour and Fred Wright – playing an elderly professor with a penchant for aquariums – to the South of France, where Balfour not only saves the professor from blackmailers but also breaks a strike at the hotel. Her reward is to be made hotel manager. Balfour was said to have sparkled as the drudge with the heart of gold and spirit to match; shortly after the film's release she was named top world star in yet another poll.[64]

Mercanton also directed *Coquette*, which was released in Britain as *Monkeynuts* (1928). The film initially failed to find a renter, despite Mercanton's long association with the British industry and the presence of Britain's most popular female star:

> For many months a film called Monkey Nuts, starring Betty Balfour … was offered to distributors in Wardour Street and else-where. Nobody wanted it. Eventually it was bought by a Mr Hall

of Cardiff, and taken up by International Cine. New shots were put in and Pat Mannock wrote some bright sub-titles ... it went down with a bang and Betty scored a personal success in the film.[65]

The film was a comedy-drama set in a circus with Balfour's character graduating from programme-seller to trapeze artiste with alacrity. Drama was provided by escaping lions, with Balfour rescuing the infant son of a widowed baronet from the jaws of some overweight feline circus performers. The ending is inevitable: Balfour in wedding attire. *Bioscope* described Balfour's circus make-up as 'a combination of David Lloyd George, a golliwog, and the white-eyed musical kaffir',[66] but *Cinema* praised the film as a 'piquant comedy' and *Kine Weekly* enjoyed Balfour's 'bright entertaining performance'.[67]

Balfour was quoted as saying the work had exhausted her as there had been no stunt-double for her circus scenes, filming had taken up to twelve hours a day, and at other times she had to learn and rehearse the gymnastic moves integral to her character's role.[68] The *East London Mirror* said the film was 'a strong story of circus life ... good entertainment and gives Betty many opportunities to display her unlimited versatile talents',[69] but after completing the film Balfour temporarily deserted the cinema for the stage because, she claimed, stage work was less taxing, touring a musical comedy based on the film *The Glad Eye*, set, like her recent films, in France.[70] That *Monkeynuts* was so difficult to distribute indicates the bias of Wardour Street and its umbilical ties to the American film industry.

Of particular historical interest is Balfour's only film directed by Alfred Hitchcock, *Champagne* (1928). The extant print, shown at the National Film Theatre in London, confirms it to be a dazzling comedy of errors, but reviews at the time of its initial release were decidedly mixed. That much was expected of the collaboration is evident: 'With Alfred Hitchcock producing and Betty Balfour as star, one had a right to expect a better picture than Champagne turned out to be. The characterisation is inadequate but Miss Balfour's performance makes Champagne a film to see.'[71] Balfour played an American heiress, Betty, who runs off to France with a suitor deemed unsuitable by her father. To teach his daughter a lesson – that money has its drawbacks as well as advantages – Betty's father fakes bankruptcy so she will have to earn her own living. Predictably she does so as a cabaret performer, and her father's desire, that she should see 'the other side of life', is satisfied.

True love and financial responsibility follow as night follows day and all ends happily. One of the main criticisms of the film concerned its storyline: 'it is a pity that a film which was so excellently produced should have been based on a story so lacking in imagination';[72] and Hitchcock himself admitted to Truffaut, 'There is no story!'[73] *Bioscope* commented that it was fortunate that 'the volatile Betty was rarely off the screen'[74] and the champagne analogy was not lost on reviewers: 'More bubble than "body"',[75] 'as a whole, Champagne has been allowed to get a little flat'.[76] Hitchcock 'touches' were noticed, one being where a room thronged with thrashing dancers fades to reveal a field of sheep.[77] The *Daily Sketch* thought the film 'the cleverest, cruellest satire on night club life as it is that has ever been shown on the screen',[78] and Balfour was said to have 'never done better work in her screen career'.[79]

The important trade paper *Kine Weekly* did not like the film at all, commenting that it had a 'distinct pseudo-American flavour', and that it was 'a feeble imitation of the type of entertainment at which the Americans are unsurpassed'.[80] The review accused Hitchcock of attempting to emulate American 'high speed comedy drama' and American attitudes to popular entertainment, and the concomitant belief that the British industry should be producing an entirely different genre of film was an issue frequently raised; for instance, some time later *Screen Pictorial* suggested the British industry should specialize in historical films, with perhaps a few excursions into West End farcical comedy, and leave other topics to Hollywood.[81] But audiences could connect to such films as *Champagne*. They would have known exactly whose side they were on when Balfour's character is 'victimized by snobbery' when she gives carnations to members of a dance band rather than handing them to the privileged club clientele.[82] It has been argued that the mass audience's enjoyment of films in which class barriers are breached indicates an 'equable acceptance of the class structure', but this fails to allow for the fact that it is just as likely that the acts of social dissonance themselves – Betty defining herself as 'one of us' with musicians, rather than with the club's affluent patrons – were what audiences responded to, perhaps enjoying the fact that on film, at least, such barriers were not impenetrable.[83]

A similar confusion may be noted in some reactions to Hitchcock's British films. What Hitchcock understood was audience's emotions; to accuse him of possessing a manipulative technique, as some did, was the equivalent of accusing Dickens of using too many words when telling a story. Spending large sums of money on stars, sets and costumes was meaningless unless a film connected with its audience by way of images and, later, words. And so a film like *Blackmail* (1929), which Hitchcock described as being about 'the conflict between love and duty – a human problem', gained a social and artistic value in its own right by appealing to universal values.[84] And that value is subject to a reciprocative process; initially a film's value may be determined by finance, by personnel, by journalists, sometimes by intellectuals, but, ultimately, accrued value – audience approval – must have at least equal status with critical and artistic veracity.[85] Hitchcock's inclusion of the commonplace, the familiar, the universal, in his films was, in one sense, an act of respect for his audience, an acknowledgement of the value of 'bums on seats'. His films were not insular like so many British films: the film star posters on Anny Ondra's bedroom walls and the advertisements for 'penny dreadfuls' and film magazines in the tobacconist's shop in *Blackmail* would have been familiar sights to audiences everywhere; the Disney cartoon playing in the cinema in *Sabotage* (1936) was a universal symbol. What parent could not identify with the children's uncontrolled familiarity with Herbert Marshall in *Murder* (1930)? Who, but the most dour abstainer, could help but laugh at the drunk in *Champagne* who walks with a steady gait on a storm-tossed ship but falls down when all is calm? This was film-making for audiences who went to the movies to be entertained; it was film-making for a generation bred in film culture.

Although *Champagne* has been regarded as only a minor Hitchcock film, Balfour's name and the young director's reputation were sufficient to make it a 'big hit with the public' and, as noted, Balfour's portrayal was praised. As she completed the film nursing a broken rib, credit must be given to her professionalism.[86] Part of Hitchcock's cinema education at this time was gained in Europe, with co-productions with the German Emelka Company, and Balfour's film career continued to thrive, thanks to France and, to a lesser degree, Germany. There was a negative response to another of Balfour's French films, *Le Diable au Coeur*. The British title was *Little-Devil-May-Care*, and if the press and public alike expected the usual light-hearted, warm-spirited Balfour performance they were in for a surprise. The film, and her characterization, marked a turning point in Balfour's career, at which her usual cheerful gamine persona was almost completely deconstructed. Scripted and directed by Marcel L'Herbier, it was the film he made prior to the extraordinary *L'Argent*. Set in the channel port of Honfleur, the film was a dark and rainswept tale of revenge, drunkenness, marital discord and youthful rebellion. L'Herbier altered Balfour's image completely; he changed her usually fluffy halo of curls to a severe short and straight style, in order that she could convincingly play Ludivine, a violent, alienated young woman who, after a broken heart, attempted rape and much stormy weather, is happily married off to the young man who had been the object of her hatred at the outset of the film.

Le Diable au Coeur was the first French film to be shot on panchromatic stock and much was made of the lighting, with 'fantastic' nightclub shots and picturesque scenes of studio-built fishermen's cottages. There were major problems with the film; both Balfour and the French leading man contracted pneumonia due to regular drenching – they had to stand for hours in front of churning aeroplane propellers which, with water cascading from hoses, were used to create the windswept, rainsodden atmosphere of the film. Balfour was said to have worked for thirteen hours a day, seven days a week, for eight weeks, on the film. One commentator noted that Ludivine was Balfour's 'most difficult role, but somehow she accomplished it as a true professional'.[87] The role was certainly different to the kind of parts she was used to playing in England. No British director had given her the opportunity of playing such a dark character and Balfour ably demonstrated, as she had in *Reveille*, that she was more than just a pert and pretty comedienne.

A Sister to Six (1927), adapted from a farcical French novel, was made jointly with the German Isepa Company and was said to be 'easily the best film comedy made outside America'.[88] The director, Carl Hoffmann, took a pan-European approach to its casting with competitions in Hungary, Sweden, Denmark, Russia and Germany to find young women to play Balfour's sisters.[89] The film's plot was simple: how to find husbands for six daughters. In one scene Balfour, dressed as a man, 'made love' to an actress, persuading her to undress so that she could steal the performer's costume, and there is a fluid sexuality underpinning a number of Balfour's performances. In *Squibs* she was a lively tom-boy, skipping about Piccadilly like a boisterous child, and in the opening reels of *Le Diable au Coeur* she was a juvenile delinquent before the term was coined. In *Satan's Sister* she masqueraded as a man and in *A Sister to Six* she went further: pretending physical attraction for another woman. This ambiguous sexuality is matched in some of the film magazines of the time: *Photobits and Cinema Star* published a long-running series on

'Women who lived as Men', there are articles which pose the question 'Would you rather by a Boy?', and letters from 'Man Haters' which, perhaps unwittingly, exposed the fragility of male–female relations at the time.[90]

More than a thousand women had been imprisoned for fighting for the vote, some had died.[91] Thousands of women had made personal and financial sacrifices in order to have a say in the running of society, and yet there were commentators, especially those with a bent for eugenics, who unhesitatingly declared that the demand for the vote was evidence of women's dereliction of duty, and 'that no possible good could come from Feminism, that it offered no hope for a better world, and that it was a quack remedy for our sickness'.[92] As late as the 1929 general election, the *Daily Mail* ran a virulent campaign against what it called 'the flapper vote' and there was by no means a consensus as to women's role in society.[93] One unemployed hotel servant, deprived of the luxury of the music hall and cinema because of poverty, took to visiting her local cathedral instead, 'But I always come away now feeling that ministers are still living in a pre-war world of their own making. They either will not or dare not step out into the real, terribly real, post-war world where the battle is being fought in grim earnest by poor respectable men and women.'[94]

The debate about women's place in society was primarily couched in traditional terms, as were their roles in the majority of films. *This Freedom*, shown during British Film Weeks, was a cinematic tract attacking working women and was also said to express typical British values.[95] Starring Fay Compton, the film detailed the degradation brought upon a family by a mother choosing to work rather than stay at home bringing up her family, and would appear to be about as realistic, and as contemporary, as one of Corelli's lengthy tomes: *The Mighty Atom* detailed the depths of despair to which children sank if their parents allowed them to be over-educated; *Boy* told the story of a youth destined for alcoholism and death because his slatternly mother failed in her maternal duty.[96] Similarly, *Afraid of Love* (1925), in which a wife leaves a faithless husband to manage her lover's dress shop, was deemed 'disreputable', especially as the woman who wrote the screenplay had been party to the situation depicted in the film.[97] But, in the real world, women worked. Women had to work, they had no choice.

One of the more memorable films in which a woman's place was illuminated is *Hindle Wakes* (1927). The film, based on Stanley Houghton's pre-war stage success, was directed by the veteran Maurice Elvey, and it exemplifies both Elvey's considerable talent and the sometimes realized potential of British silent films. Elvey opened up the play, made the most of a small but effective set of terraced houses, and included some mesmerizing material, shot in Blackpool, of swirling crowds in the Tower Ballroom whose unrehearsed patterns rival anything choreographed by Busby Berkeley. He also captured the brittle, desperate gaiety of factory workers intent on escaping the mills' grim routines. The story, of Fanny's holiday fling with her boss's son and her subsequent refusal to marry him to satisfy convention, provided Elvey with a text to which he attached a series of genuinely moving images which show the silent cinema at its most eloquent. The film is a tense and beautifully detailed commentary on the independence of Lancashire working women, the gulf between the 'haves' and the 'have-nots', and the hypocrisy of respectable opinion. The 'nervous artificiality' of the American-born Estelle Brody's performance is beguiling and the film was impressively boomed.[98]

The film ends on a more dramatic note than the play, with Fanny leaving home because of the so-called disgrace she has brought upon her parents. To a background of pulsing looms and shuttles, her last speech from the play appears as titles: 'I'm a Lancashire lass, and so long as there's a weaving shed in Lancashire I shall earn enough brass to keep me going ... I'm going to be on my own in the future.'[99] Elvey altered the final titles to read, 'I'm an *independent* Lancashire lass ... ' and the film remains one of the few films of the period to recognize the changed and changing status of women to which Virginia Woolf alluded when she wrote:

> The younger generation had the audacity to say that Queen Victoria was no better than an honest charwoman who had brought up her children respectably. They had the temerity to doubt whether to sew straight stitches into men's hat brims should be the sole aim and end of a woman's life ... Strange ideas indeed were seething in their brain. A girl, for instance, would reason, as she walked along the streets of a factory town, that she had no right to bring a child into the world if that child must earn its living in a mill. A chance saying in a book would fire her imagination to dream of future cities where there were to be baths and kitchens and washhouses and art galleries and museums and parks.[100]

The investigators whose philanthropic sensibilities bore down on the problem of unemployment after the 'crash' of 1929 attacked such distracting notions, castigating the working women of Liverpool and Blackburn for their 'indifferent or bad household management'.[101] They dismissed the dreams of would-be kindergarten teachers, children's nurses, dancers or stewardesses, as 'phantasy'. When one young woman refused to countenance the thought of domestic service, her inappropriate response was reckoned to indicate her 'lack of quality': 'Do you think it's pleasant to spend one's whole life with people who make one feel inferior to them?' This 'lack of quality' was blamed on the cinema and dance halls which were frequented by such women. 'Unrealistic dreams' were also the fault of the cinema: 'an appetite for the unreal and the shoddy can be commercially exploited while genuine sensibility cannot.' Such was the chasm between the sensibility, and class, of investigators and subject that protests against poverty, the means test and other indicators of social neglect were cited as evidence of an unhealthy propensity for self-pity.[102]

Both Estelle Brody and Mabel Poulton specialized in 'lack of quality' roles in British films. Both projected verve and energy, a wayward femininity which was a variant on Betty Balfour's Cockney gamine. Estelle Brody lit up the screen in *Hindle Wakes* and Mabel Poulton also had an eye-catching screen presence. In such vehicles as *The Alley Cat* (1929), *The Hellcat* (1928) and *Taxi for Two* (1929), Poulton portrayed perky working-class characters with much charm, and reviewers often praised her performances even when they did not like her films.[103] The apogee of Mabel Poulton's career was *The Constant Nymph* (1928). The plot concerns the 'doings' of a musician named Sanger and his 'Bohemian' family, 'none of them with any moral sense except where instrumental music was concerned'.[104] The *British Film Catalogue* describes the plot in spare terms: 'Composer leaves dominating wife for school-girl.'[105] Set in the Tyrol, the stage production had been *the* play to see of 1926 and had started a fashion for Austrian dresses and Austrian summer holidays, which is, in itself, a comment on the financial status of those attending its performances.[106] In his own uniquely socio-sexual manner, D. H. Lawrence summed up the plot as 'pure sacrifice' and of course the nymph, Mabel Poulton at her most winsome, died, just in time to avoid technical adultery. This may well have reassured those who plumped for *The Constant Nymph* as 'best film' of 1928.[107] It was the film, apparently, which finally reconciled the suburbs to 'Bohemia'; they were reconciled, it is presumed, because death alleviated guilt, and morality triumphed at the behest of the grim reaper.[108] A review commented that nothing remained of the story 'but the dry bones ... clothed in respectability and refinement ... Perhaps too much was expected for Basil Dean's first picture ... it takes something wider, faster and more broadly understanding than stage technique to obtain satisfactory effects on the vivid canvas of the screen.'[109]

The 'vivid canvas' was also lacking from some of Balfour's last films of the silent age. She appears to have been trapped between repeating endless variations on her past triumphs and the development of new roles which would bring future success. *The Brat* (1930), *Bright Eyes* and *The Vagabond Queen* (1929) were silent films made at the tail-end of the 1920s; sound, in varying decrees, was added to them. Synchronized songs were added to *Bright Eyes*. *The Vagabond Queen*, frothy Ruritanian nonsense with Balfour playing a queen and her Cockney double, was in production at Elstree when Alfred Hitchcock was re-shooting *Blackmail* with sound. *The Vagabond Queen* was released with a musical score but no dialogue and it was said that 'it passes well as a silent film if there is a breezy orchestral accompaniment'.[110] *The Brat* cast Balfour as a petty thief who is taken under the wing of a film producer; of course she becomes a star. No distributing company would take an option on the film because it was silent, so Balfour produced an 'all-talkie' version of it in three and a half weeks. The strain evidently told on her as she was reported to be ill in hospital again.[111] With the advent of sound on film, and the rush to capture what many considered to be the industry's role as guardian of the English language, it is a surprise to find the star so inactive in the early 1930s.[112] Her voice was suited to sound and her accent acceptable. A short publicity film showcasing Elstree stars, which premièred at the *New Empire* at the end of 1928, evidently surprised audiences who suspected that Balfour's Cockney screen persona was real.[113]

After her first 'all-talking, all-dancing musical', *Raise the Roof* (1930), which was hailed as 'the first British Film Musical', Balfour was away from the screen for nearly four years.[114] She played a soubrette in the Jessie Matthews hit musical *Evergreen* (1934) and although the part was small her performance was praised; Matthews was, of course, the star of the film.[115] *My Old Dutch* (1934) was more in line with Balfour's past screen performances. She was teamed with Gordon Harker and the cast included the redoubtable Florrie Forde, who was rarely given the opportunity to make the same impact on screen as she did 'on the 'alls'. *Kine Weekly* described the film as 'a pageant of life during the last forty years', and 'many scenes familiar to Londoners are used as background … the theme is the struggles of a typical workman and his wife to make a career for their son, and afterwards for a grandson when he is killed [in the war]'.[116] Not only did the film manage to incorporate asides about the development of electricity, the telephone, radio and air travel, it depicted 'a number of heart-rending situations – unemployment, strikes, air-raids … '[117] The family in the film was shown to be righteous but impecunious and part of the film's tension was provided by class and familial conflict. *My Old Dutch* came down firmly on the side of the work-worn angels. Balfour played an unmarried mother, her lover having been killed in the war, and the film's themes were similar to those explored by Auden in *The Dance of Death*, published the same year: the bitterness of women widowed by war, young women deprived of companionship, the almost constant struggle to ward off poverty, to make ends meet.

> I was a girl that had nice young men,
> But they've all gone abroad since then,
> If you can bring them back again,
>   I'll follow thee.
>
> For five years now I've been out of a job,
> I don't care whether you're a Jew or a nob,
> If you will promise me a bob,
>   I'll follow thee.[118]

Balfour's performance in *My Old Dutch* was said to be consistent with 'the stellar screen work' she had done in the past; the direction, by the veteran Sinclair Hill, was said to 'leave little or nothing to be desired' and 'unusual care was taken with regard to detail for a relatively un-pretentious picture'.[119] Even if the film only groped at the possibilities of film as a medium responsive to its audience, the glorification of working-class resilience in *My Old Dutch* demonstrates an awareness of the limits within which the British industry worked whereby a huge proportion of the British audience was denied connection with its own films because of the exclusivity of the film-makers' language, denied even 'the faintest dribble of real English life'.[120] There was at least a glimmer of recognition of the fact that there was value in the lives of those who were familiar with the insides of public houses, who lived in difficult conditions in industrial towns, and this indicates a tenuous understanding that film must spread its net, must ingest as many ideas, from as many disparate sources, as possible. To limit subject matter, source material, location or characters by class leads, inevitably, to artistic sterility and commercial disaster.

G. K. Chesterton noted that 'foreigners can often appreciate what we cannot ... some European judge will discover the vigour of our Cockney comic songs; and publish them, as we should have done in a companion to the Golden Treasury',[121] and John Grierson argued that many of the spectacular British successes of the 1930s drew on working-class culture, rather than excluding it: 'Whenever British films have followed in the old English music-hall tradition – with all its reflection of the life and humour of working people – we get zip and zingo, and everything that makes a good picture.'[122] *My Old Dutch* was released at the same time as *Sing as We Go*, Gracie Fields' naive but sprightly contribution to the war against unemployment, and both stars were similarly defined as 'ours'. A title from Balfour's *Squibs* characterization, 'Ain't we sisters', was indicative of the connection between star and audience. A production worker commented that she was 'a pal' to everyone, a fact Balfour was proud of, and there was undoubtedly a bond between audiences and 'their own', like Balfour and Fields, which goes completely against common practice: the hiring of middle-brow performers to film middle-brow plays for middle-brow audiences.[123]

Balfour's role in *Forever England* (1935) was secondary to that of John Mills, but it was pivotal portrayal of an aspect of British womanhood which was beyond the scope of Gracie Fields' ebullient persona or the fey charm of Jessie Matthews. Once more Balfour played an unmarried mother who, across time and classes, sacrifices her son for the sake of his father and England; as *Kine Weekly* noted in its review, 'Breed will tell.'[124] During the Great War Balfour's son becomes a hero by holding a German cruiser at bay single-handedly until a British ship arrives; he loses his life, and in death his identity is discovered by his father, who finds on the boy's body the pocket-watch he gave his lover, years before, as a keepsake.[125] The film was made with the co-operation of the Admiralty and was premièred in the presence of the King and Queen.[126] It was said to be 'a magnificent piece of work – splendid popular entertainment' and it was, one reviewer noted, 'a relief to have the English language spoken as ordinary people speak it'. Balfour was said to be 'as convincing and as prominent as the story treatment will permit'.[127] The same review regretted that 'a grand opportunity to consolidate feminine appeal is missed', and an American review also noted that 'the human element doesn't count for much'.[128] The film was based on one of C. S. Forester's macho sea-faring novels, *Brown on Resolution*, so the fact that the principal female character was only a thumbnail sketch should have been expected. In New York the film was accorded the status of one of *Movie Mirror*'s 'Films of the Month', and was said to be an 'exceptional production ... the scenes of action are thrilling and well worth seeing and the acting of John Mills, the boy, suggests that you will be hearing from him in the future'.[129] In both *My Old Dutch* and *Forever England* Balfour personified women's duty to their country; romance was incidental, with passion defined in terms of male need rather than joint commitment; as both films were set in the past, with war a central motif, there was the suggestion, once again, that national identity was fully realized only when it was isolated from contemporary references and under threat. In such cicumstances even unwed motherhood was excused.

The film marked Balfour's last significant performance in a long and varied career. In 1935 she remade *Squibs* at Julius Hagen's tiny Twickenham studio and even if the lack of finance and cramped conditions show in the film, there are hints of the excitement which must have greeted the first appearance of the Cockney flower-seller back in 1921. The new version was not without its admirers; Balfour contributed 'a performance of tireless resource and energy', and she was 'in her element, and has no difficulty in meeting the entertainment's wide demands'.[130] The film is no masterpiece, but it is a jolly little film with much in it to enjoy. The less said about Balfour's last starring role, in *Eliza Comes to Stay* (1936), the better. The film is based on a pre-war melodrama, and Balfour was said to have given 'an intelligent rendering' of the part of a 'frightened little ward who descends on the home of a susceptible bachelor', played 'with less finesse than usual', by Sir Seymour Hicks. Balfour was already in her thirties and too old for the role, which may well explain why she was hidden behind enormous dark glasses and hideous 'Orphan Annie' clothes. There was said to be 'a slowness in the whole proceedings that won't help people forget the vintage of the comedy'.[131] A less than flattering reviewer declared that 'Eliza would have been far wiser to have stayed where she was, honourably buried in the past'.[132]

To conclude the account of Betty Balfour's career on such a negative note fails to do her justice, given her contribution to British films over two decades. That she was the one female home-grown star of the silent era to have truly connected with British audiences is a triumph in itself and the fact that she survived the changes that significantly altered the process of film-making during the period is a small miracle. Miracles, where the British film industry is concerned, should be celebrated, whatever their size.

There were plans to star Balfour in the story of a 'nippy' working in a Lyons Corner House; the publicity material claimed she was going to spend a month working in one of the restaurants so that her portrayal would do justice to the character in the film and to the young women in real life.[133] Nothing appears to have come of the project, but in broaching such a subject, in recognizing that screen and real life were not confined to country houses or to Mayfair, that 'the world before our eyes' – a slogan prominently displayed in the cinema's formative years – could serve as an inspiration for the British industry rather than as an indictment of it, at least some British producers were warily facing up to the challenges regularly made by those who cared about film.[134] The majority of Betty Balfour's films confirm Arthur Dent's contention that 'film entertainment should be based on democratic principles', that success could be gained from making films about 'factory workers, about the Yorkshire Dales, about Saturday football matches and Sunday teas',[135] that the streets of London, Manchester and Birmingham, 'the concrete pavements, and not ye olde cobbled stones, are trod by a panorama of plots'. For fifteen years Balfour sustained a relationship with British audiences by doing just that; few British performers, without the benefit of Hollywood, have ever matched that relationship.[136]

8

George Pearson: Hollywood Dreams, Twickenham Nightmares

In Julius Hagen's studio at Twickenham, on the single sound-stage where Betty Balfour resurrected *Squibs* in 1935, George Pearson all but ended his long and creative career in film. Working on 'quota quickies' – some of them shot at night to keep the studio's production facilities busy – was a long way from the heady days of the early 1920s. Then, Pearson's reputation was second to none; his films with Balfour had made him a very rich man with a prestige to match, and he was the one British director who, while accepting the arcadian myth, attempted to broach the subject of life as it was lived by working-class audiences, albeit with a schoolmaster's eye for the educational potential of the medium.[1] The pessimism which prompted one commentator to write, 'British Film Weeks were eminently successful [but] there is hardly likely to be another for the simple fact there will be hardly any British Films to show', did not appear to apply to Pearson.[2] In 1924 Pearson could do no wrong: 'In a class by themselves are Love, Life and Laughter, and the Squibs pictures, and George Pearson, whose personality is as indelibly stamped upon his delightful creations as is Griffith's on his, has made in the first named what may be hailed as the most charming British picture of the year.'[3]

Love, Life and Laughter was celebrated in terms which suggest that it was one of the first British films to look lovingly at London, with an eye for the potential of the city as a background. Pearson was said to have 'found as much beauty in the flare of a street light, the ill-lit doorway of a garret, or the reflection of candlelight in a cracked window pane, as all the poets before have found in honeysuckle and a moon'.[4] This is a long way from the baronial residences and gallops of Walter West and the agrarian idylls of Hepworth:

> Pearson has filled his canvas with remarkable character types, which might have stepped straight out of a London scene ... lit and photographed with a beauty to dream of, common sights and things of every day take on a new meaning, and carry one back to childhood days when even the smallest things and the most trivial had an enormous importance.[5]

Pearson was said to be 'the composer of our London screen' with Betty Balfour as 'the songster'.[6] No director, it was said, had done more to raise the standard of British pictures (without resorting to period costume, peers and landscapes, it should be stressed) and by some miracle of timing Pearson combined artistic integrity with popular taste to forge a career that stood head and shoulders above those of his contemporaries.

To say that Pearson took film-making seriously would be to under-estimate the gravitas of the man. An excerpt from a lecture he delivered in 1923 illustrates his passionate espousal of his chosen medium of expression:

> I plead for the art of the screen which is something so great that I ache with longing to free this great dumb things that is with us, this great dumb giant. To strike off the gyves of the spoken word and all its puny conventionality. The kinema is the greatest, the most tremendously powerful force for the bringing together of that universal brotherhood of the world that mankind has ever known and only by living for it, giving oneself to it, housing it, seeing it, and believing in it, can great things from it be achieved.[7]

It is difficult not to place considerable emphasis on the creative partner-ship of Pearson and Balfour; it was, perhaps, her bright spirit which leavened Pearson's serious vision. Once their partnership was over Pearson attempted to re-create their celluloid alchemy with the Franco-Argentinian actress Mona Maris, and later with the legendary music-hall entertainer Harry Lauder, but failed to replicate his past successes with either.

In terms of technique *The Little People*, made in 1926 with Maris, was said to be Pearson's most adventurous film, but it was rejected by many critics and the public as well. The story has a familiar ring to it – a dancer gives up her career to marry her poor stepbrother – but *Bioscope* called it 'vague … thin and wearisome'. The film had been trade-shown in April, but in July a re-edited version, with 'less sententious' sub-titles, was shown.[8] Pearson savoured one review, from the *Illustrated London News*, but it was in the minority in praising the film: 'The same quality of imagination, of merging the real and the unreal, lends glamour to the simple story, beautifully told.'[9] The film may have been, according to Pearson, 'a breeze blowing in the right direction' but it did not produce queues at the box-office. Possibly the problem was Pearson's former association with Balfour. Audiences may have expected a re-run of *Squibs*, instead the film was an ostensibly foreign story, with Italian locations and a less popular star.[10] Given Pearson's assertion that 'you will find more sincerity about the making of a picture than you will find on the legitimate stage about the making of a new play', it was a surprising choice for him to film a less than well-known play, *Mr Preedy and the Countess*. The film was made in Paris, with Mona Maris again, but it evidently failed to find a renter in Britain.[11]

A number of films Pearson made for the American production company Paramount – *Love's Option* (1928), *Yellow Stockings* (1928) and *The Broken Melody* (1929) – did not rate a serious review in the trade papers, but *The Silver King* (1929), based on a hit Victorian melodrama, was praised for its 'sympathetic direction, sound acting and technical excellence'. The film was produced by Pearson but directed by the American T. Hayes Hunter. It was said to contain the best snow scene yet filmed and the story, of a man framed for murder who goes on the run, strikes it rich, and then can only support his struggling wife by remaining incognito, was said to be of 'strong emotional flavour accentuated by brilliant acting'.[12] The strength of the story was enough, *Bioscope* claimed, to secure 'a gratifying reception with popular audiences' but as the film was silent, released after the first sound films had caused something of a sensation, it did very little for the finances of the Welsh-Pearson-Elder production company.[13]

The two films Pearson made with the venerable Scots entertainer Harry Lauder, *Huntingtower* (1927) and *Auld Lang Syne* (1929), failed to persuade the public that the comedian had what it took for screen stardom. *Auld Lang Syne* included synchronized songs and was regarded as an important release, especially at a time when British sound films were still a rarity, but it did very little for the company's increasingly precarious financial state and even less for Pearson's reputation.[14] It cannot have helped the cause of the film, or the star, to have shown the film with the songs and lip movements out of synchronization, which sometimes happened.[15] The direction was said to be even better than *Love, Life and Laughter*, an early triumph still, evidently, clear in the reviewer's mind six years after its 1923 release.[16] Lauder was said to be the vibrant centre of the film, especially after his son, a boxer, and his daughter, a dancer, had introduced him to a bohemian life in London. There was evidently some beautiful scenery to admire, a prolonged joke about a salmon which did not impress reviewers, and, on the whole, the film was thought suited to Harry Lauder's admirers rather than to the general public.[17]

A review of *Huntingtower* illustrates both the strengths and weaknesses of Pearson's work; the settings, exteriors, location, cast and photography were said to be 'first class', but the film was 'curious' and lacking in 'conviction and appeal'.[18] Given Pearson's former repudiation of socialism in *Reveille*, John Buchan's novel was, perhaps, a logical choice of material although the story's anti-Soviet plot was far from an automatic crowd-puller as anti-Russian newsreels were highly unpopular with cinema audiences.[19] And of course one of Buchan's 'pukka' heroes was a long way from Balfour's down-at-heel Cockneys, even further when it is noted that Buchan was a member of the ruling class whose certainties about the anathema of socialism were reinforced by 'the bold experiment of Fascism'.[20] The story concerns a middle-aged Glasgow grocer going to the rescue of a Russian princess holed up in a deserted castle in order to escape the clutches of vicious Bolsheviks.[21] Apart from Harry Lauder as the grocer, there is a hero named Captain Heritage, and with a plot involving an alien culture and ideology, Pearson built on the exploration of human and national angst he had painted in *Reveille*. As previously noted, in *Reveille*, Betty Balfour's character, Mick, saves a poor ex-soldier, Nutty, from the doctrinal infamy of socialism; the key to Pearson's resolution of the threat to stability by alien solutions was to reduce the issue to a question of humour. When Mick discovers the embittered, out-of-work Nutty reacting vehemently to the rhetoric of 'a wild-eyed orator preaching rebellion', her solution is to take him home, adding a demand: 'but for Gawd's sake, Larf.'[22]

This attitude to social disruption, to crisis resolution, was not confined to Pearson; Victor Saville, in discussing what aspects of British identity could be utilized in British films, was quoted as saying: 'It should show the problems and ambitions of our people. It should also show such characteristic touches as the Englishman's sense of humour, which he exercises even in the most trying circumstances'; inevitably Saville then regaled the journalist with a war story and it seems to be a peculiarly narrow view of what constitutes humour to locate it within the specific confines of a life-threatening situation. Once again, a key element of national identity is linked to an exterior force; British character is at its best, is most clearly defined, when threatened.[23] In *Huntingtower*, with its communist threat, Harry Lauder and the kilted youngsters of the Gorbals plump wholeheartedly for the Russian aristocracy for the sake of past and future privilege. One review claimed that 'a merrier entertainment has never been produced', and the film is far from boring, but it was not popular and Pearson's agreement with Famous Players-Lasky to produce that company's quota films was abruptly terminated.[24]

Pearson had been the only British film director deliberately to accentuate the innate values of the ordinary; his films lent credence to elements of British life which were, in peacetime, excluded from any definition of national identity. The titles lists of the *Squibs* films are full of sassiness, expressions of familial disrespect and an earthy lack of consideration for convention.[25] With *Huntingtower*, Pearson moved decisively closer to the refined, respectable notion of national identity, closer to a paternal vision of conflict resolution. It is the aptly named Captain Heritage, a representative of privilege and history, who harnesses the latent forces of the ordinary folk of Glasgow to thwart the communist menace in much the same way as feudal lords employed their serfs and other dependents in the waging of wars. The film divorced Pearson from the natural exuberance which had permeated his earlier films, from the integrity of humour and courage as class-blind concepts; he was becoming just another British director making just the same kind of films other directors made; everything he touched now turned into a 'frightening loss'.[26]

The leitmotif of *Huntingtower* was also present in *The Flight Commander* (1927), directed by Maurice Elvey, which was released a few months before Pearson's film. Elvey's film fused the heroic, triumphant part of national identity with a slightly different kind of threat by telling the story of a British pilot thwarting the plans of Bolsheviks in China – mocked-up in Hendon – and having the character played by a real-life hero, Captain Alan Cobham, who had broken records for flights to Capetown and Australia. On Cobham's return from Australia his seaplane landed on the River Thames, near Westminster Bridge, and he was met by an official delegation from the House of Commons.[27] If Cobham's presence in an anti-Soviet story signified tacit establishment approval – a review noted that the director had laboured under the handicap of propaganda 'which seems to be the film's aim'[28] – neither Pearson's nor Elvey's efforts were appreciated at the box-office, surprisingly in the case of Elvey as he had always appeared to have a clear idea of what constituted popular entertainment.[29]

Pearson appears to have concentrated on producing at this time – he was far from happy with the coming of sound because of the extra costs it involved – and he found himself bidding against Michael Balcon for the rights to R. C. Sherriff's highly successful play, *Journey's End*. A gentleman's agreement was reached by which Pearson and Balcon would jointly produce the film. The relationship was further enlarged to include the American company Tiffany, which was a 'Poverty Row independent which entertained day dreams of moving up the ladder'.[30] It may well have been a second-rate studio in Hollywood but it had facilities for making sound films at a time when conversion to sound had not been completed in Britain. The industry in Britain was tardy in appreciating the importance of sound. *The Jazz Singer* had been trade-shown in October of 1927. Louis Levy, the musical director on countless British films, had seen earlier examples of sound films as well as the Al Jolson film in New York and had reported back to London; his enthusiasm was met with laughter and derision, and only a few members of the industry, among them Maurice Elvey, always the professional, shared Levy's appreciation of the changing medium.[31] In November 1929 all the films on release in London were either synchronized with sound recordings or 'full talkie'; that only one-tenth of the cinemas in Britain were equipped for sound films was said to be an example of 'the wishes of the few ... dictating the supply to the majority'.[32] The New Commodore, Hammersmith, opened in November 1929, was the first theatre to be built entirely for the presentation of talking pictures, although the New Gallery in Regent Street was the first cinema to be fitted with a sound system.[33] The impact of sound on film attendance may be gauged, in London, from the Astoria which, after its conversion to sound, was 'pulling in 60,000 patrons a week'.[34]

The Tiffany studio in Hollywood had recently parted from one of its founder directors, John M. Stahl, and was desperately looking around for a hit movie. Pearson's future was uncertain and his company floundering; of such an inauspicious partnership one of the most successful films of 1930 was born. It was the American company which insisted on James Whale directing *Journey's End* (1930); he had a reputation for sensitive direction of actors, both on the stage and for film. He had recently worked as dialogue coach on the Richard Dix vehicle, *The Love Doctor*, and was assisting Howard Hughes in adding sound to the epic, and silent, *Hell's Angels*.[35] Whale was the embodiment of the personal transformation necessary before success could be had in the West End of London. From an impoverished background in Dudley, Whale resolved to lose his accent and gain respect from those who defined social and theatrical acceptability in terms of accent and diction; 'storming the snobbish fortress of the West End and its elite became an all encompassing goal.'[36]

Elsa Lanchester remembered Whale telling stories of his 'poverty-stricken family', of 'the tiny little fire in the tiny little grate in the rooms where he was brought up', but when he arrived in London, via the Oxford Playhouse, he had become 'Bohemian upper-class with very precise, clear speech patterns'.[37] After serving a theatrical apprenticeship which included stage managing, scene designing and acting – notably with Charles Laughton in *The Man with Red Hair* – Whale took the amateur dramatist Sherriff's play *Journey's End* on a journey to the heights of popularity in London and New York. The success of the play on Broadway led to a rapid decamping to Hollywood, where Whale enjoyed 'pouring the gold through my hair'. This new wealth was, evidently, only a temporary salve to his desire for acceptance by his social superiors for when Pearson informed him of a rumour in London that Sherriff was about to be knighted Whale was devastated; such was the extent of his anger and envy he was physically sick and unable to work.[38] At a later date he returned to England and, at an industry function at the Dorchester Hotel, was seated next to Lord Portal; having enjoyed a few glasses of wine Whale gave a speech in which he acknowledged, with some irony, the absurdity of his deep-seated desire to be taken to the bosom of the British establishment: 'I've always wanted to find myself sitting next to a real Lord. And now it's happened. Unfortunately, we neither of us have anything to say to each other.'[39]

George Pearson's diary, written when he was in Hollywood producing *Journey's End*, makes salutary reading for any would-be producer or director trying to make sense of the perversely erudite box-office mentality motivating Hollywood studio executives. At one point before the filming of *Journey's End* began, someone at Tiffany's decided that a love interest would improve the film's chances of success. As the play was set in the trenches of the Great War, a female love interest had been obviously missing from the stage production. With some eloquence Pearson stood his ground, arguing that the spirit of woman, 'the unseen presence of Woman', motivated the characters, lent power to the actions of the male characters. He supervised the daily filming and floated new ideas in what he obviously found to be a stimulating, frustrating and challenging environment. He was excited by the prospect of directing Paul Robeson in a screen version of *Othello*, but nothing came of the project. After watching Estelle Brody's performance in *Hindle Wakes*, Pearson's thoughts turned back to *Squibs*; the nervous energy Brody projected would have been perfect for an updated version of his great success. Pearson was pleased to have Colin Clive play the leading role in *Journey's End*, as Clive had made a huge success of the part in the theatre. There was so much riding on the film – finance, reputation, personal integrity – that Pearson was 'haunted by the fear of failure'. There were scathing reports in the London trade papers about the imminent collapse of his company, and his diary entries reflect the depression that sometimes consumed him. He was keenly aware of 'the injustices of human judgement in the film business', and recorded his 'Thoughts re my wasted years in England. What I could have done here as a director!'[40]

When *Journey's End* was completed, a preview was arranged at a cinema in Glendale, a working-class suburb of Los Angeles, which would clearly indicate how Joe Public would take to the film. *Variety* was the first trade paper to review the film and Pearson must have taken heart from what he read: 'One might say that if the English would leave their talkie making to these two men England would have talkies for world-wide distribution.'[41] Further reviews confirmed that the film was at least a critical success. *Film Mercury* wrote: 'It is a breathing document of men on the front line trenches. After the realism of this cinema I cannot see how any other war film would not seem trivial … occasionally a piece of work is so perfect that even the mob recognises its beauty and sincerity.'[42] *Hollywood Diary* noted: 'It is an English story of English officers and such expression is essentially British – its "toppings", "cheerios" and "Oh I says" are typical and not effeminate, as some critics have been silly enough to insinuate.'[43]

The issue of masculinity, of the supposed effeminacy of British actors and heroes, was not confined to the trade papers; it was an issue also raised by correspondents to film magazines, especially once sound reproduced the 'the "precious" clipped voices which are so prevalent among our young actors'.[44] Wyndham Lewis's homophobic appraisal of British men, 'the bashful and dreamy, young-lady like "spoilt child" has always, as a type, been an anglo-saxon speciality',[45] appears to have been at the heart of some of the criticism and British film fans were unhappy about 'the erroneous conception of the unfortunate Englishman who wears a monocle and emits inane remarks like "Bai Jove", "Perfectly topping", "Quaite, my dear fellah" ... studios prefer caricatures to characters'.[46]

Even British stars whose fortunes were assured by Hollywood did not escape criticism. Leslie Howard, known as 'whimsy' to his friend Douglas Fairbanks Junior, was characterized as 'Simperin' Through' after his performance in the archetypal Hollywood–England melodrama, *Smilin' Through*.[47] The performance prompted one English film fan to write: 'His fans have called Leslie Howard "the perfect type of English gentleman". On behalf of my race I repudiate the horrid imputation. He may be English, but he is not typical, and before being a gentleman it is necessary to be a man. Leslie Howard is not my idea of manliness.'[48] Another fan's ire was raised by the kind of roles in which British actors specialized: 'Naturalism and charm, as personified by Herbert Marshall and Leslie Howard are appealing qualities in an actor, but caviare as a staple diet would be definitely dull. Let's have subtlety, well-bred reserve and undertone, but there's always room for that authentic dash and verve that adds glamour to almost any picture.'[49] Such exquisite refinement, such well-bred reserve were, it seems, the stock-in-trade of so many British actors. Young leading men seemed predisposed to a technique of self-effacement, with any notable characteristics silk-screened by an embarrassment of self-sacrifice and a surfeit of impeccable manners. Where was the 'dash', the 'verve'?

Both *Journey's End* and another war film, *Tell England* (1930) were similar in that they both featured an essential Englishness which was anathema to some and a cause for celebration to others. Pearson's notes about how he envisaged the opening frames of *Journey's End* illuminate the lyricism, and sharply-framed limits, of his definition of national identity:

It might be a good thing to open with a beautiful English meadow – a brook – old trees – perhaps a vista of hills and rolling clouds – and then the delicious poignancy of a boy's young voice ... the hearty laughter of youth – the quick pad of young feet on grass – the breathless chase of the lads to the river bank – the [illegible word] of a quick ... stripping of clean young bodies for the plunge ... and we know at once that two youths – a few years apart – are English.[50]

Both *Journey's End* and *Tell England* were paeans to the upper classes, and to the public school system in particular. *Tell England* displays an almost homoerotic compulsion to set the friendship of the two principal characters above the carnage and death of the Gallipoli campaign and there is the sense that the mother country is the only female entity with an existence worth recognizing. In the bookish banter of the public school heroes there is a reassurance, an echo of the cloistered all-male domain of the public school, which not war nor marriage nor career will ever replace as long as there are clubs in St James's, hymns to the alma mater and old school ties.[51]

These male-dominated films, these portrayals of Englishness, of British social relations, were, according to J. B. Priestley, why Hollywood thought contemporary Britain was still largely inhabited by 'the fading world of aristocratic landowners and hat-touching tenancy'.[52] The treatment of the officer-class in both films was not far short of idolatry; conversely, the treatment of members of the rank and file was, in the traditions of West End farce, and most British films, far from realistic. *Journey's End* was a significant employer of stereotypes; Mason, the cook, and Trotter, the obligatory suburban character dreaming of his hollyhocks growing in the garden ('the carefree Trotter retains his smile and appetite through it all'), provide comic relief much in the same way as Gordon Harker provided hilarity, scenes of social embarrassment and sometimes lower-case menace, in innumerable Edgar Wallace productions on film and stage. As was noted of the working-class characters in *Tell England*, there was no justification for portraying 'the rank and file of the British Army as comic idiots'.[53] Such characters were not permitted the dramatic luxury of imaginative heroism, or introspection; that was reserved for officers, who were much given to whimsy, world-weariness and valiant acts of studied emotional rigidity. In the true blue manner, death and the ability to pull oneself together resolved the plot contrivances of *Journey's End* and evidently sent many a tearful picture-goer contently to their beds, secure in the knowledge that democracy was safe in the hands of the self-sacrificing class.

In one sense self-sacrifice may be a negative personal characteristic: D. H. Lawrence claimed it was 'the vilest act a man can do [because] the self that we are, at its best, is all that we are'.[54] The glorification of an act which devalues 'the individual flame of life itself', is, in the world of the cinema, antithetical to the whole process of personal projection, where individuality is a core component of popularity, of the relationship between star, character and audience.[55] It is, therefore, tempting to equate the national predilection for self-denying heroism with the failure of scores of British actors to project any indication of that elusive flame on to celluloid; for all that they really were, at their core, made up of their accent, their class and regional background, had been sacrificed on the altar of reinvention for the benefit of London theatre-goers and the arbiters of cultural correctness. There is a more prosaic form of self-sacrifice also at work: from the published recollections of notable actors of the period, and from biographies of the same, there is hardly a positive expression to be found regarding film. It is evident that in the battle between pecuniary rewards and artistic integrity, stiff upper-lips were regularly employed; given such an attitude it is likely that self-sacrifice, in this instance in the cause of money earned in the crass world of the cinema, was apt to produce less than satisfactory performances.

There had scarcely been a break in the cycle of war films from Hollywood as well as Britain. *What Price Glory, All Quiet on the Western Front, The Big Parade* and *Hell's Angels* were American views of the Great War, ranging from the hostilities being shown in the context of soldiers 'fighting over a bunch of dames' to Lewis Milestone's version of Remarque's classic pacifist novel.[56] *Blighty, Mademoiselle from Armentieres* and *Roses of Picardy* were notable British war films and Michael Balcon and Victor Saville produced a 15-minute film entitled *Armistice* (1929) which was a compilation of images set against wartime songs, inspired by the poem *In Flanders Field*.[57] *Remembrance* (1927) posited a peculiarly Victorian solution to the bitter reality of lives broken by the war; a builder and a clerk enlist, are wounded and find themselves on the unemployment scrapheap at the end of the war, a situation familiar to many servicemen returning from Europe: 'We were told Your King and country needs you! It is no consolation now to be told: Your King and

Country don't need you.' On screen the British Legion comes to the rescue – charity is the salve which dresses the wounds of hopelessness.[58]

Mumsie (1927), for which Herbert Wilcox imported 'the screen's greatest tragedienne' from Hollywood, Pauline Frederick, who had been born in Preston, Lancashire, while her father, a music-hall clown of some repute, was performing there, ran against the anti-war theme of other films by portraying a pacifist as a dupe of foreign powers, ultimately so compromised by a flawed nature that spying for the enemy – betrayal of his own country – becomes a logical extension of pacifism. This scenario had more in common with the hysterical outbursts of Lady Houston, who bought the *Saturday Review* in order to have a platform for her 'England is in deadly peril' message, than it did with the growing numbers of people, of all classes, whose memories of the Great War and fears for the future were to have their apotheosis in the Peace Pledge Union of the 1930s.[59] The film was effective in so far as 'a number of female hard-boiled eggs wiped away channels in their face powder as they came out' of the theatre and another review noted that 'the story is of great interest and charm and will be appreciated none the less for its omission of the horrors of the front line'.[60]

High Treason (1929) depicted, with some imagination, a future, circa 1940, in which the world is driven to the brink of war again. The film unites women under the banner of the World Peace League to prevent another worldwide conflagration, and their attempts to avert war are portrayed as a battle with the forces of unscrupulous capitalism whose profits depended on armaments and for whom war is simply an entry on the credit side of their double-entry book-keeping.[61] This argument had some basis in truth, as one of the first reports issued by the League of Nations accused armaments firms of fomenting war scares in the name of profit.[62] The film was shot silent but was hastily remade with sound by Maurice Elvey who was anxious to explore the possibilities of the latest technical developments.[63] Its futurist trappings were favourably compared to *Metropolis* and Elvey was praised for confirming the impression that 'the talking picture is the medium in which Britain is qualified to lead the world'.[64]

Journey's End became, in one sense, a world leader. It appeared on the list of the top ten films released in the United States in 1930, polling fewer votes than *All Quiet on the Western Front*, *Abraham Lincoln* and *Holiday*, but outscoring Howard Hughes' *Hell's Angels* and Greta Garbo's first talkie, *Anna Christie*.[65] The play's author, R. C. Sherriff, was sufficiently impressed by the success of the film in America to encourage George Pearson to use the following correspondence as publicity in Britain:

> I went to see the film, in fact, with a prejudice against it; so great was my fear least certain liberties had been taken which I could not reconcile. My first feeling after seeing the picture was one of relief, followed by admiration for a very beautiful piece of work. I say without hesitation that it is the finest achievement in photography and recording that it has been my privilege to witness. The photography is the work of an artist, the sound recording is uncanny in its perfection ... When I think of the difficulties you faced, and the infinite patience demanded for such perfection of detail, I can only repeat my admiration and thanks to all concerned, I am glad to think my play has inspired such a beautiful picture.[66]

The financial returns for *Journey's End* were considerable but they had to be split three ways – with Pearson, Tiffany and Gainsborough – and they were insufficient to stabilize Pearson's production company. The subsequent demise of the company was devastating to a man who had given up a respectable and secure profession to embark on what was still regarded as a rather suspect venture. Michael Balcon attempted to assuage the damage by offering Pearson the chance to co-produce *The Good Companions* (1933). The film was a prestige production, based on a picaresque novel, and play, by J. B. Priestley, which enhanced the reputations of those associated with it, including Jessie Matthews, Edmund Gwenn and John Gielgud.[67] Pearson regarded the venture as a personal favour from Balcon, and Pearson does not seem to have been a man who would readily accept favours. His own efforts to resuscitate a flagging career almost inevitably took him into the realms of the small production companies which had sprung up in the wake of the quota legislation. These companies have largely been dismissed by historians who have, like British audiences before them, squirmed at the ineptitude on show. Many of the films were, like Michael Powell's *His Lordship* (1932), hissed off the screen by British audiences.[68] Others had their dialogue drowned out by booing.[69] But not all companies producing these 'quota quickies' were controlled by men with stunted imaginations. Julius Hagen's studio at Twickenham was exceptional in so far as it was not content with mediocrity.

Screen Pictorial described Hagen as 'the great pioneer and producer'[70] and John Paddy Carstairs, director and scriptwriter, noted that Hagen 'has by sheer determination and ability become one of our better British producers. His flair, not for expensive but for average-priced pictures and his ability is, I think, greatly underappreciated.'[71] In a period when success was often measured against Alexander Korda's extravagance, it is not difficult to understand why Hagen's contribution to film has been underestimated. But watch such simple films as *Music Hall* and *Say it with Flowers*, made by the humanitarian John Baxter at Twickenham, or more expansive productions like *The Wandering Jew*, *Vintage Wine*, *Squibs*, *Scrooge* and *The Private Secretary* and it is apparent that the producer was no celluloid charlatan. *Bella Donna* (1934), featuring Conrad Veidt, played at the Acme Theatre in New York and *Variety* praised Hagen's 'attempt to keep production values and artistic integrity to the fore'.[72] Another review acknowledged that Hagen was making a genuine effort to give the public what they wanted: 'Picturegoers will revel in Veidt's Machiavellian "cave-man" stuff. Flappers will revel in the treat-me-rough tactics … a lavish, but tasteful production … with artistic appeal throughout … its appeal is universal.'[73]

Hagen's production of *The Morals of Marcus* (1935), featuring the 'Mexican spitfire', Lupe Velez, was said to be a good vehicle for Velez's tempestuous charms: 'smooth direction and attractive settings make this an acceptable feature of general consumption';[74] and there is more artistry, more brilliance in the photography and sets in *Death on the Set* (1935) than in many of Korda's lavish films of the time. One scene, shot from above, with the actor Henry Kendall, a regular Hagen face, lounging on a bed with his mistress, is full of menace and passion – pure cinema. There can be little doubt that *The Lodger* (1932) and *I Lived With You* (1933) are as interesting as any of Herbert Wilcox's historical charades and Ivor Novello, in both, is a compelling screen presence as always. *I Lived with You* is a fascinating exploration of hypocrisy and double standards and remains one of the few British films of the period to look, with a jaundiced eye, at the inconsistencies and pretences in British society.[75] *Dusty Ermine* (1936) is a little musty now, but there is some impressive location work by the European photographer Otto Martini and some clever ski-ing stunts which are as effective in their own way as those later choreographed for James Bond films. *Variety* called *Dusty Ermine* a 'nice gentle, matter-of-fact British picture … direction is good and camera work expert'. The review outlined the usual reservations about British actors: 'all were gentlemen, everything and everybody is quite dignified.'[76]

Hagen's most extraordinary project was to enlist the services of D. W. Griffith in the remake of Lillian Gish's great triumph, *Broken Blossoms*. Griffith worked on the script in a suite at the Dorchester Hotel where, one day, a call from the front desk informed him of a visitor. The visitor was the neon-named Ariane Borg who tearfully told Griffith she had been working in a laundry in Paris, blistering her hands, exhausting her body, but sustaining her spirit with the certain knowledge that the great Griffith would discover her and make her a star. Griffith immediately told Hagen, 'I must have her for the Gish part.' Unfortunately for Ariane Borg, and Griffith, Hagen's production supervisor, Hans (John) Brahm, and Brahm's actress wife Dolly Haas were contracted for *Broken Blossoms* (1936) and they were both intent on making the film a calling card for Hollywood. So ended Griffith's association with Twickenham Films.[77] As directed by Brahm, *Broken Blossoms* is a bizarre film, with Dolly Haas playing Lucy Burrows of Limehouse with a middle-European accent and Emlyn Williams emoting with a Welsh lilt as Chen the Chinese hero of the piece. It certainly holds the attention, and one review suggested the film contained 'moments unbelievably harrowing to audiences'. It is not clear if the reviewer was referring to the mixed bag of accents.[78]

Pearson's principal quota assignments were part of Julius Hagen's celluloid *mélange*. The studio's motto was 'Economy is All' and films were made, according to Pearson, 'by the stop watch'.[79] The Real Art logo which adorned some Twickenham productions was accompanied by the slogan 'Looking Forward/Backward Looking' and it is ironic that the company's motto, epitomizing a mind-set which had, for decades, informed British film-making, should be used to specify the cheapest nooks and crannies of the British industry. In a later film, *Command Performance* (1937), co-scripted by Pearson, there is an amusing reference to the conditions under which he worked at Twickenham, with a scene in which a star's time before the cameras, and its cost, is counted down on a clock. Pearson also betrays what he undoubtedly felt about the way his career had dipped while foreign directors, many with lesser reputations and less talent than his own, were finding ample work in Britain. *Command Performance* contains some sly digs at foreigners, with fun poked at a 'wop' director's broken English and his re-shooting, time after time, of scenes which he has just declared 'perfect'. There was a sign at Hagen's studios which read, 'English spoken here' and it is likely that Pearson's personal style of film-making allowed him at least a reference or two to his own experiences.[80]

In twelve months Pearson directed eight films for Hagen, three of them at night, and despite their limitations – finances were scarce and there was only one sound-stage – there are moments in some of them which recall the vision and enterprise of his early work. *River Wolves* (1934) was Pearson's favourite film of this period; it was an adaptation of a play about blackmail and assorted skulduggery in a London boarding house. John Mills played a supporting role in the film and the milieu in which the film was set harked back to Pearson's earlier films with Betty Balfour.[81] *Open All Night* (1934) is a dark little melodrama set in a hotel; it was advertised as showing 'Behind the Scenes in a Great Hotel … Romance … Love … Tragedy … Murder!'[82] As with *Huntingtower*, the film concerns a member of the dispossessed Russian aristocracy: Frank Vosper plays an exiled Grand Duke who works as night manager in a West End hotel. The complicated plot does not bear detailing but Pearson deftly portrays the disparate strands of a multi-layered story with considerable perception and honesty. Most of the characters live cramped and desperate lives and at Pearson's behest the camera catches that desperation, setting it against the noisy gaiety of the hotel. He succinctly sketches in the alienation of a woman, no longer young, selling herself for the sake of a good time so as to distract herself from an uncertain future, and the moral dilemma of a young husband debating whether or not sacrifice his ideals, everything he values, for the sake of his bride's life.

When Vosper's character, Anton, is sacked from his position at the hotel, because new blood, youth, is preferred, he is deprived of his dignity, and the identity he has created for himself after being driven from his homeland. He also loses the will to live, having had his dreams of a little cottage with a garden, somewhere in the country, shattered. His suicide, in a poignant scene in which he lovingly caresses the relics of his past life, lights candles before the icons which are among the few items remaining from his Russian heritage, draws together the various strands in the plot – absolving one character from a charge of murder, providing hope for the newlyweds battling illness and despair, and leaving the 'good time girl' with a message of her own worth. Once again there is the element of self-sacrifice. Anton's suicide liberates the other characters from the consequences of their own mistakes. The film has more emotional layers, more movement, more cinematic finesse, more atmosphere and more humanity than many of the prestige productions from more important studios, and it was given positive reviews: 'Frank

Vosper, in the role of the old man, gives a sincere and moving performance. The women are far above the average, and despite the improbabilities of some of the situations, the picture is interesting and a credit to director and cast.'[83] Another review referred to it as 'good popular entertainment', and praised Pearson's 'resourceful direction'.[84] The film makes a statement about human values, about the lack of respect accorded those whose experience and age are undervalued, and, with hindsight, it is possible to see the film's theme as mirroring Pearson's career and status at that time.

Given Pearson's triumphs, his association with the great and good in film, in various branches of the arts, and the possibilities he saw in his beloved medium, it is difficult to feel anything less than regret when reading the opening passage in his own collection of jottings and press clippings: 'In this Mss Book is an Ironic Record of a Failure.'[85] As a pioneering director he was anything but a failure, but perhaps the rapid changes in the industry overtook him as they did so many other directors who learned their craft in the heyday of silent movies. In everything Pearson wrote, in the material which exists written about him, there is the sense that he was an honest, patient, caring director, who genuinely wished to show the lives of real people on the screen and thought he could turn the everyday into art; sometimes he was able to do that, at other times he was less successful. But he never stopped trying to make film more than an artistic expedient, more than mere celluloid. He had faith in film, in British films, which he never lost. When the fledgling director Penn Tennyson, whose brief life and promising career were destroyed in the Second World War, was given his first assignment, Pearson wrote to him:

> Good luck to you, Pen – go all out for it – draw heavily on all
> that varied store of experience gained by helping in the making
> of the really good pictures on which you have worked – mix this
> (with your own ideas) as leaven and make a film that is more than
> 'just another'. It's going to help you and help Mickey [Balcon] and
> help the Old Country. Don't pass phoney stuff. The most treacher-
> ous word in our work is 'compromise' – avoid all that it embraces
> like the very devil.[86]

The Old Country – be it Squibs' tenement, the cramped apartments of *Open All Night*, the Gorbals of *Huntingtower*, the dimly lit doorways of *Love, Life and Laughter*, the dockside dives of *River Wolves* or God's own English countryside in *Mord Em'ly* – was Pearson's inspiration, and unlike other British directors, who limited their vision to select addresses at which resided the pure, the primped and the richly potty attended by a freak-show of flunkies who fell over furniture, spilt tea and dropped their 'h's with the precise timing of a mesmerist's stooge, Pearson shone a torch-light on the lives of ordinary people, depicting them as stars, as heroes and heroines, and in so doing validated their existence, both in real and reel life, recognised their talents, loves and hates, their joys and sorrows, allowed their often mundane niceties screen credence and, perhaps, most importantly, testified to their inherent right to equal status in that longest-running saga of all, national identity. He ignored Cecil Day Lewis's advice, which appears as a cinematic codicil to so many British films: 'history, like God in the past, is a certain winner; and once on the bandwagon you can be promised almost anything with confidence.'[87] Pearson's template was, for the most part, the here and now.

During his stay in Hollywood supervising the production of *Journey's End*, Pearson and the director James Whale shared considerable frustrations as well as the occasional triumph. At a moment of deep depression, when everything seemed to be going badly, when Pearson was desperate and homesick for 'the old country', Whale sent him some lines of poetry. Seeing photographs of Pearson – an intense, determined, bookish-looking man, the archetypal schoolmaster – and viewing the deeply humane films he made, the lines seem to sum him up, to specify his long and honourable career more accurately than any retrospective analysis.

> Each well born soul must win what it deserves.
> Let the fool prate of luck. The fortunate
> Is he whose earnest purpose never swerves,
> Whose slightest action or inaction serves
> The one great aim. Why even Death stands still,
> And waits an hour sometimes for such a will.[88]

If there is a Hollywood or Elstree, Twickenham or Real Art heaven, it is likely that George Pearson is still working. Probably he's just completed *Squibs*, again, or maybe he's preparing for a mammoth documentary on the history of British films; he would probably call it 'The Ones That Got Away'.

Notes

Introduction

1. Victoria de Grazia, 'Mass Culture and Sovereignty: the American Challenge to European Cinemas 1920–1960', *Journal of Modern History* 61 (Chicago, March 1989), 53–87.

2. Allen Eyles and David Meeker (eds), *Missing Believed Lost: the Great British Film Search* (London, 1992).

1. Branding British Films: 'Quite English, you know'

1. *Cinema Chat* 22 (1919), p. 33; *Cinema Chat* 24 (1919), p. 25.
2. Rachael Low, *The History of the British Film 1918–1929* (London, 1971), p. 39.
3. *Kine Monthly* (June 1919), p. 3.
4. *Kine Monthly* (April 1919), p. 2.
5. Langford Reed and Hetty Spiers (eds), *Who's Who in Filmland* (London, 1928).
6. Low Warren (ed.), 'Who's Who in the Cinema Industry', in *Exhibitors' Diary* (London, 1929); Reed and Spiers (eds), *Who's Who*.
7. *Kine Monthly* (May 1919), p. 2.
8. *Trade Show Critic Annual* (1922), p. 38; *Trade Show Critic Annual* (1924), p. 25.
9. *Trade Show Critic Annual* (1922), p. 38; *Trade Show Critic Annual* (1924), p. 4.
10. HLRO Historical Collection 184, Beaverbrook H/277, Internal Memo, 19 August 1921.
11. *Trade Show Critic Annual* (1923), p. 6; *Kine Monthly* (August 1919), p. 2.
12. HLRO Historical Collection 192, Lloyd George B12, 20 July 1920.
13. *Kine Monthly* (April 1919), p. 2.
14. *Kine Monthly* (April 1919), p. 89.
15. *House of Lords Journals*, 11 February 1919, p. 30.
16. HLRO Historical Collection 191, Bonar Law 114/10/22.
17. John Hodge, *From Workman's Cottage to Windsor Castle* (London, 1931), pp. 214, 218, 219.

18. HLRO Collection 191, Bonar Law 114/10/24.

19. Hodge, *From Workman's Cottage*, pp. 236–8.

20. *Daily Herald,* 7 November 1922.

21. *Picture-Play Magazine* (February 1919), p. 227; (March 1919), pp. 18–23.

22. *Cinema Chat* 27 (1919), p. 6.

23. *Cinema Chat* 25 (1919), p. 6.

24. *Cinema Chat* 31 (1920); *Cinema Chat* 33 (1920).

25. *Film Fiction* (August 1921), p. 4.

26. *Cinema Chat* 35 (1920), pp. 3, 4.

27. *Cineshows,* 19 December 1919, p. 3.

28. *Cinema Chat* 14 (1919), p. 8.

29. *Stoll's Editorial News* (December 1919), p. 3.

30. *Kine Monthly* (March 1921), p. 39.

31. *Cinema Chat* 34 (1920), p. 2.

32. *Variety,* 11 July 1919.

33. Low, *British Film 1918–1929,* p. 124.

34. Edward S. Van Zile, *That Marvel – The Movie* (New York and London, 1923), p. 61.

35. *Trade Show Critic Annual* (1920), p. 61.

36. Reed and Spiers (eds), *Who's Who.*

37. *Kine Monthly* (June 1920), p. 18.

38. *Kine Monthly* (November 1919), p. 48.

39. *Cinema Chat* 43 (1920), p. 28.

40. *Kine Monthly* (May 1920), p. 40.

41. *Cinema Chat* 35 (1920), p. 26

42. *Cinema Chat* 25 (1919), p. 24.

43. Iris Barry, *Let's Go to the Pictures* (London, 1926), pp. 240, 241.

44. Kenelm Foss, *Cinema, A Practical Course* (London, 1920), p. 20.

45. *Cinema Chat* 40 (1920), p. 1.

46. *Trade Show Critic Annual* (1922), p. 30.

47. *Cinema Chat* 1 (1919), p. 6.

48. Cecil M. Hepworth, *Came the Dawn: Memories of a Film Pioneer* (London, 1951), p. 144.

49. Martin J. Wiener, *English Culture and the Decline of the Industrial Spirit 1850–1980* (London, 1981), p. 55. For a fuller exposition of Hepworth's films see Andrew Higson, *Waving the Flag: constructing a national cinema in Britain (London,* 1995).

50. Low, *British Film 1918–1929,* p. 114.

51. Hepworth, *Came the Dawn,* pp. 184, 151.

52. *Bioscope,* 16 October 1919, p. 67.

53. Hepworth, *Came the Dawn,* pp. 193, 194; *Variety,* 31 December 1924.

54. Barry, *Let's Go to the Pictures,* p. 242.

55. Sir Philip Gibbs, Introduction to Mrs Desmond Humphreys ('Rita'), *Recollections of a Literary Life* (London, 1936), p. 5.

56. Eileen Bigland, *Marie Corelli, the Woman and the Legend* (London, 1953), pp. 90, 128.

57. *Variety,* 29 August 1919.

58. Penelope Dell, *Nettie and Sissie* (London, 1977), p. 61.

59. Ibid., p. 148.

60. *Kine Monthly* (June 1920), p. 23; *Unrest* was unfavourably reviewed because it did not use English scenery.

61. Wiener, *English Culture*, p. 6.

62. C.E. Carrington, *The Life of Rudyard Kipling* (New York, 1956), p. 286.

63. Wiener, *English Culture*, pp. 105, 121.

64. Ibid., p. 105; Aubrey Rees, *The Heroic Spirit* (London, 1918), p. 36.

65. *Cinema Chat* 47 (1920), p. 7.

66. *Kine Monthly* (January 1921), p. 10.

67. *Kine Monthly* (April 1920), p. 30.

68. *Kine Monthly* (November 1919), p. 35.

69. *Kine Monthly* (July 1920), p. 21.

70. *Kine Monthly* (April 1920), p. 10; *Bleak House* was praised for its accurate representation of the past.

71. Barry, *Let's Go to the Pictures*, p. 243.

72. *Kine Monthly* (March 1920), p. 38; *Kine Monthly* (February 1921), p. 38.

73. *Cinema Chat* 37 (1920), p. 7.

74. *Kine Monthly* (February 1920), p. 46.

75. *Cinema Chat* 53 (1920), p. 54.

76. *Kine Monthly* (June 1920), p. 20.

77. *Cineshows*, 15 December 1919, pp. 1, 2.

78. *Kine Monthly* (June 1920), p. 11.

79. *Cinema Chat* 65 (1920), p. 6.

80. *Kine Monthly* (June 1920), p. 20.

81. *Kine Monthly* (November 1919), p. 22.

82. François Bedarida, *A Social History of England 1851–1990* (London, 1991), pp. 130, 131.

83. *Kine Monthly* (September 1919), p. 60.

84. Kenneth Muir, *Arnold and the Victorian Dilemma* (London, 1947), p. 106.

85. *Kine Monthly* (August 1919), p. 42.

86. W. M. Thackeray, 'On Some Country Snobs', in *The Book of Snobs* (London, 1899), pp. 127–58.

87. *Cinema Chat* 61 (1920), p. 2.

88. *Cinema Chat* 24 (1919), p. 4.

89. *Kine Monthly* (August 1919), p. 77.

90. *Cinema Chat* 67 (1920), p. 7.

91. *Cinema Chat* 61 (1920); much of the issue is given over to publicity for *I Will*.

92. *Kine Monthly* (March 1920), p. 32.

93. *Kine Monthly* (June 1921), p. 11.

94. L. C. B. Seaman, *Life in Britain Between the Wars* (London, 1970), p. 6.

95. *Cinema Chat* 33 (1920), p. 28; Barry, *Let's Go to the Pictures*, p. 243.

96. *Cinema Chat* 51 (1920), p. 5.

97. *Cinema Chat* 50 (1920), p. 2.

98. *Cinema Chat* 51 (1920), p. 5.

99. *Cinema Chat* 39 (1920), p. 35.

100. *Cinema Chat* 73 (1920), p. 4.

101. *Cinema Chat* 70 (1920), pp. 30–2.

102. *Cinema Chat* 78 (1920), p. 16.

103. *Cinema Chat* 62 (1920), p. 29.

104. *Kine Monthly* (August 1919), p. 90; Bedarida, *A Social History*, p. 26; Robert Graves and Alan Hodge, *The Long Weekend; A Social History of Great Britain 1918–1939* (London, 1940), p. 112.

105. *Cinema Chat* 53 (1920), p. 4.

106. *Kine Monthly* (May 1920), p. 36.

107. *Cinema Chat* 39 (1920); Seaman, *Life in Britain*, p. 57.

108. *Cinema Chat* 50 (1920), p. 31.

109. *Trade Show Critic Annual* (1924), p. 39.

110. *Cinema Chat* 85 (1920), p. 14.

111. *Cinema Chat* 77 (1920), p. 2.

112. *Kine Monthly* (May 1920), p. 29.

113. H. Durant, *The Problem of Leisure* (London, 1938) p. 91.

114. Barry, *Let's Go to the Pictures*, pp. 241, 242.

115. *Trade Show Critic Annual* (1921), p. 11.

116. *Kine Monthly* (December 1919), p. 33.

117. *Cinema Chat* 60 (1920), p. 5.

118. Constance Collier, *Harlequinade* (London, 1929), p. 283; Van Zile, *That Marvel – The Movie*, pp. 160, 161.

119. Irene Clephane, *Ourselves 1900–1930* (London, 1933), pp. 161–3.

120. Graves and Hodge, *The Long Weekend*, p. 134.

121. Frank Owen, *Tempestuous Journey, Lloyd George, His Life and Times* (London, 1954), p. 511.

122. John Collier and Iain Lang, *Just the Other Day: An Informal History of Great Britain Since the War* (London, 1932), p. 125.

123. *Cinema Chat* 62 (1920), p. 3.

124. *Cinema Chat* 72 (1920), p. 28.

125. *Kine Monthly* (June 1919), p. 51.

126. *Cinema Chat* 4 (1919), p. 19.

127. *Cinema Chat* 25 (1919), p. 5.

128. Guy Newall, *Husband Love* (London, 1924), p. 195; a character in the actor's novel voices that opinion.

129. *Trade Show Critic Annual* (1920), p. 11.

130. *Kine Monthly* (July 1921), p. 12.

131. *Kine Monthly* (October 1919), pp. 1, 2.

132. *Kine Monthly* (October 1919), p. 10.

133. *Kine Monthly* (July 1921), p. 11.

134. *Kine Monthly* (September 1919), p. 20.

135. Langford Reed, *The Picture Play* (London, (1920), Book 2, pp. 3, 4; *Cinema Chat* 32 (1920), p. 9.

136. Collier and Lang, *Just the Other Day*, p. 188.

137. *Kine Monthly* (August 1919), p. 1.

138. *Film Chats*, presented to the patrons of the Queen's Hall cinema, Cricklewood, with the compliments of the management, January 1922.

139. Low, *British Film 1918–1929*, p. 137.

140. *Kine Monthly* (August 1919), p. 1.

141. *Film Chats*, presented to the patrons of the Shaftesbury Pavilion on the occasion of the first presentation of Mary Pickford in her latest entertainment *Through the Back Door*, February 1922.

142. *Cinema Chat* 67 (1920), p. 1.

143. *Cinema Chat* 17 (1919), p. 31.

144. *Cinema Chat* 45 (1920), p. 6.

145. *Cinema Chat* 40 (1920), p. 2.

146. *Cinema Chat* 22 (1919), p. 27.

147. *Cinema Chat* 38 (1920), p. 5.

148. *Trade Show Critic Annual* (1921), p. 12.

149. *Trade Show Critic Annual* (1922), p. 38.

150. *Trade Show Critic Annual* (1923), pp. 5, 35; and *Trade Show Critic Annual* (1924), p. 28.

151. Hepworth, *Came the Dawn*, p. 186.

152. *Trade Show Critic Annual* (1924), p. 6.

153. *Trade Show Critic Annual* (1923), p. 41.

154. *Trade Show Critic Annual* (1922), p. 45; a reference to product made by Progress Films.

155. *Trade Show Critic Annual* (1922), p. 38; *Cinema Chat* 26 (1919), p. 22; Low, *British Film 1918–1929*, p. 77.

156. *Kine Monthly* (May 1919), p. ii.

157. George Pearson, 'Memories – Into the Twilight Twenties, and What Then?' *Royal Academy Bulletin* 13 (London, 1951), p. 11.

158. *Cinema Chat* 24 (1919), p. 26.

159. F.A. Talbot, *Moving Pictures: How They are Made and Worked* (London, 1923), p. 158.

160. Adrian Brunel, *Nice Work* (London, 1949), p. 52.

161. Brunel, *Nice Work*, pp. 90, 91; Hannen Swaffer, *Hannen Swaffer's Who's Who* (London, 1929), p. 58; Seymour Hicks, *Between Ourselves* (London, 1930), p. 185.

162. Peter Noble, *Ivor Novello: Man of the Theatre* (London, 1951), pp. 94, 95; *Picture Show Annual* (1926), p. 14.

163. Herbert Wilcox, *25,000 Sunsets* (London, 1967), pp. 58–60, 107.

164. *Daily Mail*, 16 April 1925.

165. *Variety*, 1 July 1921: *Carnival*.

166. *Variety*, 1 December (1920): *A Rank Outsider*.

167. *Variety*, 29 November 1924: *The Eleventh Commandment*.

168. *Kine Monthly* (July 1919), p. 54.

169. *Variety*, 1 July 1921.

170. *Variety*, 9 September 1921: Guy Newall in *The Bigamist*.

171. *Cinema Chat* 61 (1920), pp. 30, 31: *I Will*.

172. *Cinema Chat* 26 (1919), p. 24: *The Chinese Puzzle*.

173. *Variety*, 26 February 1924.

174. *Pictures*, 2 July 1921, p. 10.

175. Dell, *Nettie and Sissie*, p. 62: *The Knave of Diamonds*.

176. *Cinema Chat* 56 (1920), p. 21: *The Forest on the Hill*.

177. *Variety*, 14 May (1920).

178. *Kine Monthly* (August 1921), p. 23: *Nance*.

179. *Picture Show Annual* (1926), p. 93.

180. *Kine Monthly* (March 1920), p. 13: *The Hour of Trial*.

181. *Kine Monthly* (July 1921), p. 10.

182. *Kine Monthly* (April 1920), p. 22.

183. *Kine Monthly* (August 1920), p. 23: *The Toilers*.

184. Denis Gifford, *The British Film Catalogue 1895–1970. A Guide to Entertainment Films* (Newton Abbot, 1973): no. 06962 *In Borrowed Plumes*.

185. W.A. Darlington, *Alf's Button* (London, 1919); *Pictures*, 30 July 1921, p. 90.

186 *Kine Monthly* (August 1919), p. 77, noted how ordinary people were caricatured by 'too distinguished' stage actors.

187. Paul Swann, *The Hollywood Feature Film in Postwar Britain* (London, 1987), p. 38.

188. *Picture Show Annual* (1928), p. 116; Stella Margetson, *The Long Party: High Society in the Twenties and Thirties* (London, 1976).

189. Walter Southgate, *That's the Way it Was: A Working-Class Autobiography 1890–1950* (London, 1952), p. 79.

190. *Kine Weekly*, 3 January 1924, p. 14.

191. *Kine Weekly*, 3 January 1924, p. 12.

192. J. B. Priestley, *Midnight on the Desert* (London, 1937), p. 194.

2. Roles for Women: 'Ladies ... right through'

1. *Newcastle Chronicle*, undated letter from 'a disappointed picture-goer' complaining that no matter what happened to characters in British films they remained 'ladies and gentlemen right through', in BFI, Betty Balfour Collection.

2. *Cinema Chat* 36 (1920), p. 23.

3. *Cinema Chat* 27 (1920), pp. 22, 23.

4. *Kine Monthly*, (October 1919), p. 54.

5. Rachael Low, *The History of the British Film 1918–1929* (London, 1971), p. 136.

6. *Pictures*, 20 August 1921, p. 174.

7. *Cinema Chat* 25 (1919), p. 21.

8. *Variety*, 3 October 1919, p. 174.

9. *Pictures*, 20 August 1921, p. 152.

10. Irene Clephane, *Ourselves 1900–1930* (London, 1933), p. 170.

11. *Pictures*, 22 January 1921, p. 152.

12. *Cinema Chat* 68 (1920), p. 12.

13. *Pictures*, 2 July 1921, p. 10; Luke McKernan, *Topical Budget: The Great British News Film* (London, 1992), p. 116.

14. *Cinema Chat* 65 (1920), p. 3.

15. *Cinema Chat* 42 (1920), p. 24.

16. *Pictures*, 5 February 1921, p. 148.

17. *Pictures*, 20 August 1921, p. 152.

18. *Cinema Chat* 56 (1920), p. 25.

19. *Pictures*, 21 May 1921, p. 502.

20. *Kine Monthly* (October 1921), p. 11.

21. *Cinema Chat* 67 (1920), p. 1; *Cinema Chat* 41 (1920), p. 3.

22. *Pictures*, 20 August 1921, p. 152.

23. *Cinema Chat* 27 (1920), p. 6.

24. Roy Armes, *French Cinema* (London, 1985), p. 138.

25. George Pearson, 'Memories – Into the Twilight Twenties and What Then?', *Royal Academy Bulletin* 13 (London, 1951), p. 11.

26. Ivan Butler, *Silent Magic: Rediscovering the Silent Film Era* (London, 1987), p. 50.

27. *Kine Monthly* (June 1921), p. 14.

28. Armes, *French Cinema*, pp. 43–5, 52; Pearson, 'Memories', p. 11.

29. *Kine Monthly* (August 1919), p. 70.

30. *Kine Monthly* (November 1919), p. 47.

31. *Kine Monthly* (May 1920), p. 19.

32. Armes, *French Cinema*, pp. 47–9; *Cinema Chat* 62 (1920), p. 5.

33. Ian Christie, *Arrows of Desire* (London, 1985), p. 23; George Perry, *The Great British Picture Show* (London, 1974), pp. 341, 342; David Quinlan, *The Illustrated Guide to Film Directors* (London, 1983), pp. 213, 214.

34. Perry, *The Great British Picture Show*, p. 36.

35. *Cinema Chat* 62 (1920), p. 19.

36. *Kine Monthly* (October 1920), p. 19.

37. *Close-up* (May 1928), p. 34; Low, *British Film 1918–1929*, pp. 139, 140; Perry, *The Great British Picture Show*, p. 50.

38. *Cinema Chat* 9 (1919), p. 3.

39. *Kine Monthly* (August 1919), p. 15.

40. *Cinema Chat* 7 (1919), p. 26.

41. *Cinema Chat* 66 (1920), p. 25.

42. Robert Graves and Alan Hodge, *The Long Weekend: A Social History of Great Britain 1918–1939* (London, 1940), p. 34.

43. *Pictures*, 16 July, 1921, p. 58.

44. *Cinema Chat* 5 (1919), p. 9; *Trade Show Critic Annual* (1924), p. 29; L. Reed and H. Spiers, *Who's Who in Filmland* (London, 1928), entry for Poppy Wyndham.

45. *Pictures*, 23 July 1921, p. 78.

46. *Kine Monthly* (August 1921), p. 7.

47. Stella Margetson, *The Long Party: High Society in the Twenties and Thirties* (London, 1976), p. 106.

48. *Kine Monthly* (September 1920), p. 17.

49. *Pictures*, 12 August 1921, p. 129.

50. Diana Cooper, *The Rainbow Comes and Goes* (London, 1958), p. 231.

51. Butler, *Silent Magic*, pp. 60, 61.

52. Cooper, *The Rainbow Comes and Goes*, p. 232.

53. *Trade Show Critic Annual* (1923), p. 12.

54. Cooper, *The Rainbow Comes and Goes*, p. 231.

55. Arrar Jackson, *Writing for the Screen* (London, 1929), p viii.

56. *Kine Monthly* (November 1920), p. 16: review of *Testimony*.

57. *Pictures*, 22 January 1921, p. 34.

58. *Variety*, 2 September 1924.

59. *Kine Monthly* (September 1919), p. 23.

60. *Variety*, 2 September 1924.

61. *Pictures*, 30 July 1921, p. 98.

62. *Kine Monthly* (September 1919), p. 23.

63. James Corbett, 'English Girls on the Screen', in BFI, Betty Balfour Collection.

64. *Pictures*, 5 February 1921, p. 149.

65. *Trade Show Critic Annual* (1923), p. 16.

66. *Pictures*, 29 January 1921, p. 127.

67. *Picture Show Annual* (1926), p. 61.

68. *Kine Monthly* (October 1921), p. 12.

69. *Variety*, 31 December 1924.

70. Low, *British Film 1918–1929*: film listings.

71. Corbett, 'English Girls on the Screen'.

72. Pearson, 'Memories', p. 8.

73. *Kine Monthly* (January 1921), p. 11; *Variety*, 1 December 1920.

74. *Kine Monthly* (November 1920), p. 47.

75. *Cinema Chat* 62 (1920), p. 4.

76. *Variety*, 22 July 1921.

77. *Kine Monthly* (January 1921), p. 10.

78. *Variety*, 22 July 1921.

79. *Pictures*, 30 July 1921, p. 89.

80. *Picture Show Annual* (1926), p. 24.

81. *Cinema Chat* 12 (1919), p. 4; *Cinema Chat* 44 (1920), p. 15.

82. *Variety*, 16 April 1924.

83. *Picture Show Annual* (1926), p. 26.

84. *Kine Monthly* (June 1920), p. 18.

85. *Kine Monthly* (July 1920), p. 16.

86. *Variety*, 29 October 1924.

87. Langford Reed, *The Picture Play* (London, 1920)), Book 4, p. 11.

88. *Bioscope*, 16 February 1928.

89. Gladys Cooper, *Gladys Cooper* (London, 1931), pp. 181, 268; Sewell Stokes, *Without Veils, the Intimate Biography of Gladys Cooper* (London, 1953), p. 139.

90. *Trade Show Critic Annual* (1921), p. 44.

91. *Kine Monthly* (September 1920), p. 14.

92. BFI, Betty Balfour Collection: from undated newspaper extract entitled 'How I Cried Over My First Film'.

93. Peter Stead, *Film and the Working Class: The Feature Film in British and American Society* (London, 1989), p. 30.

94. *Film Weekly*, 29 July 1929.

95. Garth Pedlar, 'Betty Balfour', *Classic Images* 108 (June 1984), p. 29.

96. Fenn Sherie, 'Betty Balfour: A Personal Close-up of Britain's Favourite Film Star', in BFI, Betty Balfour Collection; undated extract from the *Sketch* (1924), p. 170.

97. Sherie, 'Betty Balfour', pp. 170, 171.

98. Pedlar, 'Betty Balfour', p. 29.

99. *Dundee Telegraph*, 25 September 1926.

100. Sherie, 'Betty Balfour', p. 173.

101. *Newcastle Chronicle*, undated letter, BFI, Betty Balfour Collection.

102. Pearson, 'Memories', p. 10.

103. George Pearson, *Nothing Else Matters*; trade show programme notes in BFI, George Pearson Collection.

104. Pearson, 'Memories', p. 10.

105. Pearson, 'Memories', p. 11.

106. *Kine Monthly* (December 1920), p. 10.

107. *Picture Show*, 21 August 1926, p. 19; *Westminster Gazette*, 29 September 1926.

108. Sherrie, 'Betty Balfour', p. 171.

109. W. Pett Ridge, *A Story Teller* (London, 1923)), pp. 22, 173, 301.

110. *Cinema Chat* 65 (1920), p. 1.

111. *Cinema Chat* 24 (1919), p. 25.

112. *Kine Monthly* (February 1920), p. 17.

113. *Kine Monthly* (March 1921), p. 42.

114. *Kine Monthly* (June 1920), p. 11.

115. *Evening Standard*, 16 July 1928.

116. BFI, Betty Balfour Collection.

3. Roles for Men: 'Gentlemen ... right through'

1. *The Times*, 19 March 1929.

2. Kine Monthly (October 1920), p. 19.

3. *Cinema Chat* 87 (1920), p. 19.

4. *Pictures*, 4 June 1921, p. 550.

5. *Kine Monthly* (June 1921), p. 10.

6. *Cinema Chat* 89 (1920), p. 9.

7. Rachael Low, *The History of the British Film 1918–1929* (London, 1971), p. 267.

8. *Cinema Chat* 22 (1919), p. 9.

9. *Pictures*, 31 July 1921, p. 58.

10. *Variety*, 18 June 1924.

11. *Pictures*, 16 July 1921, p. 58.

12. Don Miller, *B Movies* (New York, 1987), p. 111.

13. *Trade Show Critic Annual* (1922), p. 42.

14. Victor McLaglen, *Express to Hollywood* (London, 1933).

15. *Pictures*, 25 June 1921, p. 622; *Picture Show Annual* (1926), p. 123.

16. *Kine Monthly* (August 1921), p. 7.

17. *Kine Monthly* (November 1920), p. 10.

18. *Trade Show Critic Annual* (1923), p. 35.

19. Ivan Butler, *Silent Magic: Rediscovering the Silent Film Era* (London, 1987), p. 93.

20. *Kine Monthly* (February 1921), p. 39

21. *Kine Monthly* (October 1920), p. 20.

22. Low, *British Film 1918–1929*, p. 120.

23. *Cinema Chat* 11 (1919), p. 31.,

24. *Picture Show Annual* (1927), p. 30

25. *Pictures* 30 July 1921, p. 98.

26. *Kine Monthly* (October 1920), p. 10.

27. *Cinema Chat* 47 (1920), p. 1.

28. *Picture Show Annual* (1928), p. 18.

29. *Picture Show Annual* (1928), p. 80.

30. *Kine Monthly* (November 1919), p. 35.

31. *Variety*, 23 April 1924.

32. *Variety*, 1 December 1924.

33. *Pictures*, 23 July 1921, p. 78.

34. John Parker (ed.), *Who's Who in the Theatre* (London, 1925).

35. Alex Matheson Lang, *Mr Wu Looks Back: Thoughts and Memories* (London, 1941), pp. 117, 152, 153.

36. *Kine Monthly* (November 1919), p. 64.

37. Lang, *Mr Wu Looks Back*, p. 156.

38. Reginald Denham, *Stars in My Hair* (London, 1958), p. 139.

39. Peter Noble, *Ivor Novello: Man of the Theatre* (London, 1951), p. 90.

40. *Kine Monthly* (July 1921), p. 12.

41. *Kine Monthly* (July 1921), p. 3.

42. *Variety*, 1 July 1921.

43. *Variety*, 5 August 1921.

44. Michael N. Druxman, *Basil Rathbone: His Life and His Films* (London, 1975), pp. 37–9.

45. *Variety*, 5 August 1921.

46. Noble, *Ivor Novello*, p. 85.

47. Roy Armes, *French Cinema* (London, 1985), p. 22.

48. Noble, *Ivor Novello*, p. 81.

49. *Cinema Chat* 28 (1919), p. 6.

50. *Cinema Chat* 36 (1920), p. 7.

51. *Kine Monthly* (May 1920), p. 30.

52. *Kine Monthly* (March 1921), p. 34.

53. *Pictures*, 26 February 1921, p. 218.

54. *Cinema Chat* 41 (1920), p. 32.

55. *Kine Weekly*, 11 November 1920; Noble, *Ivor Novello*, p. 89.

56. Noble, *Ivor Novello*, pp. 97, 98, 103.

57. *Variety*, 7 February 1924.

58. Noble, *Ivor Novello*, p. 103; *Variety*, 7 February 1924.

59. *Kine Monthly* (August 1920), p. 5; *Kine Monthly* (June 1921), p. 8.

60. Noble, *Ivor Novello*, p. 102.

61. *Variety*, 12 March 1924.

62. *Variety*, 7 February 1924.

63. *Picture Show Annual* (1926), pp. 2, 6.

64. *Pictures*, 4 June 1921, p. 550.

65. *Cinema Chat* 62 (1920), p. 1.

66. *Variety*, 31 January 1924.

67. Walter Southgate, *That's the Way it Was: A Working-Class Autobiography 1890–1950* (London, 1952), pp. 75–7.

68. Penelope Dell, *Nettie and Sissie* (London, 1977), p. 164.

69. *Cinema Chat* 65 (1920), p. 19.

70. *Kine Monthly* (November 1921), p. 9.

71. *Kine Monthly* (June 1921), p. 11.

72. *Pictures*, 4 June 1921, p. 550.

73. H. F. Maltby, *Ring up the Curtain* (London, 1950), p. 221.

74. D. Gifford, *British Film Catalogue 1895–1970. A Guide to Entertainment Films* (Newton Abbot, 1973): no. 06929 *A Temporary Gentleman*.

75. Maltby, *Ring up the Curtain*, p. 150.

76. 'C.T.', *Penrose Tennyson* (London, 1943), p. 83.

77. *Cinema Chat* 50 (1920), p. 2.

78. *Cinema Chat* 83 (1920), p. 9.

79. *Kine Monthly* (July 1920), p. 22.

80. Jeffrey Richards, T*he Age of the Dream Palace: Cinema and Society in Britain 1930– 1939* (London, 1984), p. 186.

81. *Cinema Chat* 26 (1919), p. 22.

82. *Cinema Chat* 5 (1919), p. 3.

83. *Variety*, 3 October 1919.

84. *Picture Show Annual* (1928), p. 20.

85. *Cinema Chat* 2 (1919), p. 20: *The Great Gay Road*.

86. *Pictures*, 8 January 1921, p. 47.

87. *Cinema Chat* 40 (1920), pp. 1, 2: *A Son of David*.

88. *Cinema Chat* 41 (1920), p. 21.

89. *Pictures*, 1 January 1921, p. 9.

90. *Kine Monthly* (July 1921), p. 11.

91. *Cinema Chat* 44 (1920), p. 30.

92. *Kine Monthly* (October 1921), p. 9.

93. *Kine Monthly* (February 1920), p. 26.

94. *Kine Monthly* (November 1919), p. 48.

95. *Kine Monthly* (November 1919), p. 26.

96. *Cinema Chat* 12 (1919), p. 31.

97. *Pictures*, 5 February 1921, p. 142.

98. *Film Chats* (Queen's Hall cinema, Cricklewood); *Cinema Chat* 12 (1919), p. 31; *Kine Monthly* (July 1920), p. 15.

99. *Film Chats* (Shaftesbury Pavilion).

100. *Pictures*, 21 February 1921, p. 78.

101. *Kine Monthly* (May 1919), p. 11; *Picture Show Annual* (1928), p. 16.
102. *Pictures*, 29 February 1921, p. 127.
103. *Cinema Chat* 37 (1920), p. 23.
104. *Bioscope*, 11 November 1919, p. 62; *Variety*, 2 January 1920.
105. *Kine Monthly* (December 1919), p. 28.
106. *Kine Monthly* (August 1919), p. 10.
107. *Kine Monthly* (June 1921), p. 34.
108. *Picture Show Annual* (1928), p. 16.
109. Low, *British Film 1918–1929*, pp. 109, 110.
110. *Trade Show Critic Annual* (1921), p. 30.
111. Low, *British Film 1918–1929*, p. 147.
112. J. Park, *British Cinema: The Lights that Failed* (London, 1990), p. 30.
113. *Kine Monthly* (March 1920), p. 13.
114. *Variety*, 12 November 1924.
115. *Variety*, 9 September 1921.
116. *Kine Monthly* (August 1919), p. 77.
117. *Kine Monthly* (October 1919), pp. 17, 18.
118. *Variety*, 31 January 1924.
119. *Morning Post*, 29 September 1927.
120. *Kine Monthly* (October 1919), p. 47.
121. *Kine Monthly* (November 1919), p. 50.
122. K. Rockett, L. Gibbons, and J. Hill, *Cinema and Ireland* (Dublin, 1987), p. 23.
123. *Kine Monthly* (March 1920), p. 19.
124. *Kine Monthly* (September 1920), p. 18.
125. *Trade Show Critic Annual* (1924), p. 10.
126. *Variety*, 22 July 1921.
127. *Cinema Chat* 24 (1919), p. 26.

4. The Audience Votes: 'Far from the Promised Land of Public Esteem'

1. *Kine Monthly* (October 1919), p. 3.
2. BFI, newspaper clippings, folder dated 1924–26.
3. Herbert Wilcox, *25,000 Sunsets* (London, 1967), p. 51.
4. George Robey, *Looking Back on Life* (London, 1933), p. 266.
5. F. M. Speed (ed.), *Film Review* (London, 1948), p. 149.
6. Victor McLaglen, *Express to Hollywood* (London, 1933), p. 246.
7. *Kine Monthly* (January 1921), p. 3.
8. Basil Dean, *Seven Ages. Vol. 2: 1927–1972* (London, 1973), p. 111.
9. *Kine Monthly* (October 1919), p. 17.
10. *Kine Monthly* (December 1919), p. 28.
11. *Kine Monthly* (December 1919), p. 39.
12. *Kine Monthly* (October 1919), p. 47.
13. *Kine Monthly* (October 1919), p. 25.
14. *Kine Monthly* (November 1920), p. 16.
15. *Kine Monthly* (August 1920), p. 15.
16. Edward S. Van Zile, *That Marvel – The Movie* (New York and London, 1923), p. 67.
17. *Kine Monthly* (December 1919), p. 46.

18. Cecil M. Hepworth, *Came the Dawn: Memories of a Film Pioneer* (London, 1951), p. 130.

19. *Kine Monthly*, (March 1920), p. 21.

20. *Kine Monthly* (November 1919), p. 60.

21. *Cinema Chat* 66 (1920), p. 3.

22. Tom Gallon, *Young Eve and Old Adam* (London, 1913), fly-leaf advertisement.

23. *Kine Monthly* (October 1919), p. 3.

24. *Cinema Chat* 8 (1919), p. 9.

25. G. Pearson, 'Memories – Into the Twilight Twenties, and What Then?', *Royal Academy Bulletin* 13 (London, 1951), p. 9.

26. *Kine Monthly* (May 1920), p. 16.

27. Gertrude de St. Wentworth-Jones, *Scarlet Kiss* (London, 1910), p. 35.

28. James Agate, *On an English Screen* (London, 1926), p. 43.

29. *Kine Monthly* (October 1919), p. 26.

30. *Kine Monthly* (August 1921), p. 9.

31. Penelope Dell, *Nettie and Sissie* (London, 1977), pp. 61, 109.

32. *Kine Monthly* (August 1921), p. 10.

33. *Kine Monthly* (October 1920), p. 19.

34. *Kine Monthly* (September 1920), p. 14.

35. *Kine Weekly* (February 1921), p. 28.

36. *Kine Monthly* (April 1921), p. 40.

37. *Kine Monthly* (June 1920), p. 20.

38. *Kine Monthly* (January 1921), p. 38; 'Rita', *Calvary* (London, 1909), introduction.

39. *Kine Monthly* (August 1920), p. 20; *Kine Monthly* (September 1919), p. 61.

40. *Kine Monthly* (June 1920), p. 23.

41. *Kine Monthly* (September 1919), p. 52.

42. *Kine Monthly* (August 1920), p. 20.

43. *Kine Monthly* (September 1921), p. 9.

44. David C. Murray, *Aunt Rachel: A Rustic Sentimental Comedy* (London, 1886), p. 2; *Kine Monthly* (August 1920), p. 11.

45. *Kine Monthly* (August 1920), p. 12.

46. *Kine Monthly* (June 1920), p. 13.

47. *Kine Monthly* (September 1921), p. 6.

48. *Kine Monthly* (February 1920), p. 25.

49. *Kine Monthly* (November 1920), p. 12.

50. *Kine Monthly* (August 1920), p. 14.

51. *Kine Monthly* (September 1921), p. 6.

52. *Cinema Chat* 73 (1920), p. 18.

53. Reginald Denham, *Stars in My Hair* (London, 1958).

54. *Kine Monthly* (May 1920), p. 11.

55. *Kine Monthly* (October 1920), p. 20.

56. *Kine Monthly* (February 1920), p. 15.

57. *Kine Monthly* (July 1921), p. 24.

58. *Kine Monthly* (October 1919), p. 55.

59. *Kine Monthly* (August 1920), p. 24.

60. *Cinema Chat* 48 (1920), p. 2.

61. Langford Reed, *The Picture Play* (London, 1920), Book 10, p. 5.

62. Ibid., Book 8, p. 13.

63. *Cinema Chat* 52 (1920), p. 6.

64. *Cinema Chat* 24 (1919), p. 26.

65. HLRO Historical Collection 184, Beaverbrook; letter from the novelist Hall Caine to Beaverbrook.

66. Denis Gifford, *The British Film Catalogue 1895–1970. A Guide to Entertainment Films* (Newton Abbot, 1973); calculated using plot precis, character lists, novels and plays on which films were based.

67. *Cinema Chat* 48 (1920), p. 2.

68. *Kine Monthly* (October 1921), pp. 18, 114; *Cinema Chat* 24 (1919), p. 1.

69. *Kine Monthly* (July 1921), p. 34.

70. E. Newton-Bungay, *The Fordington Twins* (London, 1913), pp. 31, 34; Gifford, *British Film Catalogue*: no. 06982.

71. Ivan Butler, *Silent Magic: Rediscovering the Silent Film Era* (London, 1987), p. 93.

72. Maurice Drake, *The Salving of A Derelict* (London, 1906), p. 51.

73. George Pearson, trade show programme notes for *Nothing Else Matters* (London, 23 July 1920), in BFI, George Pearson Collection.

74. Sewell Stokes, *Without Veils, the Intimate Biography of Gladys Cooper* (London, 1953), pp. 85, 86.

75. *Kine Monthly* (July 1920), p. 16.

76. J. B. Priestley, *Midnight on the Desert* (London, 1937), p. 120.

77. *Film Renter*, 19 January 1924.

78. *Bioscope*, 20 October 1919, p. 29.

79. *Kine Monthly* (October 1920), p. 19.

80. Norman Lee, *Log of a Film Director* (London, 1949), pp. 15, 16.

81. *Trade Show Critic Annual* (1924), p. 6.

82. Rachael Low, *The History of the British Film 1918–1929* (London, 1971), p. 276.

83. *Cinema Chat* 65 (1920), p. 19.

84. *Cinema Chat* 7 (1919), p. 27.

85. *Kine Monthly* (February 1921), p. 30.

86. Ronald Blythe, *The Age of Illusion* (London, 1965), p. 7.

87. Robert Graves and Alan Hodge, *The Long Weekend: A Social History of Great Britain 1918–1939* (London, 1940), p. 33.

88. Jack Common (ed.), *Seven Shifts* (London, 1938), p. 97.

89. Ibid., p. 43; George Lansbury, *Jesus and Labour*, Independent Labour Party Pamphlet no. 60 (London, 1924), pp. 3, 4.

90. Graves and Hodge, *The Long Weekend*, pp. 35, 69.

91. Common (ed.), *Seven Shifts*, p. 105.

92. *Cinema Chat* 73 (1920), p. 19.

93. *Kine Monthly* (November 1920), p. 10.

94. *Kine Monthly* (February 1921), p. 30.

95. Graves and Hodge, *The Long Weekend*, p. 68.

96. Luke McKernan, *Topical Budget: The Great British News Film* (London, 1992), p. 129, 130.

97. Miles Malleson, *The Independent Labour Party Arts Guild*, Independent Labour Party Pamphlet no. 67 (London, 1925); Ethel Carnie Holdsworth, *This Slavery* (London, 1926).

98. *Cinema Chat* 68 (1920), p. 1.

99. *Cinema Chat* 32 (1920), p. 3.

100. *Trade Show Critic Annual* (1922), p. 4.

101. BFI, Betty Balfour Collection.

102. Priestley, *Midnight on the Desert*, pp. 76, 99, 130.

5. Responses to the Slump: 'Reclaiming the Stolen Soul of England'

1. *Film Renter and Moving Picture News*, 5 January 1924, p. iii.
2. *Kine Weekly*, 3 January 1924, p. 65.
3. *Morning Telegraph*, 10 February 1924.
4. *Pictures* (February 1924), p. 54; G. K. Chesterton, *G. K. Chesterton Explains the English* (London, 1936), p. 2.
5. *Film Renter*, 2 February 1924.
6. *Film Renter*, 5 January 1924.
7. *Film Renter*, 29 March 1924
8. *Film Renter*, 8 March 1924.
9. *Film Renter*, 26 January 1924.
10. *Film Renter*, 1 March 1924; *Film Renter*, 8 March 1924.
11. *Kine Weekly*, 28 February 1924.
12. *Film Renter*, 2 February 1924.
13. *Variety*, 23 April 1924; *Kine Weekly*, 23 January 1924, p. 42.
14. Rachael Low, *The History of the British Film 1918–1929* (London, 1971), p. 183; *Kine Monthly* (September 1919), p. 31; *Variety*, 4 June 1924.
15. *Kine Monthly*, June 1921, p. 11.
16. *Kine Weekly*, 23 January 1924, p. 90; *Kine Weekly*, 1 February 1924, p. 39.
17. *Film Renter*, 29 March 1924.
18. *Kine Weekly*, 1 March 1924, p. 12
19. *Film Renter*, 29 March 1924.
20. *Film Renter*, 15 March 1924.
21. Ibid.
22. *Cinema World* (October 1927), p. 31.
23. D. H. Lawrence, 'Is England Still a Man's Country?', in *Assorted Articles* (London, 1930), pp. 77–82; and 'Film Passion', in *Collected Poems* (London, 1926) p. 538.
24. *Film Renter*, 8 March 1924.
25. *Variety*, 9 February 1938.
26. *Girl's Cinema*, 19 March 1927, p. 4.
27. Donald P. Costello, *The Serpent's Eye: Shaw and the Cinema* (New York, 1965), p. 22.
28. Alfred Hitchcock, interviewed in *Screen Pictorial* (June 1935), p. 14.
29. Wyndham Lewis, 'Film-Filibusters', in E. W. F. Tomlin (ed.), *Filibusters in Barbary: an Anthology of Wyndham Lewis's Prose* (London, 1969), p. 365.
30. *Pictures* (February 1924), p. 61.
31. Caradoc Evans, 'Should the Cinema Be Abolished?', *Kine Weekly*, 17 January 1924.
32. James Agate, *On an English Screen* (London, 1926), p. 35; *Pictures* (November 1924), p. 36.
33. Anthony Hope, quoted in Graham Greene, *The Lost Childhood and Other Essays* (London, 1951), p. 102.
34. *Pictures* (February 1924), p. 7.
35. Ibid., p. 53; *Pictures* (May 1924), p. 11.
36. *Pictures* (February 1924), p. 7.
37. Ibid.
38. *Cinema Chat* 61 (1920), p. 32.
39. *Kine Weekly*, 1 February 1924.
40. *Bioscope*, 13 November 1921, p. 45.

41. *Girl's Cinema*, 19 March 1927, p. 4.

42. *Variety*, 28 March 1926; *Pictures, Pleasures and Past-times* (November 1929), p. 17.

43. *Bioscope*, 18 March 1926, p. 61; *Pictures, Pleasures and Past- times* (November 1929), p. 17.

44. *Pictures, Pleasures and Past-times* (October 1929), p. 6; Low Warren, *The Film Game* (London, 1937), p. 186.

45. Victor McLaglen, *Express to Hollywood* (London, 1933), p. 238.

46. Hannen Swaffer, *Hannen Swaffer's Who's Who* (London, 1929).

47. Miles Mander, *Gentleman by Birth* (London, 1933), p. 89.

48. *Pictures* (February 1924), p. 43.

49. *Pictures* (March 1924), p. 66.

50. Oliver Sandys, *Full and Frank: the Private Life of a Woman Novelist* (London, 1941), p. 92.

51. *Best of British: The Heroes* (BBC Production, 1987).

52. *Film Renter*, 5 January 1924.

53. J. B. S. Haldane, *The Inequality of Man, and Other Essays* (London, 1932), p. 62.

54. *Film Renter*, 5 January 1924.

55. *Hollywood Chronicles: The American Hero* (Cabin Fever Productions, 1991), interview with King Vidor.

56. W. H. Auden, 'The Initiate, Part II – Argument', in *Poems* (New York, 1934), pp. 102, 103.

57. Geoffrey Smith, quoting Rudyard Kipling, *Sunday Times*, 28 June 1992, p. 5.

58. G. K. Chesterton, 'A Case for Main Street', in *Sidelights on New York and Newer York, and Other Essays* (London, 1932), p. 134.

59. D. H. Lawrence, 'The State of Funk' in *Assorted Articles*, p. 99.

60. James Harding, *Gerald du Maurier* (London, 1989), pp. 62, 63; Denis Gifford, *The British Film Catalogue 1895–1970. A Guide to Entertainment Films* (Newton Abbot, 1973): no. 07273 *Mr Justice Raffles* and no. 09207 *The Return of Raffles*.

61. Harding, *Gerald du Maurier*, pp. 112, 114.

62. E. M. Forster, 'Notes on the English Character', in *Abinger Harvest* (London, 1936), p. 11.)

63. G. K. Chesterton, 'On Facing Facts', in *Avowals and Denials* (London, 1934), p. 184.

64. Forster, 'Notes on the English Character', p. 9.

65. Graham Greene, 'The Last Buchan', in *The Lost Childhood*, p. 104.

66. Wyndham Lewis, *Doom of Youth* (London, 1932), p. 260.

67. *Variety*, 9 January 1938; *Screen Pictorial* (February 1939), p. 61: *Crackerjack*.

68. *Screen Pictorial* (November 1938); *Screen Pictorial* (February 1939): *Strange Boarders*.

69. G. K. Chesterton, 'Keeping Your Hair On', in *Sidelights on New York and Newer York*, p. 30; *Screen Pictorial* (February 1939), pp. 25, 22.

70. Hilaire Belloc, *The Contrast* (London, 1923), p. 138; and *An Essay on the Nature of Contemporary England* (London, 1937), p. 30.

71. S. J. Woolf, *Drawn from Life* (London, 1932), in conversation with G. K. Chesterton.

72. Chesterton, *Avowals and Denials*, p. 184

73. Chapman Cohen, *Opinions* (London, 1930), p. 142; Haldane, *The Inequality of Man*, p. 43.

74. E. W. Bakke, *The Unemployed Man* (London, 1933), p. 240.

75. George Lansbury, *My England* (London, 1934), p. 82; G. C. Heseltine, 'The Change', in *Essays on the Land* (London, 1927), pp. 61, 71, 105.

76. Lewis, *Doom of Youth*, p. 33.

77. G. K. Chesterton, 'The New Jerusalem', in *Avowals and Denials*, p. 238.

78. W. H. Auden, *The Dance of Death* (New York, 1933), pp. 197, 217.

79. Marina Warner, *The Crack in the Teacup* (London, 1979), p. 62; Luke McKernan, *Topical Budget: The Great British News Film* (London, 1992), p. 134.

80. George Lansbury, *Outside the Right* (London, 1963): letter from George Bernard Shaw, pp. 210, 211.

81. Auden, *Poems*, p. 197.

82. E. A. Baughan, drama and film critic of the *Daily News*, in *Film Renter*, 5 January 1924.

83. J. B. Priestley, 'The Wicked People', in *Apes and Angels* (London, 1929), p. 61.

84. Stella Margetson, *The Long Party: High Society in the Twenties and Thirties* (London, 1976), p. 46.

85. James Laver, 'The Twenties', in *The Saturday Book* (London, 1952), p. 231.

86. Ibid., p. 228.

87. Charles MacKay, quoted in ibid.

88. J. H. Thomas, quoted in J. Collier and I. Lang, *Just the Other Day: An Informal History of Great Britain Since the War* (London, 1932), p. 65.

89. D. H. Lawrence, 'Change of Government', in *Collected Poems*, p. 571.

90. *Morning Telegraph*, 10 February 1924.

91. *Film Renter*, 5 January 1924.

92. *Kine Weekly*, 31 January 1924, p. 37.

93. Fenner Brockway, *Pacifism and the Left* (London, 1938), p. 8.

94. Margetson, *The Long Party*, pp. 162, 178.

95. Woolf, *Drawn from Life*, p. 171.

96. Auden, *Poems*, p. 215.

97. *Film Renter*, 5 January 1924.

98. Lansbury, *My England*, p. 88.

99. Robert Graves and Alan Hodge, *The Long Weekend: A Social History of Great Britain 1918–1939* (London, 1940), p. 147; Patrick Wright, *On Living in an Old Country: The National Past in Contemporary Britain* (London, 1985), pp. 108, 109.

100. John Betjeman, *Antiquarian Prejudice*, Hogarth Pamphlet no. 3 (London, 1939), p. 19.

101. *Pictures*, 8 January 1921, p. 38.

102. *Pictures*, February 1924, p. 10.

103. *Pictures*, December 1924, p. 11.

104. C. M. Hepworth, *Came the Dawn: Memories of a Film Pioneer* (London, 1951), pp. 193, 194; *Trade Show Critic Annual* (1924), p. 36.

105. Ernest Betts, *Heraclitus*, or the Future of Film (London, 1928), p. 15.

106. *Film Renter*, 5 January 1924.

107. *Kine Weekly*, 3 January 1924, p. 89; and *Kine Weekly*, 10 January 1924, p. 55; *Film Renter*, 5 January 1924.

108. *Film Renter*, 5 January 1924.

109. *Screen Pictorial* (April 1936), pp. 10, 11.

110. *Picture-Play Magazine* (September 1919).

111. *Fame and Fortune* 24 (November 1928), p. 44.

112. H. J. Forman, *Our Movie-Made Children* (New York, 1933), p. 138; Wyndham Lewis, 'America and Cosmic Man', in *Filibusters in Barbary*, p. 382.

113. Isaac Rosenberg, 'The Pre-Raphaelite Exhibition', in I. Parsons (ed.), *Collected Works of Isaac Rosenberg* (London, 1984), pp. 283, 284.

114. D. H. Lawrence, *Lady Chatterley's Lover* (London, 1928), p. 1; David Shipman, *The Good Film and Video Guide* (London, 1984): review of *Lady Chatterley's Lover*; Susan Sontag, *Against Interpretation* (London, 1987), p. 45.

115. D. H. Lawrence, 'The Factory Cities', in *Collected Poems*, p. 586.

116. Reginald Denham, *Stars in My Hair* (London, 1958), p. 135: titles from *The Silver King*.

117. W. H. Auden, *On this Island* (New York, 1937), p. 42.

118. Caradoc Evans, *My People* (London, 1919), pp. 48, 49.

119. *Romance* 8 (London, 1890), pp. 143 et al; this publication carried numerous stories warning women of the terrible fate awaiting them in cities e.g. 'Made Mad in Liverpool', 'Lost in Liverpool', 'Revelations of Horrible London'.

120. *Screen Pictorial* (September 1936), p. 28.

121. *Film Renter*, 5 January 1924.

122. J. Nuttall and R. Carmichael, *Common Factors/Vulgar Fraction* (Lancashire, 1977), p. 24.

123. *Pictures* (February 1924), p. 53.

124. *Variety*, 6 June 1919: *A House Divided.*

125. Terry Ramsaye, *A Million and One Nights* (New York, 1926), p. 775.

126. Cohen, *Opinions*, p. 20.

127. Ramsaye, *A Million and One Nights*, p. 776; Ivan Butler, *Silent Magic: Rediscovering the Silent Film Era* (London, 1987), p. 58..

128. Low, *British Film 1918–1929*, p. 126.

129. *Film Renter*, 5 January 1924.

130. *Film Renter*, 1 March 1924.

131. *Film Renter*, 2 February 1924.

132. *Film Renter*, 29 March 1924.

6. Government Intervention: Legislating the Intangible

1. Sir Philip Cunliffe-Lister, *Parliamentary Debates* (Commons), Fifth Series, Volume 203, Column 2039.

2. *Parliamentary Debates* (Commons), Vol. 203, Col. 252.

3. *Daily Express*, 18 March 1927.

4. *Parliamentary Debates* (Commons), Vol. 203, Col. 266; Cinematographic Films Act (1927).

5. *Cinematograph Exhibitors' Diary* (London, 1931), p. 18.

6. *Parliamentary Debates* (Commons), Vol. 203, Col. 293.

7. Ibid.

8. C. A. Lejeune, 'Eyes and No Eyes', in R. S. Lambert, (ed.), *For Film-goers Only* (London, 1934), p. 88.

9. E. M. Forster, *Abinger Harvest* (London, 1936), p. 5.

10. Ernest Betts, *Heraclitus, or the Future of Films* (London, 1928), p. 79.

11. Hilaire Belloc, *An Essay on the Nature of Contemporary England* (London, 1937), p. 39

12. C. E. M. Joad, *Diogenes* (London, 1928), p. 14.

13. Stephen Spender, *The New Realism*, Hogarth Pamphlet no. 2 (London, 1939), p. 13.

14. *Royal Screen Pictorial* (August 1935), p. 51.

15. *Movie Mirror* (August 1934), p. 5.

16. Mass Observation, *May the Twelfth Survey* (London, 1937), p. 148.

17. Ibid., p. 119.

18. Ibid., p. 201.

19. Ibid., pp. 143, 203.

20 Ibid., pp. 202, 313.

21. Ibid., p. 273.

22. Ibid., p. 401.

23. Ibid., p. 211.

24. *Screen Pictorial* (June 1937), p. 66.

25. *Screen Pictorial* (March 1939), p. 9.

26. *Screen Pictorial* (November 1937): 'The Cinema in the Suburbs', based on Bernstein's surveys.

27. John Betjeman, *Antiquarian Prejudice*, Hogarth Pamphlet no.3 (London, 1939), p. 7.

28. David Quinlan, *British Sound Films 1928–1959* (London, 1984), p. 14.

29. Basil Dean, *Seven Ages. Vol. 2: 1927–1972* (London, 1973), p. 204.

30. Ibid., p. 231; Rachel Low, *The History of the British Film 1929–1939* (London, 1985), pp. 164, 165.

31. Seton Margrave, *Successful Screen Writing* (London, 1936), p. 8.

32. John Paddy Carstairs, *Movie Merry-Go-Round* (London, 1937), p. 170.

33. *Parliamentary Debates* (Lords), Vol. 9, Cols. 291, 292.

34. Keane, John, *Tom Paine: A Political Life* (London, 1996), pp. 468, 469.

35. Ivor Montagu, *The Political Censorship of Films* (London, 1929), p. 32: Hilaire Belloc, *The Contrast* (London, 1923), p. 137.

36. *Royal Screen Pictorial* (January 1935), p. 17.

37. *Screen Pictorial* (March 1939), p. 37: review of *Goodbye, Mr Chips*.

38. *Films and Fiction* (December 1932), p. 19.

39. Ivor Montagu, *Political Censorship*, p. 32.

40. *Screen Pictorial* (November 1937), p. 34.

41. *Screen Pictorial* (February 1937), p. 38.

42. *Screen Pictorial* (October 1936), p. 34

43. *Screen Pictorial* (November 1936), p. 34; *Screen Pictorial* (July 1939), p. 35.

44. George Arliss, *By Himself* (London, 1940), p. 127.

45. Graham Greene, *The Pleasure Dome: The Collected Film Criticism 1935–1940* (London, 1972), p. 138; review of *Thunder in the City*.

46. *Screen Pictorial* (February 1938), p. 53.

47. *Movie Mirror* (April 1935), p. 97.

48. *Movie Action Magazine*, 1, nos 2 and 3 (1935).

49. John Strachey, in C. Caudwell, *Studies in a Dying Culture* (London, 1938), introduction, p. xv.

50. Personal correspondence; of sixty-nine hereditary peers who would have been of an age to have started seeing films between 1919 and 1939, fifty-nine cited American films and/or actors as being their first memory of the cinema (100 peers were circularized; 69 replied).

51. J. B. Priestley, *Midnight on the Desert* (London, 1937), p. 99, 100.

52. Caradoc Evans, *My People* (London, 1919), p. 281.

53. W. H. Auden, Poem xiv, in *On This Island* (New York, 1937), p. 34.

54. Henry Durant, *The Problem of Leisure* (London, 1938), p. 145.

55. E. W. Bakke, *The Unemployed Man* (London, 1933), pp. 219, 220, 224.

56. Luke McKernan, *Topical Budget: the Great British News Film* (London, 1982), p. 131.

57. *Daily Mail*, 3 May 1926.

58. William Plomer, in Graham Greene (ed.), *The Old School* (London, 1934), p. 146; Plomer claims the government treated the strike as if it was a game played at a public school.

59. Ronald Blythe, *The Age of Illusion* (London, 1965), p. 165.

60. Patrick Wright, *On Living in an Old County: The National Past in Contemporary Britain* (London, 1985), p. 105.

61. Stella Margetson, *The Long Party; High Society in the Twenties and Thirties* (London, 1976), p. 47, 52.

62. J. Symons, *The General Strike* (London, 1957), p. 158.

63. Personal viewing; see also Jeffrey Richards, *The Age of the Dream Palace: Cinema and Society in Britain 1930–1939* (London, 1984), p. 270.

64. *Parliamentary Debates* (Commons), Vol. 203, Col. 689.

65. *Parliamentary Debates* (Commons) Vol. 203, Cols. 741, 742.

66. *Variety*, 21 December 1927.

67. *Parliamentary Debates* (Commons), Vol. 203, Col. 743.

68. *Parliamentary Debates* (Commons) Vol. 203, Col. 259.

69. *Variety*, 28 December 1927.

70. *Bioscope*, 16 September 1926; *Mademoiselle from Armentieres* was praised for its sincerity, as was *Mons*, in *Bioscope* 23 September 1926. *Bioscope*, 5 May 1927, praised *Roses of Picardy* for being both truthful and restrained and *The Flag Lieutenant* was lauded for stirring up 'the emotion and patriotism of every class of audience'; *Bioscope*, 4 November 1926.

71. *Bioscope*, 6 September 1926.

72. *Parliamentary Debates* (Commons), Vol. 203, Cols. 262, 263.

73. *Variety*, 28 March 1928.

74. *Variety*, 7 December 1927.

75. *Variety*, 21 December 1927: review of *The Flag Lieutenant*.

76. Beverley Nichols, *Cry Havoc!* (London, 1933) p. 216.

77. *Parliamentary Debates* (Commons), Vol. 203, Cols. 744, 748.

78. *Parliamentary Debates* (Commons), Vol. 203, Cols. 751, 862, 863.

79. *Parliamentary Debates* (Commons) Vol. 203, Col. 258.

80. *Parliamentary Debates* (Commons), Vol. 203, Col. 250.

81. See, for instance, Low, *British Film 1929–1939*; Geoff Brown, *Walter Forde* (London, 1977); Herbert Wilcox, *25,000 Sunsets* (London, 1967); and Monja Danischewsky (ed.), Michael Balcon's *Twenty-Five Years in Films* (London, 1947).

82. *Biograph*, 16 September 1926; *Kine Weekly*, 16 September 1926.

83. *Bioscope*, 9 September 1926.

84. *Bioscope*, 27 May 1926.

85. *Bioscope*, 10 February 1927.

86. Herbert Wilcox, *25,000 Sunsets*, p. 69.

87. *Bioscope*, 7 February 1924; *Kine Weekly*, 31 January and 7 February 1924.

88. Greene, *The Pleasure Dome*, p. 247; review of *Nurse Edith Cavell*.

89. *Variety*, 27 January, 1926.

90. Gilbert Adair and Nick Roddick, *A Night at the Pictures: Ten Decades of British Films* (London, 1985), pp. 19, 20; David Quinlan, *The Illustrated Guide to Film Directors* (London, 1983): entry for Wilcox.

91. *Movie Mirror* (September 1935), p. 8.

92. *Pictures* (January 1924), p. 60.

93. *Kine Weekly* (1 February), 1924, p. 27.

94. *Variety*, 2 April 1924.

95. *Parliamentary Debates* (Commons), Vol. 203, Col. 2051.

96. *Kine Weekly*, 21 February 1924.

97. *Variety*, 21 March 1928.

98. *Parliamentary Debates* (Lords), Vol. 69, Col. 293.

99. *Parliamentary Debates* (Lords) Vol. 69, Col. 278.

100. *Bisoscope*, 28 April 1927, p. 23.

101. *Parliamentary Debates* (Lords), Vol. 69, Col. 286.

102. *Bioscope*, 28 April, 1927, p. 23.

103. *Parliamentary Debates* (Commons), Vol. 203, Col. 698.

104. *Screen Pictorial* April 1938, p. 23.

105. Virginia Woolf, 'The Cinema' (1926), in *The Captain's Death Bed and Other Essays*, (London, 1959), p. 171.

106. Belloc, *Contemporary England*, p. 42.

107. *Movie Action Magazine* no. 4 (1936), p. 4: *Ah Wilderness*.

7. The Betty Balfour Connection: 'Ain't we sisters'

1. *Halliwell's Film Guide* (London, 1991 edn): *29 Acacia Avenue*.

2. *Pictures*, 5 February 1921, p. 142.

3. *Pictures*, 2 April 1921, p. 334.

4. Iris Barry, *Let's Go to the Pictures* (London, 1926), p. 96.

5. *Film Renter*, 5 January, 1924.

6. BFI, Betty Balfour Collection: letter from Raymond Hague, Prestwich.

7. George Pearson, 'Memories – Into the Twilight Twenties, and What Then?'; *Royal Academy Bulletin* 13 (London, 1951), p. 14.

8. *Squibs Wins the Calcutta Sweep*; print of film held in Museum of Modern Art, New York.

9. James Park, *British Cinema: The Lights that Failed* (London, 1990), p. 33.

10. George Pearson, *Flashback: The Autobiography of a British Film-maker* (London, 1957), pp. 97, 98.

11. BFI, George Pearson Collection: hand-written diary from period when Pearson was producing *Journey's End* in Hollywood (1929/30).

12. Park, *British Cinema*, p. 33.

13. Pearson, *Flashback*, p. 94.

14. Pearson, 'Memories', p. 13.

15. Jeffrey Richards, 'Gracie Fields: Consensus Personified', in *The Age of the Dream Palace: Cinema and Society in Britian 1930–1939* (London, 1989), pp. 169–90.

16. BFI, George Pearson Collection: titles list from *Squibs MP*.

17. *Film Renter*, 2 February 1924.

18. Fenn Sherie, 'Betty Balfour; A Personal Close-up of Britain's Favourite Film Star', in *The Sketch* (1924) p. 170, in BFI *Betty Balfour Collection* (1924).

19. BFI, George Pearson Collection: titles list for *Squibs' Honeymoon*.

20. Richards, *The Age of the Dream Palace*, pp. 189, 190.

21. *Film Renter*, 2 February 1924.

22. *Sussex County Herald*, 14 July 1928.

23. Pearson, 'Memories', p. 11; *Bioscope*, 31 May 1923, p. 57.

24. *Film Renter*, 2 February 1924.

25. *Bristol Times*, 16 July 1928; *Sussex County Herald*, 14 July 1928.

26. W. Pett Ridge, *I Like to Remember* (London, 1925), p. 251.

27. *Birmingham Daily Mail*, 7 June 1928; *Picture Show Annual* (1929) p. 8.

28. BFI, George Pearson Collection: notes for trade show of *Reveille*.

29. Pearson, *Flashback*, p. 14.

30. *Cinema World*, undated extract in BFI, *George Pearson Collection*.

31. *Film Renter*, June 28 1924.

32. *Girl's Cinema*, 8 October 1927, p. 19.

33. *Cinema World*, 15 October 1927, p. 31.

34. Sherie, 'Betty Balfour' in *The Sketch*, p. 167, in BFI, Betty Balfour Collection.

35. *Picture Show Annual* (1928), p. 16.

36. *Daily Telegraph*, 15 October 1927; *Westminster Gazette*, 15 October 1927.

37. The *Times*, 19 March 1929.

38. *Film Weekly*, 2 September 1929.

39. *Daily Express*, 21 April,1925.

40. *Daily Film Renter*, 1 March 1924.

41. *Girl's Cinema*, 2 April 1927.

42. Garth Pedlar, 'Betty Balfour', *Classic Images* 108 (June 1984) pp. 29, 30 and 50.

43. Pearson, *Flashback*, p. 143.

44. *Daily Telegraph*, 24 May 1926.

45. *Bioscope*, 31 September 1926.

46. Rachael Low, *The History of British Film 1918–1929*, (London, 1971) p. 163; *Daily Mail*, 19 September 1926.

47. Ada Reeve, *Take it for a Fact* (London, 1954), p. 179.

48. Pearson, *Flashback*, p. 143.

49. John Simon, quoted in Robert Graves, and Alan Hodge, *The Long Weekend: A Social History of Great Britain 1918–1939* (London, 1940), p. 186.

50. Denis Gifford, *The British Film Catalogue 1895–1970. A Guide to Entertainment Films* (Newton Abbot, 1973): no. 08041 *Sea Urchin*.

51. *Daily Film Renter*, 11 September 1928.

52. *Cinema*, 27 October 1927.

53. *The Lady*, 20 September 1928.

54. *Daily Mirror*, 23 May 1928.

55. *Catholic Herald*, 2 June 1928.

56. *Weekly Dispatch*, 27 May 1928.

57. *The Lady*, 20 September 1928.

58. *Daily Film Renter*, 11 September 1928.

59. *Kine Weekly*, 12 July 1928.

60. *Cinema*, 12 September 1928.

61. *Sunday Graphic*, 16 September 1928; Low, *British Film 1918–1929*, p. 264; *Daily Film Renter*, 11 September 1928.

62. *Pictures* (January 1924), p. 36.

63. Pedlar, 'Betty Balfour'.

64. Ibid.

65. *Weekly Dispatch*, 28 May 1928.

66. *Bioscope*, 24 May 1928.

67. *Cinema*, 23 May 1928; *Kine Weekly*, 24 May 1928.

68. *Girl's Cinema*, 14 June 1927.

69. *East London Mirror*, 23 May 1928.

70. *Girl's Cinema*, 14 June 1927, p. 4.

71. *Birmingham Gazette*, 21 September 1928.

72. *Morning Post*, 21 August 1928.

73. François Truffaut, *Hitchcock* (London, 1969), p. 57.

74. *Daily Film Renter*, 22 August 1928; *Bioscope*, 22 August 1928.

75. *Daily Sketch*, 21 August 1928.

76. *Cinema*, 22 August 1928.

77. *Irish Independent*, 25 August 1928.

78. *Daily Sketch*, 21 August 1928.

79. *Daily Film Renter*, 21 August 1928.

80. *Kine Weekly*, 23 August 1928.

81. *Royal Screen Pictorial* (March 1935), p. 52.

82. Maurice Yacowar, *Hitchcock's British Films* (New York, 1977), p. 79.

83. Arthur Marwick, *Class: Image and Reality in Britain, France and the USA Since 1930* (London, 1990), p. 164.

84. *Screen Pictorial Winter Annual* (1938).

85. *Hollywood Chronicles: The Depression Years* (Cabin Fever Productions, 1991); interview with King Vidor.

86. *The Star*, 21 July 1928.

87. Garth Pedlar, 'Betty Balfour and her silent films that survive on 9.5mm home-movies only in French' *Flickers* 49 (1982).

88. *Sunday Pictorial*, 10 June 1927.

89. *Girl's Cinema*, 19 January 1927, p. 4.

90. *Photobits and Cinema Star*, 17 November 1923, p. 11, 19 January 1924, p. 10 and 3 May 1924, p. 3; *Girl's Cinema*, 2 February 1927, p. 16.

91. Midge Mackenzie, *Shoulder to Shoulder* (London, 1988), pp. ix, x.

92. Anthony Ludovici, *Lysistrata. On Woman's Future and Future Woman* (London, 1924), p. 82.

93. Graves and Hodge, *The Long Weekend*, pp. 246, 252.

94. H. L. Beales and R. S. Lambert, *Memoirs of the Unemployed* (London, 1934), pp. 261, 262.

95. *Film Renter*, 5 January 1924; Gifford, *British Film Catalogue* no. 07660: 'Cleric's daughter marries but stays in business so that neglected children grow up perverted.'

96. Eileen Bigland *Marie Corelli, the Woman and the Legend* (London, 1953), pp. 167, 187.

97. Low, *British Film 1918–1929*, pp. 62, 147.

98. *Cinema World* (September 1927); Pearson, *Flashback*, p. 127.

99. Stanley Houghton, *Hindle Wakes* (London, 1912), p. 107.

100. Virginia Woolf, introduction to M. L. Davies (ed.), *Life as We Have Known It*, by Co-operative Working Women (London, 1931), p. xxxiv.

101. Pilgrim Trust, *Men Without Work* (London, 1938), pp. 232, 240.

102. Ibid., pp. 261, 235, 277, 295.

103. *Bioscope*, 22 March 1928 and *Bioscope*, 27 March 1929.

104. Graves and Hodge, *The Long Weekend*, p. 147.

105. Gifford, *British Film Catalogue*: no. 08314 *The Constant Nymph*.

106. Graves and Hodge, *The Long Weekend*, p. 147.

107. David Lodge (ed.) 'D. H. Lawrence: Morality and the Novel', in *Twentieth Century Literary Criticism* (London, 1972), p. 130.

108. Graves and Hodge, *The Long Weekend*, p. 147; Ivan Butler, *Silent Magic: Rediscovering the Silent Film Era* (London, 1987), p. 78.

109. *Variety*, 21 March 1928.

110. *Evening Standard*, 13 May 1929; Pedlar, 'Betty Balfour'.

111. BFI, Betty Balfour Collection; unattributable newspaper clipping.

112. *Pictures, Pleasures and Past-times* (November 1929), p. 15.

113. *Daily Film Renter*, 9 November 1928.

114. P. Warren, *Elstree, the British Hollywood* (London, 1983), p. 50

115. *Variety*, 8 May 1934.

116. *Kine Weekly*, 13 September 1934.

117. *Variety*, 25 September 1934.

118. W. H. Auden, *The Dance of Death* (New York, 1933), pp. 196, 197.

119. *Variety*, 25 September 1934; *Kine Weekly*, 20 September 1934 and *Kine Weekly*, 4 October 1934.

120. Peter Stead, 'The Faintest Dribble of Real English Life' in *Film and the Working Class*: the Feature Film in British and American Society (London, 1989), pp. 99–119.

121. G. K. Chesterton, *G. K. Chesterton, Explains the English* (London, 1936), p. 4.

122. *Screen Pictorial* (June 1938), p. 4.

123. Sherie, 'Betty Balfour' in *The Sketch*, p. 137, in BFI, Betty Balfour Collection; BFI, George Pearson Collection: titles list for *Squibs' Wins the Calcutta Sweep*, personal viewing.

124. *Kine Weekly*, 23 May 1935.

125. Jeffrey Richards, *The Age of the Dream Palace*, p. 193; Marcia Landy, *British Genres*, pp. 122, 123.

126. *Kine Weekly*, 9 May 1935

127. *Kine Weekly*, 23 May 1935; *Screen Pictorial* (July 1934), p. 62.

128. *Movie Mirror* (November 1935), p. 40.

129. *Movie Mirror* (October 1935), p. 97.

130. *Kine Weekly*, 23 May 1935.

131. *Kine Weekly*, 22 April 1936.

132. *Kine Weekly*, 9 April 1936

133. *Screen Pictorial* (November 1935), p. 40.

134. Simon Rowson, *British Influence Through the Films* (London, 1933), p. 8.

135. *Screen Pictorial* (March 1939), p. 7.

136. *Screen Pictorial* (June 1935), p. 5.

8. George Pearson: Hollywood Dreams, Twickenham Nightmares

1. Victor McLaglen, *Express to Hollywood* (London, 1933), p. 247; *Pictures* (December 1924), p. 34.

2. *Film Renter*, 28 June 1927.

3. *Kine Weekly*, 24 January 1924, p. 81.

4. *Pictures* (February 1924), p. 53.

5. *Pictures* (February 1924), p. 16.

6. *Pictures* (February 1924), p. 53.

7. *Pictures* (December 1924), p. 3.

8. *Bioscope*, 29 April 1926; *Bioscope*, 1 July 1926.

9. George Pearson, *Flashback: The Autobiography of a British Film-maker* (London, 1957), p. 143.

10. Rachael Low, *The History of the British Film 1918–1929* (London, 1971), p. 163

11. George Pearson, 'Memories – Into the Twilight Twenties and What Then?' *Royal Academy Bulletin* 13 (London, 1951), p. 14.

12. *Cinema*, 3 April 1929.

13. *Bioscope*, 10 June 1929; Reginald Denham, *Stars in My Hair* (London 1958), p. 135.

14. *Pictures, Pleasures and Past-times* (December 1929), p. 16.

15. Pearson, *Flashback*, p. 156.

16. *Kine Weekly*, 4 April 1929.

17. *Cinema*, 4 May 1929.

18. *Variety*, 21 March 1928.

19. Luke McKernan, *Topical Budget: The Great British News Film* (London, 1992), p. 133.

20. Robert Graves and Alan Hodge, *The Long Weekend: A Social History of Great Britain 1918–1939* (London, 1940), p. 248.

21. George Pearson, *Flashback*, p. 148.

22. Ibid., p. 128

23. *Royal Screen Pictorial* (March 1935), p. 37.

24. *Variety*, 21 March 1928; Pearson, *Flashback*, p. 149.

25. BFI, George Pearson Collection: titles list for *Squibs*.

26. Pearson, *Flashback*, p. 157.

27. Graves and Hodge, *The Long Weekend*, p. 229.

28. *Variety*, 12 October 1927.

29. Low, *British Film 1918–1929*, p. 173.

30. J. Curtis, *James Whale* (London, 1982), pp. 39, 40; Pearson, *Flashback*, pp. 157ff.

31. Louis Levy, *Music for the Movies* (London, 1948), p. 29.

32. *Pictures, Pleasures and Past-times* (November 1929), p. 15.

33. Levy, *Music for the Movies*, p. 30.

34. *Pictures, Pleasures and Past-times* (October 1929), p. 75.

35. Don Miller, *B Movies* (New York, 1987), pp. 16, 17.

36. J. Curtis, *James Whale*, pp. 3, 15.

37. Elsa Lanchester, *Herself* (London, 1969), p. 105; Curtis, *James Whale*, p. 46.

38. Lanchester, *Herself*, p. 15; George Pearson, *Hollywood Diary*, entry for 26 November, 1929, in BFI, George Pearson Collection.

39. *Screen Pictorial* (August 1938), p. 34.

40. Pearson, *Hollywood Diary*, entries for 21 and 28 September, 16 and 26 October, 1929.

41. Curtis, *James Whale*, pp. 55, 56.

42. *Film Mercury*, 21 March 1929.

43. Pearson, *Hollywood Diary*; entry for 27 March 1929.

44. *Screen Pictorial* (January 1936), pp. 22, 23.

45. Wyndham Lewis, *Doom of Youth* (London, 1932), pp. 218, 219.

46. *Screen Pictorial* (July 1935), p. 62.

47. *Movie Mirror* (March 1934), p. 24: interview with Douglas Fairbanks Junior.

48. *Movie Mirror* (July 1933), p. 90.

49. *Movie Mirror* (September 1934), p. 84.

50. Pearson, *Hollywood Diary*.

51. Marcia Landy, *British Genres* (Oxford, 1991), p. 121.

52. J. B. Priestley, *Midnight on the Desert* (London, 1937), p. 101.

53. Paul Rotha, *Celluloid: The Film Today* (London, 1933), p. 180; E. M. Forster, *Abinger Harvest* (London, 1936), p. 165;

54. D. H. Lawrence, in D. Lodge (ed.), *Twentieth Century Literary Criticism* (London, 1982), p. 678.

55. Priestley, *Midnight on the Desert*, p. 170.

56. *Film Mercury* 21 March, 1930

57. Denis Gifford, BFI 1895–1970. *A Guide to Entertainment Films* (Newton Abbot, 1973): no. 08741 *Armistice*; *Bioscope*, 16 September 1926; *Bioscope*, 5 May 1927.

58. H. L. Beales and R. S. Lambert, *Memoirs of the Unemployed* (London, 1934), p. 182; Gifford, *British Film Catalogue* no. 08256 *Remembrance*.

59. Low, *British Film 1918–1929*, p. 177; Graves and Hodge, *The Long Weekend*, pp. 200, 328, 329; *Bioscope*, 8 September 1927.

60. *Variety*, 5 October 1927; *Bioscope*, 8 September 1927.

61. Jeffrey Richards, *The Age of the Dream Palace: Cinema and Society in Britain 1930–1939* (London, 1984), pp. 284–6; *Close-up* (September 1929); *Bioscope*, 14 August 1929.

62. Beverley Nichols, *Cry Havoc!* (London, 1933), p. 28.

63. Levy, *Music for the Movies* (London, 1948), p. 30.

64. *Bioscope*, 14 August 1929.

65. *Film Daily Yearbook* (1938), pp. 213, 214.

66. BFI, George Pearson Collection: telegram from R. C. Sherriff.

67. Richards, *The Age of the Dream Palace*, pp. 213, 214.

68. *Film and Fiction* 7 (1932), p. 6.

69. Henry Kendall, *I Remember Romano's* (London, 1960), p. 115.

70. *Screen Pictorial* (January 1937), p. 25.

71. John Paddy Carstairs, *Movie Merry-Go-Round* (London, 1937), p. 175.

72. *Variety*, 13 May 1935.

73. *Variety*, 14 August 1935.

74. *Variety*, 10 April 1935.

75. Richards, *The Age of the Dream Palace*, pp. 312, 313.

76. *Variety*, 27 April 1938.

77. Rodney Ackland and Elspeth Grant, *The Celluloid Mistress* (London, 1954), pp. 63–5.

78. *Screen Pictorial* (August 1935), p. 45.

79. Pearson, *Flashback*, p. 193.

80. H. F. Maltby, *Ring Up the Curtain* (London, 1950), p. 214.

81. Pearson, George, *Flashback*, p. 195.

82. *Kine Weekly*, 18 October 1934.

83. *Variety*, 6 Novemeber 1934.

84. *Kine Weekly*, 25 October 1934.

85. BFI, George Pearson Collection.

86. 'C.T.', *Penrose Tennyson* (London, 1943), p. 131.

87. Cecil Day Lewis, quoted in J. Symons, *The Thirties. A Dream Resolved* (London, 1960), p. 20.

88. Pearson, *Hollywood Diary*, entry dated 14 October 1929.

Select Bibliography

British Film Institute

Betty Balfour Collection; George Pearson Collection; Folder of press clippings 1924–1926.

House of Lords Record Office

Parliamentary Debates
HLRO Historical Collection 184, Beaverbrook
HLRO Historical Collection 191, Bonar Law
HLRO Historical Collection 192, Lloyd George
House of Lords Journals

Miscellaneous

The Best of British (television series)
Hollywood Chronicles (television series)
South Bank Show; Terence Davies interviewed by Melvin Bragg (5 April 1992)
Personal correspondence

Periodicals

Bioscope; Cinema; Cinema Chat; Cinema Pie; Cinema World; Cinematograph Exhibitors' Diary; Cineshows; Close-up; Daily Express Film Book; Daily Film Renter; Exhibitors' Diary; Fame and Fortune; Film and Fiction; Film Chats; Film Daily Yearbook of Motion Pictures; Film Fiction; Film Renter and Moving Picture News; Film Review; Girl's Cinema; Kinematograph Monthly Record; Kinematograph Weekly; Movie Action Magazine; Movie Mirror; Photobits and Cinema Star; Picture Show Annual; Picture-Play Magazine; Pictures; Pictures, Pleasures and Past-times; Romance; Royal Screen Pictorial; Screen Pictorial; Trade Show Critic Annual; Variety

Fiction

Annesley, Maude, *The Wine of Life* (London, 1908).

Applin, Arthur, *Wicked* (London, 1920).

Askew, Alice and Claude, *Testimony* (London, 1909).

— *God's Clay* (London, 1913).

Ayres, Ruby M., *Castles in Spain: The Chronicles of an April Month* (London, 1912).

Barcynska, Countess, *The Honey Pot* (London, 1916).

Barrett, Frank, *The Woman of the Iron Bracelets* (London, 1893).

Besant, Walter, Sir, *The Children of Gibeon* (London, 1886).

— *Beyond the Dreams of Avarice* (London, 1895).

Biss, Gerald, *Branded* (London, 1908).

Caine, William, *Great Snakes* (London, 1916).

Corelli, Marie, *The Sorrows of Satan, or, The Strange Experience of One Geoffrey Tempest, Millionaire* (London, 1895).

— *God's Good Man* (London, 1904).

Couch, Arthur Quiller, *True Tilda* (London, 1919).

Darlington, W. A., *Alf's Button* (London, 1919).

Deeping, George Warwick, *Unrest* (London, 1916).

Dell, Ethel M., *The Rocks of Valpre* (London, 1914).

— *Bars of Iron* (London, 1916).

— *The Hundreth Chance* (London, 1917).

— *The Tidal Wave, and Other Stories* (London, 1919).

Drake, Maurice, *The Salving of a Derelict* (London, 1906).

Edgar, George, *The Pride of the Fancy* (London, 1914).

Ewer, Monica, *Not for Sale* (London, 1923).

Farnol, Jeffery, *The Money Moon* (London, 1911).

— *The Amateur Gentleman* (London, 1913).

— *The Definite Object* (London, 1917).

Gallon, Tom, *The Great Gay Road* (London, 1910).

— *Young Eve and Old Adam* (London, 1913).

Garvice, Charles, *Nance* (London, 1900).

— *Linked by Fate* (London, 1905).

— *With All Her Heart* (London, 1907).

Gould, Nat, *A Dead Certainty* (London, 1900).

— *A Rank Outsider* (London, 1900).

— *The Chance of a Lifetime; the novel of the film and the play* (London, 1921).

Grundy, Mabel Barnes, *Candytuft – I Mean Veronica* (London, 1914).

— *The Mating of Marcus* (London, 1923).

Hamilton, Cosmo, *Duke's Son* (London, 1905).

— *The Princess of New York* (London, 1911).

— *Scandal* (London, 1918).

Harding, Dolores C. F., *Oranges and Lemons* (London, 1916).

Hill, Marion, *The Lure of Crooning Water* (London, 1913).

Hocking, Silas K., *Her Benny* (London, 1890).

— *The Shadow Between* (London, 1908).

Holdsworth, Ethel Carnie, *Helen of Four Gates* (London, 1917).

— *This Slavery* (London, 1926).

Houghton, Stanley, *Hindle Wakes* (London, 1912).

Hutchinson, A. S. M., *Once Aboard a Lugger. The History of George and His Mary* (London, 1908).

Jenkins, Herbert, *Patricia Brent, Spinster* (London, 1918).

Jerome, Jerome K., *Three Men in a Boat* (London, 1899).

Lawrence, D. H., *Lady Chatterley's Lover* (London 1961 edn).

Lewis, Helen Prothero, *As God Made Her* (London, 1919).

Lock, W. J., *The Usurper* (London, 1901).

Lyons, A. Neil, *A London Lot*, based on the successful play 'London Pride', by A. N. Lyons, and Gladys Unger, (London, 1913).

Mander, Miles, *Gentleman by Birth* (London, 1933).

Mason, A. E. W., *Miranda of the Balcony* (London, 1899).

— *At the Villa Rose* (London, 1910).

Mather, Helen, *Cherry Ripe* (London, 1921).

Murray, D. C., *Aunt Rachel: A Rustic Sentimental Comedy* (London, 1886).

Newell, Guy, *Husband Love* (London, 1924).

Newton-Bungay, E., *The Fordington Twins* (London, 1913).

Oppenheim, E. Phillips, *Anna the Adventuress* (London, 1904).

— *The Double Life of Mr Alfred Burton* (London, 1914).

Page, Gertrude, *Love in the Wilderness: The Story of an African Farm* (London, 1907).

— *Edge O'Beyond* (London, 1908).

Raine, Allen, *Torn Sails* (London, 1898).

— *By Berwin Banks* (London, 1899).

'Rita', *Sheba: A Study of Girlhood* (London, 1899).

— *Calvary* (London, 1909).

Roy, Olivia, *The Husband Hunter* (London, 1907).

Sandys, Oliver, *Chappy – That's All* (London, 1922).

— *Blinkeyes* (London, 1925).

Soutar, Andrew, *Snow in the Desert* (London, 1919).

Sutro, Alfred, *The Great Well* (London, 1922).

Thurston, E. Temple, *Sally Bishop* (London, 1906).

— *The City of Beautiful Nonsense* (London, 1909).

— *The Garden of Resurrection* (London, 1911).

Vachell, H. A., *The Case of Lady Camber* (London, 1916).

Wadsley, Olive, *The Flame* (London, 1913).

— *Possession* (London, 1916).

Walton, O. F. (Mrs), *Shadows; Scenes and Incidents in the Life of an Old Arm Chair* (London, 1884).

Watts, Theodore, *Alwyn* (London, 1899).

Wentworth-Jones, Gertrude de St, *Scarlet Kiss* (London, 1910).

Wilson, Augusta Evans, *At the Mercy of Tiberius* (London, 1887).

Non Fiction

Abrams, Mark, *The Condition of the British People 1911–1945* (London, 1946).

Ackland, Rodney and Elspeth Grant, *The Celluloid Mistress* (London, 1954).

Adair, Gilbert and Nick Roddick, *A Night at the Pictures: Ten Decades of British Films* (London, 1985).

Agate, James, *On an English Screen* (London, 1926).

— *The Common Touch* (London, 1926).

Allen, Walter, 'Mass Entertainment', in J. Raymond (ed.), *The Baldwin Age* (London, 1960).

Arliss, George, *By Himself* (London, 1940).

Armes, Roy, *A Critical History of British Cinema* (London, 1978).

— *French Cinema* (London, 1985).

Arnheim, R. and P. Rotha, *Film* (London, 1933).

Ashley, W., *The Cinema and the Public* (London, 1954).

Auden, W. H., *The Dance of Death* (New York, 1933).

— *Poems* (New York, 1934).

— *On This Island* (New York, 1937).

Bakke, E. W., *The Unemployed Man* (London, 1933).

Balcon, Michael, *Michael Balcon Presents: A Lifetime in Films* (London, 1968).

Balcon, M., Ernest Lindgren, Forsyth Hardy and Roger Manvell, *Twenty Years of British Films 1925–1945* (London, 1947).

Bardeche, Maurice and Robert Brasillach, *History of the Film* (London, 1978).

Barker, Felix, *The House that Stoll Built* (London, 1951).

Barr, Charles (ed.), *All Our Yesterdays: 90 Years of British Cinema* (London, 1986).

Barry, Iris, *Let's Go to the Pictures* (London, 1926).

Beales, H. and R. S. Lambert, *Memoirs of the Unemployed* (London, 1934).

Bedarida, François, *A Social History of England 1851–1990* (London, 1991).

Belloc, H., *The Contrast* (London, 1923).

— *Survivals and New Arrivals* (1926).

— *An Essay on the Nature of Contemporary England* (London, 1937).

Betjeman, John, *Antiquarian Prejudice*, Hogarth Pamphlet no. 3 (London, 1939).

Betts, Ernest, *Heraclitus, or the Future of Film* (London, 1928).

— *Inside Pictures, with Some Reflections from the Outside* (London, 1960).

— *The Film Business* (London, 1973).

Bigland, Eileen, *Marie Corelli, the Woman and the Legend* (London, 1953).

Blunden, Edmund, 'The English Countryside', in *Spectator's Gallery* (London, 1932).

Blythe, Ronald, *The Age of Illusion* (London, 1965).

Brantlinger, P., *Bread and Circuses: Theories of Mass Culture as Social Decay* (New York, 1983).

Brockway, A. Fenner, *Hungry England* (London, 1932).

— *Pacificism and the Left* (London, 1938).

Brown, Geoff, *Walter Forde,* (London, 1973).

— 'Sister of the Stage: British Film and British Theatre', in C. Barr (ed.) *All Our Yesterdays* (London, 1986).

Brownlow, Kevin, *How it Happens Here* (London, 1968).

Brunel, Adrian, *Filmcraft: the Art of Picture Production* (London, 1933).
— *Film Production* (London, 1936).
— *Nice Work* (London, 1949).
Buchanan, Andrew, 'Axes to Grind', in R. S. Lambert, et al., *For Film-goers Only* (London, 1934).
Burnett, R. G. and E. D. Martell, *The Devil's Camera* (London, 1932).
Butler, Ivan, *Silent Magic: Rediscovering the Silent Film Era* (London, 1987).
'C.T.', *Penrose Tennyson* (London, 1943).
Cameron, James R., *Motion Pictures* (London, 1929).
Carrington, C. E., *The Life of Rudyard Kipling* (New York, 1956).
Carstairs, John Paddy, *Movie Merry-Go-Round* (London, 1937).
— *Honest Injun!* (London, 1943).
— *Kaleidoscope and Jaundiced Eye* (London, 1946).
Caudwell, C., *Studies in a Dying Culture* (London, 1938).
Chanan, Michael, *Labour Power in the British Film Industry* (London, 1976).
— *The Dream that Kicks: the Prehistory and Early Years of the Cinema* (London, 1980).
Chesterton, G. K., *Sidelights on New York and Newer York, and Other Essays* (London, 1932).
— *Avowals and Denials* (London, 1934).
— *G.K. Chesterton Explains the English* (London, 1936).
Christie, Ian, *Arrows of Desire* (London, 1985).
Clephane, Irene, *Ourselves 1900–1930* (London, 1933).
Cohen, Chapman, *Opinions* (London, 1930).
Collier, Constance, *Harlequinade* (London, 1929).
Collier, John and Iain Lang, *Just the Other Day: An Informal History of Great Britain Since the War* (London, 1932).
Commission on Educational and Cultural Films, *The Film in National Life* (London, 1932).
Common, Jack (ed.), *Seven Shifts* (London, 1937).
Cooper, Diana, *The Rainbow Comes and Goes* (London, 1958).
Cooper, Gladys, *Gladys Cooper* (London, 1931).
Corelli, Marie, *Is All Well with England. A Question* (London, 1917).
— *My 'Little Bit'* (London, 1919).
Costello, Donald P., *The Serpent's Eye: Shaw and the Cinema* (New York, 1965).
Curle, J. J., 'The Flicks', in *The Saturday Book* (London, 1959).
Curtis, J., *James Whale* (London, 1982).
Dale, Edgar, *Contents of the Movies* (New York, 1935).
Dangerfield, George, *The Strange Death of Liberal England* (St Albans, 1970).
Danischewsky, Monja (ed.), *Michael Balcon's Twenty-Five Years in Films* (London, 1947).
Davies, M. L. (ed.), *Life as We Have Known It*, by Co-operative Women (London, 1931).
De Courville, Albert, *I Tell You* (London, 1928).
Deakin, B. (ed.), *Nothing of the Town* (London, 1957).
Dean, Basil, *Seven Ages. Vol. 1: 1888–1927* (London, 1970).
— *Seven Ages. Vol. 2: 1927–1972* (London, 1973).
Dell, Penelope, *Nettie and Sissie* (London, 1977).
Denham, Reginald, *Stars in My Hair* (London, 1958).

Dickinson, M., and S. Street, *Cinema and State: the Film Industry and the Government 1927–1984* (London, 1985).

Druxman, Michael B., *Basil Rathbone. His Life and Films* (London, 1975).

Durant, Henry, *The Problem of Leisure* (London, 1938).

Durgnat, R., *A Mirror for England* (London, 1970).

Evans, Caradoc, *My People* (London 1919).

Eyles, Allen and David Meeke (eds), *Missing Believed Lost: the Great British Film Search* (London, 1992).

Fleming, P. and D. Verschoyle (eds), *The Spectator's Gallery*. Essays, Sketches, Short Stories and Poems from the *Spectator* (London, 1933).

Ford, Ford Madox, *The Spirit of the People* (London, 1907).

Forman, H. J., *Our Movie-Made Children* (London, 1933).

Forster, E. M., *Abinger Harvest* (London, 1936).

— *What I Believe In* (London, 1939).

Foss, Kenelm, *Cinema, A Practical Course* (London, 1920).

Gifford, Denis, *The British Film Catalogue 1890–1970. A Guide to Entertainment Films* (Newton Abbot, 1973).

Gloversmith, Frank, 'Defining Culture; Clive Bell, R. H. Tawney and T. S. Eliot', in F. Gloversmith (ed.), *Class, Culture and Social Change: a new view of the 1930s* (London, 1980).

Glyn, Anthony, *Elinor Glyn. A Biography* (London, 1955).

Gramsci, Antonio, *Selections from the Prison Notebooks*, ed. Quinton Hoare and Geoffrey Nowell-Smith, (New York, 1978).

Graves, Robert and Alan Hodge, *The Long Weekend: A Social History of Great Britain 1918–1939* (London, 1940, 1991).

Grazia, Victoria de, 'Mass Culture and Sovereignty: the American Challenge to European Cinemas 1920–1960', *Journal of Modern History* 61 (Chicago, March 1989).

Green, Martin, *Children of the Sun: a Narrative of 'Decadence' in England after 1918* (London, 1976).

Greene, Graham (ed.) *The Old School* (London, 1934).

— *The Lost Childhood, and other essays* (London, 1951).

— *The Pleasure Dome: The Collected Film Criticism 1935–1940* (London, 1972).

Greenwood, Walter, 'Langy Road: a Salford Council School' in Greene, Graham (ed.), *The Old School* (London, 1934).

Hague, Eli, *Streets Away from Paradise: Reminiscences of a Staleybridge Lad* (Manchester, 1987).

Haldane, J. B. S., *The Inequality of Man, and Other Essays* (London, 1932).

Halliwell, Leslie, *Filmgoer's Companion* (London, 1976).

— *Seats in All Places: Half a Lifetime at the Movies* (London, 1986).

Halliwell's Film Guide (London, 1991).

Harding, James, *Gerald du Maurier* (London, 1989).

Hepworth, Cecil B., *Came the Dawn: Memories of a Film Pioneer* (London, 1951).

Heseltine, G. C., *Essays on the Land* (London, 1927).

Hicks, Seymour, *Between Ourselves* (London, 1930).

— *Night Lights* (London, 1938).

Higson, Andrew, *Waving the Flag: Constructing a National Cinema in Britain* (London, 1995).

Hodge, John, *From Workman's Cottage to Windsor Castle* (London, 1931).

Hoggart, Richard, *The Uses of Literacy* (London, 1986).

Humphreys, Desmond, Mrs ('Rita'), *Recollections of a Literary Life* (London, 1936).

Jackson, Arrar, *Writing for the Screen* (London, 1929).

Jackson, Holbrook, *The Eighteen Nineties* (London, 1913).

Joad, C. E. M., *Diogenes* (London, 1928).

— *The Horrors of the Countryside* (London, 1931).

Jones, J. Caradog, *Social Survey of Merseryside* (Liverpool, 1934).

Jones, S.G., *The British Labour Movement and Film 1918–1939* (London, 1987).

Keane, John, *Tom Paine: A Political Life* (London, 1996).

Kendall, Henry, *I Remember Romano's* (London, 1960).

Kennedy, M., *The Mechanized Muse* (London, 1942).

Kimmins, Anthony, *Half-Time* (London, 1947).

Knight, Arthur, *The Liveliest Art* (New York 1957).

Lambert, R. S., 'Why We Get the Films We Do', in R. S. Lambert (ed.), *For Film-goers Only* (London, 1934).

Lanchester, Elsa, *Charles Laughton and I* (London, 1938).

— *Herself* (London, 1969).

Landy, Marcia, *British Genres* (Oxford, 1991).

Lang, Alex Matheson, *Mr Wu Looks Back: Thoughts and Memories* (London, 1941).

Lansbury, George, *Jesus and Labour*, Independent Labour Party Pamphlet no.60 (London, 1924).

— *My England* (London, 1934).

— *Looking Backwards and Forwards* (London, 1935).

— *Outside the Right* (London, 1936).

Laver, James, 'The Twenties', in *The Saturday Book* (London, 1952).

— 'Every Picture Sells a Story', in *The Saturday Book* (London, 1956).

Lawrence, D. H., *Assorted Articles* (London, 1930).

— *Collected Poems*, ed. V. S. Pinto, and W. Roberts (London, 1964).

Leavis, F. R. and D. Thompson, *Culture and Environment* (London, 1933).

Lee, Norman, *Log of a film Director* (London, 1949).

Lehman, John (ed.), *Coming to London* (London, 1957).

Lejeune, C. A., *Cinema* (London, 1931).

— 'Eyes and No Eyes', in R. S. Lambert, (ed.), *For Film-goers Only* (London, 1934).

Levy, Louis, *Music for the Movies* (London, 1948).

Lewis, Wyndham, *Doom of Youth* (London, 1932).

— 'Film-Filibusters' (1921), in E. W. F. Tomlin (ed.), *Filibusters in Barbary: An Anthology of Wyndham Lewis's Prose* (London, 1969).

Lindgren, E., 'The Early Feature Film', in Michael Balcon et al., *Twenty Years of British Films 1925–1945* (London, 1947).

Lodge, David (ed.), *Twentieth Century Literary Criticism* (London, 1972).

Loudon, Hugh, *My Hollywood* (Upton-upon-Severn, 1991).

Low, Rachael, *The History of the British Film 1918–1929* (London, 1971).

— *The History of the British Film 1929–1939* (London, 1985).

Ludovici, Anthony, *Lysistrata: On Woman's Future and Future Woman* (London, 1924).

— *Recovery: the Quest for Regenerative National Values* (London, 1936).

MacBean, L. C., *Kinematograph Studio Technique* (London, 1922).

MacFarlane, Brian, 'A Literary Cinema? British Films and British Novels,' in C. Barr (ed.), *All Our Yesterdays* (London, 1986).

Mackenzie, Midge, *Shoulder to Shoulder* (London, 1988).

McKernan, Luke, *Topical Budget: The Great British News Film* (London, 1992).

McKibbon, Ross, *The Ideologies of Class: Social Relations in Britain 1880–1950* (Oxford, 1991 edn).

McLaglen, Victor, *Express to Hollywood* (London, 1933).

McPhail, Angus and Ian Dalrymple, *Granta Limericks*, compiled for May Week (Cambridge, 1925).

Malleson, Miles, *The Independent Labour Party Arts Guild*, Independent Labour Party Pamphlet no. 67 (London, 1925).

Maltby, H. F., *Ring Up the Curtain* (London, 1950).

Manvell, Roger, *Film* (London, 1944).

— *New Cinema in Britain* (London, 1969).

Margetson, Stella, *The Long Party: High Society in the Twenties and Thirties* (London, 1974).

Margrave, Seton, *Successful Screen Writing* (London, 1936).

Marwick, Arthur, *Class: Image and Reality in Britain, France and the U.S.A. since 1930* (London, 1990).

Mass Observation, *May the Twelfth Survey* (London, 1937).

Maxton, James, *Speech in the House of Commons on the Moving of the Second Reading of the Living Wage Bill*, Independent Labour Party Pamphlet 69 (London, 1931).

Medhurst, A., 'Music Hall and British Cinema', in C. Barr, (ed.), *All Our Yesterdays* (London, 1986).

Miller, Don, *B Movies* (New York, 1987).

Mitchison, G. R., *The First Workers' Government* (London, 1934).

Mitchison, Naomi, *You May Well Ask 1920–1940* (London, 1979).

Montagu, Ivor, *The Political Censorship of Films* (London, 1929).

— *Film World* (London, 1964).

— *The Youngest Son* (London, 1970).

Mosley, Oswald, Sir, MP, *Replies to Mr Baldwin on Industrial Problems and the Socialists*, Independent Labour Party Pamphlet no. 72 (London, 1929).

Muir, Kenneth, *Arnold and the Victorian Dilemma* (London, 1947).

Murphy, Robert, 'Under the Shadow of Hollywood', in C. Barr, (ed.), *All Our Yesterdays* (London, 1986).

Neagle, Anna, *It's Been Fun* (London, 1949).

Nichols, Beverley, *Cry Havoc!* (London, 1933).

Noble, Peter, *Ivor Novello: Man of the Theatre* (London, 1951).

Nuttall, J. and R. Carmichael, *Common Factors/Vulgar Fraction* (Lancashire, 1977).

Orwell, George, *Keep the Aspidistra Flying*, (London, 1936).

— *The Road to Wigan Pier* (London, 1937).

Osborn, E. B., (ed.) *The Muse in Arms* (London, 1917).

Owen, Frank, *Tempestuous Journey: Lloyd George, His Life and Times* (London, 1954).

Park, James, *British Cinema: The Lights that Failed* (London, 1990).

Parker, John (ed.), *Who's Who in the Theatre* (London, 1925).

Parsons, Ian (ed.), *The Collected Works of Isaac Rosenberg* (London, 1984).

Pearse, Innes H. and G. Scott Williams, *The Case for Action: A Survey of Everyday Life Under Modern Industrial Conditions, With Special Reference to the Question of Health* (London, 1931).

Pearson, George, 'Memories – Into the Twilight Twenties, and What Then?', *Royal Academy Bulletin* 13 (London, 1951).

— *Flashback: The Autobiography of a British Film-maker* (London, 1967).

Pearson, Hesketh, *Iron Rations* (London, 1928).

Pedlar, Garth, 'Betty Balfour and her silent films that survive on 9.5mm home-movies only in French', *Flickers* 49 (1982).

— 'Betty Balfour', *Classic Images* 108 (June 1984).

Perry, George, *Forever Ealing; A Celebration of the Great British Film Studio* (London, 1981).

— *The Great British Picture Show* (London, 1974).

Petley, J., 'The Lost Continent', in C. Barr, (ed.) *All Our Yesterdays* (London, 1986).

Phillips, M., *The Young Industrial Worker, a Study of his Industrial Needs* (London, 1922).

Pilgrim Trust, *Men Without Work* (London, 1938).

Plomer, William, 'The Gothic Arch' in Graham Greene (ed.), *The Old School* (London, 1934).

— 'Coming to London', in B. Deakin (ed.) *Nothing of the Town* (London, 1957).

Powell, Anthony, 'The Wat'ry Glade', in Graham Greene (ed.), *The Old School* (London, 1934).

Powell, Michael, *A Life in Movies* (London, 1986).

Priestley, J. B., *Talking* (London, 1926).

— *Apes and Angels* (London, 1928).

— *Midnight on the Desert* (London, 1937).

Pronay, Nicholas, 'The First Reality; Film Censorship in Liberal England',in K. M. R. Short (ed.), *Feature Films as History* (London, 1981).

Pronay, N. and D. Spring (eds), *Propaganda, Politics and Film 1918–1945* (London, 1982).

Quinlan, David, *The Illustrated Guide to Film Directors* (London, 1983).

— *British Sound Films 1928–1959* (London, 1984).

Ramsaye, Terry, *A Million and One Nights* (New York, 1926).

Raymond, Ernest, *Please You, Draw Nearer* (London, 1969).

Raymond, J. (ed.), *The Baldwin Age* (London, 1960).

Reed, Langford, *The Picture Play* (London, 1920).

Reed, Langford and Hetty Spiers, *Who's Who in Filmland* (London, 1928).

Rees, Aubrey, *The Heroic Spirit* (London, 1918).

Reeve, Ada, *Take it for a Fact* (London, 1954).

Richards, Jeffrey, *The Age of the Dream Palace: Cinema and Society in Britain 1930–1939* (London, 1984).

Ridge, W. Pett, *A Story Teller* (London, 1923).

— *I Like to Remember* (London, 1925).

Robb, M., 'The Psychology of the Unemployed', in H. Beales and R. S. Lambert (eds), *Memoirs of the Unemployed* (London, 1934).

Roberts, Robert, *A Ragged Schooling; Growing Up in a Classic Slum* (Harmondsworth, 1974).

Robertson, James C., *The Hidden Cinema: British Film Censorship in Action 1913–1972* (London, 1989).

Robey, George, *Looking Back on Life* (London, 1933).

Rockett, K., L. Gibbons and J. Hill, *Cinema and Ireland* (Dublin, 1987).

Rosenberg, Isaac,'The Pre-Raphaelite Exhibition', in Ian Parsons (ed.), *The Collected Works of Isaac Rosenberg* (London, 1984).

Rotha, Paul, *Celluloid: The Film Today* (London, 1933).

— *On Film* (London, 1958).

Rotha, P. and R. Griffith, *The Film Till Now* (London, 1967).

Rowson, Simon, *British Influence Through the Films* (London, 1933).

Russell, Dora, *Hypatia* (London, 1925).

Sandys, Oliver, *Full and Frank: the Private Life of a Woman Novelist* (London, 1941).

Seaman, L. C. B., *Life in Britain Between the Wars* (London, 1970).

Sellar, M., L. Jones, A. Sidaway and R. Sidaway, *The Best of British* (London, 1987).

Shadwell, A., *Industrial Efficiency* (London, 1906).

Shipman, David, *The Good Film and Video Guide* (London, 1984).

Short, K. M. R., *Feature Films as History* (London, 1981).

Smith, P. (ed.), *The Historian and Film* (Cambridge, 1981).

Sontag, Susan, *Against Interpretation* (London, 1987).

Southgate, Walter, *That's the Way it Was: A Working-Class Autobiography 1890–1950* (London, 1952).

Speed, F. M. (ed.) *Film Review* (London, 1948).

Spender, Stephen, *The New Realism*, Hogarth Pamphlet no. 2 (London, 1939).

Stead, Peter, 'The People and the Pictures' in N. Pronay and D. Spring (eds), *Propaganda, Politics and Film 1918–1945* (London, 1982).

— *Film and the Working Class; The Feature Film in British and American Society* (London, 1989).

Stokes, Sewell, *Without Veils, the Intimate Biography of Gladys Cooper* (London, 1953).

Swaffer, Hannen, *Hannen Swaffer's Who's Who* (London, 1929).

Swann, Paul, *The Hollywood Feature Film in Postwar Britain* (London, 1987).

Symons, J., *The General Strike* (London, 1957).

— *The Thirties. A Dream Resolved* (London, 1960).

Talbot, F. A., *Moving Pictures: How They are Made and Worked* (London, 1923).

Taylor, Mike, 'John Bull and the Iconography of Public Opinion in England c.1712–1929', in *Past and Present* 134 (February 1992).

Thackeray, William Makepeace, *The Book of Snobs* (London, 1889).

Thurston, E. Temple, *A Critical Study* (London, 1933).

Tomlin, E. W. F. (ed.), *Filibusters in Barbary: an Antholgy of Wyndham Lewis's Prose* (London, 1969).

Truffaut, François, *Hitchcock* (London, 1969).

Van Zile, Edward S., *That Marvel – The Movie* (New York and London, 1923).

Walker, R. Rowan, *George Pearson. An Appreciation*, in trade show programme for *Reveille* (London, 1924).

Wallace, R. H. Edgar, *People* (London, 1926).

Walton, J. K. and J. Walvin, *Leisure in Britain 1780–1939* (Manchester, 1983).

Warner, Marina, *The Crack in the Teacup* (London, 1979).

Warren, Low (ed.), 'Who's Who in the Cinema Industry', in *Exhibitors' Diary* (London, 1929).

— *The Film Game* (London, 1937).

Warren, P., *Elstree, The British Hollywood* (London, 1983).

White, Morton and Lucia White, *The Intellectual Versus the City* (London, 1977 edn).

Wiener, Martin J., *English Culture and the Decline of the Industrial Spirit 1850–1980* (London, 1981).

Williams, Emlyn, *George, an Early Autobiography* (London, 1961).

Wilcox, Herbert, *25,000 Sunsets* (London, 1967).

Wild, Roland, *Ronald Colman* (London, 1933).

Wood, Linda, *The Commercial Imperative in the British Film Industry: Maurice Elvey, a Case Study* (London, 1987).

Wood, M. and A. (eds), *Lord Grantley. Silver Spoon* (London, 1954).

Woolf, S. J., *Drawn from Life* (London, 1932).

Woolf, Virginia, 'The Cinema'(1926), in *The Captain's Death Bed and other Essays* (London, 1950 edn).

— Introduction to M. L. Davis (ed.), *Life as We Have Known It*, by Co-operative Working Women (London, 1931).

— *Collected Essays* (London, 1966).

Wright, Basil, *The Long View: an International History of Cinema* (London, 1976).

Wright, Patrick, *On Living in an Old Country: The National Past in Contemporary Britain* (London, 1985).

Yacowar, Maurice, *Hitchcock's British Films* (New York, 1977).

Young, Terence, *Beaconham and Dagenham: a Report Made for the Pilgrim Trust* (London, 1934).

Film Index

General Index